In Spite of Everything....

In Spite of Everything....
FOR THE WOMAN SHE LOVED

Leila Peters

authorHOUSE

AuthorHouse™
1663 Liberty Drive
Bloomington, IN 47403
www.authorhouse.com
Phone: 1-800-839-8640

© 2010 Leila Peters. All rights reserved.

No part of this book may be reproduced, stored in a retrieval system, or transmitted by any means without the written permission of the author.

First published by AuthorHouse 6/12/2010

ISBN: 978-1-4520-2409-7 (e)
ISBN: 978-1-4520-2410-3 (sc)
ISBN: 978-1-4520-2411-0 (hc)

Library of Congress Control Number: 2010906689

Printed in the United States of America
Bloomington, Indiana

This book is printed on acid-free paper.

To Sue Ann Ritter,
who meant everything.

Acknowledgements

First and always, thanks to the beautiful women who allowed me to enter their lives. With grace, frankness, and courage they revealed the storms as well as the sunshine of their relationships and let us understand what Love is: patient, forgiving, and supportive.

Thank you to Suzanne Kelsey, editor extrordinaire, whose encouragement kept me going, and whose razor-sharp mind cut many extraneous adjectives and redundant phrases to make the book read smoothly.

Thank you to all of my friends who were patient in proof-reading: Diana, who waded through reams of the first rough draft; Esther, Linda, Dal, Carole, Vickie, Sherry, Margot, Cheryl, Ruth, Becky, and Harriet.

Thank you to Carol Alfs, for finding Diane and Samantha.

Special thanks to Nancy Robertson who believes, as I do, that *In Spite of Everything* is a book that needed to be written. Her counsel and interest helped me from the beginning.

Contents

Chapter 1. Kate and Carol 1

In Ontario, Canada, on a warm summer evening in 1990, Kate and Carol met because of the deep sensual beat of "Black Velvet," a very popular song at the time. Kate danced on the nearly empty floor of the lesbian bar. Carol watched, spellbound. It took years of work for the runaway and the unwed mother to free themselves of their burdens and become a family with Kate's child. Kate says, "It was hard, but there wasn't ever a time when I wanted to be without her."

Chapter 2. Diane and Samantha 21

Diane and Samantha, African American women, met in 1988. With little money and four young children between them, they divorced their husbands and moved in together. Poverty, Diane's mother's constant prediction that they would go to Hell, and trying to balance their education and children's needs, were all resolved by the mantra they lived by: Love Prevails.

Chapter 3. Vida and Helena 43

Vida's favorite song the first years of their partnership began, "Just once can we finally find a way to make it right?" After years of compromise, they found that sacrificing ego was not as painful as the thought of separating. Helena says, "It's always a struggle for us, but you know what? We found out what's important. The kids, our safety, being together are important. We love the life, companionship, and the beautiful family we have made together."

Chapter 4. Jan and Xandra 69

> Jan and Xandra are both strong women, self assured and capable. Each had enjoyed the company of many women through the years, but had given up on lasting relationships. How quickly that changed when they looked into each other's eyes for the first time. Thirty-five years went by before they knew it.

Chapter 5. Laura and Kathleen 91

> Kathleen was the dutiful wife of a minister and a mother of two young boys. She was also part owner of a quilt shop where she met Laura. Kathleen was on duty that day when, angry with a difficult pattern, Laura stormed into the shop and shouted, "Fix it!" After getting to know each other *much* better they still met to quilt on Wednesdays. Laura laughs, "We just didn't do much quilting after that. Before that we accomplished great things."

Chapter 6. Ellen and Jo...109

> Jo at eighty-two and Ellen at seventy-six have spent most of their lives in South Carolina. If you sit with them awhile, you will be treated to light-hearted tales of their lives together. A Northerner will need some translation, for their accents are thick and the idioms abound. Neither of them had lived with any other woman before. They have been together fifty-four years.

Chapter 7. Faith and Ann..131

> Faith and Ann met in the Navy in the early '50s, a time when the armed forces were actively seeking to eradicate homosexuals. Their love held them together through the fear of being dishonorably discharged and disgraced. When Faith was interrogated by the Office of Naval Intelligence, the power of Ann's love reached her from miles away.

Chapter 8. Miriam and Rachael 151

> Miriam and Rachael met in a Jewish Bungalow Colony in Upstate New York in the '60s where they spent the summers with their children. The explosive attraction they experienced after ten

years of friendship was unnerving. In Miriam's words, "I was a mother with children for heaven's sake!

Chapter 9. Louise and Carol 169

Ever since Louise graduated from high school in 1948, she had tried everything to keep her parents from knowing she was "queer," even marriage. In 1958 she decided to join her gay friends who had been lured to San Francisco. When her plane settled on the runway, Louise began a twenty-six year adventure in one of the most beautiful, exciting liberal cities in the world where gay culture and entertainment was flourishing. Best of all, she began a 43 year love affair with Carol.

Chapter 10. Erin and Dena 189

Born in 1925 and 1927 respectively, Erin and Dena were raised in strict Irish Catholic families near Boston, Massachusetts. Erin went into a convent for seven years until anorexia nearly killed her. Dena, at age twenty-seven began to live a self-imposed cloistered life. She shut herself away from the gay community to please her family. They met, fell in love, and found a way to be together for forty-two years and remain loyal to their faith.

Chapter 11. Suzie and Leila 215

This chapter is the author's story and told in first person, since Suzie died before its writing. Leila had been so lonely, not fitting in with the rest of the world. Suzie showed her where she belonged and how her life could be fulfilled. They had twenty adventurous years together before they were caught in the grip of a terrible illness. Strength from their love overcame Huntington's disease and even cancer which threatened to destroy the "us" that they had become together.

Preface

Long before the idea of gay marriage surfaced as a civil rights issue, male and female gay couples were quietly living lives together which honored marriage's ceremonial vows. They remained faithful through rich times and poor, in sickness and in health, in spite of the clash of their own strong personalities and the risks of living in a society that was hostile to their very existence. *In Spite of Everything* was written to honor those lesbians whose love endured in spite of hate, degradation, oppression in the work place, and a pervading sense of isolation from family and mainstream society. Their unsanctioned commitment to one another was just as binding as the marriage vows of straight society.

In Spite of Everything is a collection of short biographies of twenty-two lesbians who have been in partnerships from nineteen to fifty-four years. Each story begins in childhood and ends in the present. The first of the biographies, Kate and Carol, is the most recent and the last begins with the birth of Erin in 1925. The timely, provocative stories give voice to the closeted, dismissed and, sometimes, persecuted women who have made lifelong commitments… in spite of everything.

My partner of thirty-five years died of an illness that took her slowly, over the course of eleven years. Suzie and I had twenty-four adventurous years of life together before she was diagnosed with the disease she had dreaded since her childhood. Huntington's disease seized us both in its grip for the next eleven years. At age forty-two her genes triggered the destruction of her cerebral cortex. She lost her small motor skills first; then the jerking of her head and arms began. Rage and depression were part of the early symptoms, while in the later stages she couldn't speak clearly or swallow even pureed food.

In those terrible years we concentrated on the best possible ways to maintain our quality of life. I struggled to keep from being overcome by the constant, inevitable decline of her body. In November 1991, she was diagnosed with breast cancer. She had a lumpectomy, then a mastectomy six months later. In the end, it wasn't HD that took her life. It was breast cancer. In 1993 she died peacefully in our home, surrounded by the things she loved.

After her death, I found that I couldn't clearly remember what we were like together when she was well. There had been so much to do, so much concentration on battling the illness, keeping it from overwhelming the "us" that we had become together. Through the healing process of writing down our life together, I began to catch glimpses of her, emerging as images through the fog: Suzie, at the rush party in 1958, the first time I saw her. Her hair was longer then, blond and curling at her neck in a page boy. Her tanned face accentuated her bright blue eyes. She looked at me and smiled and I felt an inexplicable rush of tenderness as I looked into her eyes. For all of her brightness and vitality, she seemed sad and a little lonely.

I remembered her body framed in the window of my front door. Seeing her was always brand new. She was only five-foot-two, but strong. She had muscular arms, a flat stomach, and shapely legs from summers spent swimming and diving off the high dive.

I began to hear her laughter, so spontaneous and joyful, and I saw her maddening self-assuredness and cockiness.

How could I have forgotten her touch, tender and teasing, warm and exciting, comforting and calming in times of pain? How could I have put aside the summer that meant everything, the summer when our love was realized and all of the emotions I had tried unsuccessfully to conjure up for the men I had dated came flooding, unbidden, when I was with Suzie, or thought of her, or dreamed of her.

All of the passion of our lives came flooding back as I wrote our story. I could see Suzie clearly again, vibrant and whole, the love of my life.

I shared our story with my younger friends who seemed to be in awe of anyone staying together for more than seven years. It was as if they needed to know that it was possible to find that kind of love. I was just as surprised that many of them had given up on the possibility. I decided to start gathering histories of other couples who had lived together twenty years or more.

What began as a catharsis for me became a nonfiction collection of lesbian love stories. I tell them for two reasons. One is to present role models for those who need to know that enduring lesbian relationships are possible. The other, more importantly, is to remember and honor those women from the early twentieth century to the early twenty-first century whose love endured. Their unsanctioned commitment to one another was just as binding as the marriage vows of straight society, vows that are still denied to many of us in the "land of the free."

Many of the women whose lives I documented are now in their late sixties through early eighties. There were others who didn't want me to record their histories. One couple I wanted to include had met during WWII while serving in the Army and was celebrating their fiftieth anniversary together. I couldn't wait to begin the interview, but after tentatively agreeing, one of them came back to me and said that they didn't want their families to find out. Even with the offer to change names and places, they, along with several other couples, were too fearful of the consequences. Another woman, who had been with her partner for thirty years, couldn't bear to relive the way she'd lost her children and grandchildren because of coming out. I was disappointed that I couldn't tell their stories, but more than that, I was sad that after all of the past struggles for gay rights, and the distance we have come, these women are still living with the ghosts of the past and even the fear of future consequences.

So many of the women I interviewed began their relationships thinking that they were the only ones. There were plenty of us, of course, but no one was going to tell. If you recognized that certain "thing" about another woman or couple, it would be weeks or months before any revelations were made, if they ever were. The risks were too great. There was much at stake. The forties and fifties were times for lesbians to be wary, to stay hidden, to keep secrets. The U.S. Civil Service Commission had a ban on the employment of gay men and women. U.S. Armed Forces were actively engaged in "witch hunts" to destroy homosexuals' careers. It was against federal laws to send homosexual material through the mail. Tests used in employment interviews were contrived to weed out "unsavory people." Until 1973, homosexuality was listed as a mental disorder by the American Psychiatric Association. It wasn't until 1962 that Illinois removed its sodomy statute from its penal codes, and it was another decade before other states did. Only recently, in 2003, did the Supreme Court strike down those remaining laws that ban homosexual sex.

Since very few lesbians were out in the forties and fifties, there were no role models to follow. There were few places to meet other women except in lesbian bars, and they were often raided. I started teaching in 1961 and I never entered a lesbian bar until I retired thirty-nine years later. I was still afraid of being outed in 2001! Some of my friends were braver and described the scenario of raids in Indianapolis in the fifties and sixties. The police would barge in, ask for IDs, and push the women around. Those who protested would be beaten, handcuffed, and taken to jail. The morning papers would list the names of those arrested. Families were scandalized, jobs were lost, reputations ruined. To be labeled homosexual was to be considered one who exhibited deviant sexual behavior. Many were branded as sinners condemned by God.

It was standard treatment, for those who had the means, to send their gay sons or daughters to psychiatrists to be "cured." My friend Anne was caught in a passionate embrace in her sorority dorm. For that, she and her lover were kicked out of the sorority and their parents were called. Anne's mother was nearly hysterical with grief, anger, and confusion. She sent Anne to a psychiatrist, who at least, had some sense. He asked how she felt about being a lesbian and when Anne said she didn't feel it was so wrong, the doctor said to her mother, "Anne doesn't need counseling, but maybe you would like some help through this." This was not a satisfactory answer for Anne's mother. She wanted Anne to be "fixed." When Anne started teaching, she moved in with her lover. Her mother became so upset that she had a nervous breakdown.

While Anne was lucky to get an enlightened doctor, others experienced the attempts of a "cure" which included institutionalization and shock treatment. Barbara, a lesbian Air Force nurse, was assigned to the psychiatric ward in a V.A. hospital. There she cared for a woman who had been receiving shock treatments and drugs to interrupt her homosexual tendencies. Barbara looked into her patient's vacant eyes and became suddenly aware of the fine line between patient and nurse.

The things women and men did to keep from being discovered seem extreme now, even comical. The lesbian newsletter, *The Ladder*, published by one of the first national lesbian organizations, Daughters of Bilitis, was sent to eager readers nationwide in a plain brown wrapper. An article in the May 1966 issue instructed readers how to select "the most heterosexual answers possible" on personality tests used in employment interviews. Many tried marriage as a cure for their homosexuality. One of my friends married a gay man to get away from the surveillance of her parents. Doing so got Louise out of her parents' house and gave her the freedom to associate with women. In Jo's and Ellen's case, they paid a friend to keep some of Ellen's clothes in her apartment, so that her detective uncle would think Ellen was living with her. He didn't want her to associate with Jo, whom he suspected of being queer. The more tragic choice for some women was to accept the pervading beliefs that their natural inclinations to love women were wrong, even evil, and deny themselves the joy of a nurturing relationship.

Dr. Susan E. Johnson undertook a broad study of 108 lesbian couples. All filled out a twenty-four-page questionnaire, and thirty-four of the women were interviewed. She includes her findings and interviews in her book, *Staying Power/Long Term Lesbian Couples*, which was published in 1991. One of her conclusions was, "Women can come to long-term lesbian coupling from past experiences, with either women, men or both, from many past experiences or none, and can begin their long term relationship at any age." In my small sampling of women's stories the variety of experiences that brings women together holds true. There are many paths leading to enduring relationships.

This book is *not* a study, but a collection of stories about women in love. Three of the women had lackluster marriages before they realized that life had more to offer. One couple is African American, another Puerto Rican. The self-labeled Jewish Princesses met in a bungalow colony in Upstate New York. One woman was a Catholic nun from 1943 to 1948, and her partner, also a devout Catholic, had abstained from contact with women for seven years, trying to please her family. One couple met in the Navy in 1954 and witnessed, first hand, the cruel treatment of homosexuals and anyone whom the Navy thought were homosexuals. Quilting brought Laura who was fifty at the time, together with Kathleen, who was, forty-one. One couple comes from the Deep

South, and another is Canadian. Three couples raised children together. These women are PhDs, RNs, abuse counselors, teachers, accountants, principals, hairdressers, hospital administrators, homemakers, entrepreneurs, and computer network specialists. *One* thing brings them all together. Each shared a desire so compelling that she left husband or a family, and risked the alienation of society and the anger of a wrathful God to be with the woman she loved.

Kate and Carol

Kate was sitting at one of the tables in a gay bar in London, Ontario, which served as a coffeehouse in the afternoon. Even in the midst of an unusually warm Canadian summer in 1990, Kate couldn't shake a feeling of unease that lingered like the memory of a bad dream. She had given up on sharing a lasting relationship after her recent year-and-a half love affair with Michelle ended. She was waiting for the buzz of too many drinks at lunch to subside so she could drive home. At 4:30 the first beats of "Black Velvet" filled the room.

The beat was sensuous, the rhythm, elemental, and alone on the dance floor, Kate responded to the music. Her auburn waist-length hair swayed with her body. She moved sensually, gracefully, closing her eyes, giving herself to the music. She was lost in the beat, the rhythm and the song, oblivious to the early arrivals, oblivious to Carol, a particularly appreciative observer, who absorbed every nuance of her body, the shapely breasts, graceful arms, expressive hips.

When the last measure of the music faded away, Kate noticed Carol and a few other people enjoying a laugh at the table in a corner. She thought Carol was cute, sexy, a k.d.lang look-a-like, slightly butch in a very appealing way. She went to their table, and they asked her to join the fun.

Carol could feel the heat rising from her neck to her face. One look into Kate's hazel eyes raised the temperature in the room. She had willed this woman to come near to her, and now? She forced herself to pay attention to the conversation. Someone had started a round of toasting to the things they liked best.

"Here's to the girls I left behind."

"Here's to the boss *I* left behind,"

"Here's to behinds!"

The sounds of clinking glasses and laughter floated around the table. About that time Kate leaned back in her chair and put her foot on the table. When it was Carol's turn to toast, she raised her glass and said, "Here's to small feet." They all drank to that. In the meantime, the disk jockey had arrived. The bar began to liven up, and many at the table left to dance. Carol says, "After the party atmosphere began to grow, it was as if the two of us shrank down to our own space. Immediately there was a connection and an ease with each other."

Kate adds, "Carol and I ended up sitting beside each other, just talking for hours. I was unaware of the room, the people, or anything but our conversation. What I remember is thinking I should go home, and when I looked up, the afternoon coffeehouse had turned into a night bar and was filled with people. Hours had passed, people had arrived, and I was only aware of Carol. I decided around midnight that I was sober and could drive home." Before she left, she gave Carol her phone number and said her last name was Jones.

Carol was born in 1971 in the small town of Travistock, Canada, into a family who belonged to a fellowship of fundamentalist Baptists. They emphasized punishment for the damned and salvation for those who adhered to a literal interpretation of the Bible. Being saved meant you were among the elite in God's kingdom on earth. Music was forbidden unless it was to praise God. The congregation was homophobic and the unspoken, unforgivable sin was being a homosexual.

Little Carol in kindergarten didn't know what a homosexual was. She was a bright child, musically gifted, and loved school. She liked to go to school because, in her home there were too many rules, too many punishments. "Besides," Carol says, "At recess the boys and girls made up a game called "Kiss Tag." All of the little boys chased the little girls so they could kiss them. Until my teacher stopped me I chased the little girls and kissed them."

By the time Carol was twelve, her feelings for girls had intensified. She still kissed the ones who wanted to be kissed. For her girl friends, it amounted to preadolescent experimentation. For Carol there was a thrill. At age fourteen her attachments became obsessions. "I wanted to be with my girlfriends all of the time. I wanted to buy them jewelry and call them on the phone. They didn't feel the same way about me and I wondered if something was wrong with the way I felt about them."

In 1984 a newsletter was sent out to all of the teens who belonged to a "Right to Life" organization supported by a Christian rock star that Carol liked. Carol remembers clearly, "In bold type the letters on the cover asked, 'ARE YOU GAY?' The picture on the cover depicted a figure looking out in despair, like it was a horrible thing to be gay." The contents disturbed her so much that she decided to go to the youth leader and tell him that she thought she might be gay. She knew that some of the straight members of her teen group had experimented with sex and drugs and nothing had happened to them. Even when her own father confessed to molesting her two cousins, the church had forgiven him. How could being gay be worse than that?

Carol remembers, "It was customary for the youth pastors to talk over the young people's problems in their homes after they had provided dinner." As always, the night Carol went for help, the atmosphere in Pastor Mike's home was cozy. After a pleasant meal, his children were excused to play. Mike and his wife, Naomi, sat at the cleared table with Carol. Naomi asked, "Would you like a cup of tea, dear?"

"No, thank you, I'm a little nervous." Pastor Mike was quick to reassure her. "We are here to help you, Carol. You are safe in this house." Carol breathed in and began, "I think there's something different about me. I saw something that worried me in the youth newsletter. I'm wondering if I'm gay." Except for the sound of a barking dog in the distance, there was silence. Naomi's eyes widened and the pastor's mouth opened. No words came out. Carol stopped breathing. "Well," Pastor Mike searched for words. He and his wife exchanged blank expressions. "I'm glad you came to us. I think we will need to talk with some of the church leaders about this, but I'm sure everything will be all right." A little too hastily, he ushered Carol to the door. "We'll pray for you."

She realized the magnitude of the problem she had caused when, two weeks later, she was told that the district head of the 200 churches in Ontario would talk with her in the sanctuary of the church. She felt relieved. The church was a special place for her. Its simple lines and muted colors had given her a sense of peace for as long as she could remember. There was no stained glass, no distracting ornamentation. It was the place where she had shared fellowship with friends and family.

When Carol entered the sanctuary, Willard Roberts was already there, standing at the foot of the altar. She had only seen him from a distance before. He looked taller than she remembered, and sterner. A little chill took away some of her confidence when he turned his deep-set eyes on her. It was hard to tell if he was smiling, because an enormous black brush of a mustache covered his lip. When he spoke, his manner was not unkind, but what he said that day ended Carol's trust in organized religion.

In his well-modulated voice, Roberts crushed all of Carol's illusions about church as family, stripped her of all faith in a loving God, and left her spirit dead. He began, "We are so glad that you have told us these things about yourself, because we need to separate you from the rest of the congregation. You must not be a part of the Sunday school program any longer. You will not baby sit for any members of our fellowship. You will no longer be in the choir or sit with others. You are welcome to come to church if you sit in the last pews where you will consider how you can repent and learn to change."

Carol felt like an insect in a jar. The outside world was blurred; sounds seemed far away and it was getting hard to breathe. She couldn't move, even when "the great man" held out the shredded pieces of her baptismal certificate and announced that her name had been crossed out in the register which held the names of church members.

They left her on the sidewalk in front of the church. Her mind was numb and she didn't remember how she got home. She does remember that there was no love there. She was treated as if she were a disgrace to the family and was asked over and over, "Why?"

She had no answers, no friends, no person to turn to, and no God. Without anyone else to turn to, Carol subjected herself to counseling. "I was given a lot of books. One in particular I remember well. It was really disgusting. It had cartoon representations of the act of sodomy. It was written for teens as a comic strip, but the message was, 'You're all sick. You're all disgusting. You're all going to Hell.'" It was this book that eventually saved her. Those pictures were an outrage. "Even if I was wrong, their response was not okay. They had no right to treat me like that. I felt a commitment to myself to make sure I wasn't destroyed."

"Denying my natural feelings lasted about three days, so I disappeared from my town and the people I knew for a while, to try and get a sense of independence and to find who I was. I was between fifteen and sixteen years old. I came to London, Ontario, about forty miles from Travistock, and did call my mother to tell her I was safe, but I didn't tell her where I was. I met some other misfits and realized I was not alone. Among us we had enough money to get an apartment. I became a part of the gay underground scene in London."

Carol realized very quickly that the fast-paced, reckless bar scene wasn't for her, either. "I didn't meet what I considered a healthy crowd, but at least I became aware that I wasn't the only person in trouble in the world, but I didn't want to spend my life drinking and sleeping around, either."

In time Carol reconnected with her parents but never went home. They owned flower shops in several towns and her mother gave her a job at their flower shop in London. She accepted the job, but she didn't want them to have any control over her. In the evening, she also had a job as cook at "the most happening gay bar" in London. Carol lived alone for three years, finished high school, and continued to search for harmony in her life.

Kate was born in 1963 and came from a home with a loving mother who had divorced a few years after Kate was born. Her mother raised her and her two brothers and sister alone. Kate never had any crushes on her teachers or the girls in her classes. "I never heard of anyone being gay or talking about being gay in high school until I was a senior. That wasn't something that was out there." She was petite and pretty and the boys were attracted to her. She dated, but never had any special feelings for any one person. She felt that she was an average person, just like her girlfriends.

"I found out I was different when I was eighteen. Some of my friends and I went to a gay bar to be cool. I felt an immediate sense that I liked it there. Everyone in the bar thought I was just a straight person looking in. There were no other women in the bar that looked like me." Because of Kate's petite body and femininity, her initial experiences with lesbians in that particular bar were disappointing. Even though she knew she had an attraction to the women in the bar, they made her doubt if she "qualified" as a lesbian. Later that week when Kate came back to the bar alone and tried her luck at meeting someone, her attempts at conversation were met with a variety of discouraging comments.

"What are you doing here, sweetie?"

"She's checking us out."

"We call people like you breeders."

"Yeah, you need to get a husband."

Kate considered the women in that bar to be quintessential lesbians. For a long time, she connected being a lesbian with being masculine.

Even though she did have a relationship with a woman for a short time, and found it much more intense than her feelings with a man, she felt guilty about it and tried to live the straight life. Nothing was good about that except the birth of her daughter, Emily. "I knew that Emily was the best thing that ever happened to me and that it would be a mistake to marry. Carl was very self-centered, verbally abusive and too irresponsible to raise a child. Kate agreed to let him spend some weekends with Emily and left him.

Kate had other fears. What kind of a life would Emily have if her mother were a lesbian? Reactions from people like her friend Marcy had compounded her doubt. At lunch, Kate told Marcy that she was dating women. Marcy began to cry, stood up, threw her napkin on the table, and rushed out. Later, she called Kate and said, "How could you do this to your daughter? What kind of mother are you? You can't raise a child in that kind of environment!"

Her intuition drew her toward women for love, while her conscious thoughts nagged, telling her she didn't fit into lesbian life. Kate had no church telling her that homosexuality was evil, but she knew what much of society thought. She was resistant to accepting that she was a lesbian, because, even in Canada, there was an element of society which thought that lesbians were perverse. She felt shame for having desires that were considered perverted. For too long, what the rest of the world thought meant a great deal to Kate. She was so close to being an accepted member of society. No one would ever think she was a lesbian. She looked "normal;" she wished that she could be so, because life would be so much easier. Kate said, "I didn't label myself as a lesbian," but her instincts won out.

Kate was majoring in family counseling at the university and met a woman in one of her classes. That relationship lasted about a year and a half. Michelle had never gotten over the love she had for her ex-partner. She finally told Kate that their relationship wasn't working and broke it off. Kate and Michelle's break-up precipitated a conflict for Kate that she struggled with for years. Already confused by her early rejections by the women in the bar, Kate took Michelle's rejection as confirmation that there was something lacking in her. She was twenty-seven years old and still felt confused about her orientation. Could feminine women be Lesbian? All of her university studies in psychology and family counseling could not supply the answers she needed so she labeled herself "free spirited," not lesbian which held her homophobia at bay. This gave her freedom to date women exclusively.

Last week she had danced with abandon in a lesbian bar and had met a woman she couldn't forget. There was something so compelling about Carol that she had to come to her table. "My feelings were an urgency to know her and I mean to know her deeply. I found her attractive immediately."

The first time Kate invited Carol to her home was for breakfast. They had seen each other a few times, but not in private. Carol was impressed when she entered Kate's apartment. "She had taken great care to make the place look nice. Emily's bedroom was beautiful, so creative and decorated so nicely. It had all of the little details that a child would love." Carol was delighted with breakfast, too. Kate served it in bed. All morning they sat propped against the headboard with a platter of fresh fruit between them.

In the afternoon Kate shared an essay she had completed for her university work. "I had to analyze my family, using the point of view of a family therapist. There was very personal information in the paper. I thought it might be a way for her to get to know me as well." This was not the way Carol usually got to know women. She was touched and grateful that Kate trusted her with this sensitive look at her family. It reinforced her feeling that there was going to be something unique about their relationship.

They spent most of the day in Kate's bed without touching until, as if time itself had decided, their lips met, slowly. Almost carefully, their arms encircled in a warm embrace. Heat that had been building for days ignited. Kate needed a list of adjectives to describe their first love making. "It was energizing, passionate, raw, vulnerable, sexy, and we were so in tune with each other." Of that afternoon Carol says, "There wasn't any awkwardness. There wasn't a 'What do we do next?' None of those moments when you realize this isn't working. It was an absolutely, mutually shared expression, and incredibly passionate. I knew it meant more. It was so much more than the physical pleasures. I'd never experienced hot passion along with respect before." Carol spent the night.

The next day, Kate had to pick her daughter up from Carl's house. She had plans to meet some other friends with children and go bowling. Carol rode along when Kate picked up four-year-old Emily. Kate's plan was to drop Carol off on the way to the bowling alley. Carol's plan was to stay with Kate as long as she could. When Emily climbed into the car and kissed her mother, Carol could see the love that flowed between them. She felt blessed to witness this kind of relationship between mother and child. She didn't want to go home so Kate invited her to watch the bowling.

Carol did finally have to go home and get out of the car, and to her horror, a few days later, Kate asked Carol to get out of her life. Kate remembers, "I asked her never to call me again. My life was too complicated. I had just come out of a depression. I was in school. I was a single parent and Carol was just ending a relationship. It was just too complicated." Carol wasn't about to give up on their relationship. Nothing could prevent her from calling Kate again. Since Carol didn't have a phone, she went to the variety store across the street to use their pay phone. She used that phone so much she began to get inquiring looks from the cashier. But dialing the phone didn't necessarily mean that Carol would have the courage to speak. Sometimes her throat seized up and she would hang up before Kate had time to answer. Click. Other times she would hang up after Kate responded, "Hello." Click.

"Oh, I'm such an idiot. Why don't I have the nerve to talk to her?" Carol's mute attacks were overcome by her compulsion to have contact. Even Kate's voice on the answering machine was a comfort, but it was fleeting. The ache in her chest began to grow, but she never fell into depression as she had done with her parents' and church's rejection. "I had a sense that Kate was going against what she really wanted. When she said, 'Don't call me,' I took it to mean just the opposite."

Kate missed Carol terribly. She had never met any one like her before, quietly strong, yet soft. She knew that the calls and hang-ups were Carol's. Even with Emily there, her house seemed so empty without her. The oppressive clouds that had been hanging around all day didn't help. The fear of losing Carol overcame her fear of another failed relationship.

The thunderstorm that had been threatening all day sealed her new resolve. Wave after wave of rain beat against her windows, distorting the scene in the street below. People were running for cover while Kate was preparing to enter the storm. She drove to Carol's apartment and left a sodden note in her mailbox. "Blame it on the rain, call me." After dropping off the note, Kate went to the variety store. "There was Carol in a phone booth calling me." Carol followed Kate into the storm and got in the car.

Within a few weeks, Carol was staying at Kate's apartment. She didn't leave until they both left to find a home together. She was confident that she and Kate would be together forever, but Kate was a realist. She had reasons to doubt "forever after," but because of their love for each other, her faith grew through the years. "I don't recall the exact moment when I knew I wanted to spend my life with Carol; it was steps along the way. The decision to move from my little apartment and get a condo together was one of those major steps, the decision to buy a house together, to put our money into one bank account, to buy our current house, and cars. Everything has been done jointly. Being able to talk about the future with her, all of those steps and moments were realizations."

Carol's confidence in their future was shaken by a continuing concern that Emily wouldn't like her. She wondered what her place would be in raising this beautiful, intelligent child. "Kate and Emily already had an established family unit. I was fully prepared to be rejected." In those first months she couldn't get away from the nagging question, "What if Emily hates me?" She got her answer very soon. "On one of the first times I was alone with Emily—I think her mother was at the store or something—I went to the washroom, and when I came out, there was Emily standing in front of me with her hands on her hips, staring at me." Emily said, "I don't have to like you."

"You're right, you don't have to." There was a long pause, and then Emily smiled and said, "I know, but I do."

Emily had gotten to know Michelle when she was dating her mother, but Michelle had never lived with them. She had nothing to compare to this new arrangement. Carol's decision to be very low-key at first was a good one. She talked with Emily at the dinner table. They went on vacations together, family trips, picnics. Kate adds, "We didn't ram our relationship down Emily's throat. We just lived as a family. Carol's and my relationship was not the main focus in our family. We'd come home, play with Emily, discipline her if necessary, get her involved in cello lessons, the ordinary things parents do. She was our main focus."

Of course, their professions were another focus. After graduating from university, Kate became a family counselor. Carol had become so interested in the books Kate had been studying when she first met her that she started classes at the university. She majored in child psychology and now works with children, holding a part time position teaching psychology at a community college.

Carol and Kate differed on some parenting issues along the way, but there were none of great concern. Kate agrees. "We have the same parenting philosophies." Carol adds, "We both recognized and shared the value that when you are responsible for the care and upbringing of a child, that should be the priority. While you are raising children, that's your job. We've given to our relationship in equal amounts while never letting Emily's growth and development be allotted to the back burner."

Carol says, "More than anything I struggled with, 'Where do I fit in?' Who am I? Trying to sort that out was hard."

Kate thinks that Carol represents another person on whom Emily, now a young adult, can count. "In her relationship with her father, Emily is the parent. I think she recognized that when she was very young. Carol and I were her safe haven when she was a child. We were the adults and the parents who set limits with her."

When Carol first moved in with Kate, Emily was four years old and had the habit of crawling into bed with Kate in the middle of the night. Until she was seven, she continued this habit after Carol was sleeping with Kate. Kate felt that Emily was getting big enough to stay in her own bed all night. Kate says, "I wasn't getting enough sleep, so I bribed her with stickers. If she slept in her own bed every night, she would earn a sticker. Five stickers would get her a bag of chips for recess on Fridays." Emily was thrilled. She began sleeping in her own bed all night. Carol and Kate had privacy and a good night's sleep.

One morning after Carol went to work, Emily walked into Kate's bedroom with her arms crossed over chest and a scowl on her face. Kate asked, "What's wrong, Honey?"

"When is Carol going to get *her* sticker chart?"

"Uh, Carol's bed is broken."

All day at work Kate regretted lying to Emily. She knew it was wrong, but in that moment, she couldn't think of anything else to say. There were no role models. There were few books that Kate and Carol knew of that discussed rearing a child of a same-sex couple. They didn't know any other couples who had children at that time. Kate says, "The books that I read were about children who had serious psychological problems because of the multiple partners the gay parents had over the course of their lives. I couldn't find any books about committed lesbians who raised a child from beginning to end." Kate's reliable mothering instincts gave her the answer. "I realized that I had missed the perfect opportunity to tell Emily the truth." She shared this idea with Carol who agreed.

When Emily got home from school that afternoon, Kate and Carol sat Emily down between them on the sofa. Kate began, "Emily, there are two kinds of family secrets, good ones and bad ones." Kate listed all of the bad things, emphasizing abuse. "If any of those things happen to you, you need to tell someone, even if it's Mommy or Carol who are doing them." She listed all of the good secrets, such as a gift that is a surprise. "Carol and Mommy love each other like all of your friends' Mommies and Daddies love each other. People don't understand our love, so we keep it a family secret. If you tell your friends about it, you might not be able to play with them any more. Some of the kids might make fun of you. Carol's and Mommy's love is a good family secret."

"Ok, Mommy. I will keep our secret."

She was willing to keep the secret because in the time that the three of them had lived together, Emily had already begun to accept and like

Carol. In the summer when Carol was studying at home for her classes in college, and her mother was at work, Carol and Emily spent a lot of time together. Carol would sometimes read her bedtime stories and tuck her in at night. One time when Emily was on the phone with a friend who had asked if she could come over and play, Emily said. "I'll ask my mom." Carol was alone in the house with Emily. She flushed with happiness when Emily called out, "Mom, can I go over to Sharon's house?" It was the first time she had been addressed this way and it seemed so natural.

It was Emily who found Carol's place in their family. She made up a pet name for her, Carolee. Carol liked that. She had a label. Emily called her, "My Carolee." Kate remembers, "One of the things Emily and I did for Carol was to have a Carolee Day that would publicly acknowledge Carol. It is on Labor Day. Just like on Mother's Day, Carol gets a card and a gift from Emily honoring her as her other parent."

Kate and Emily especially want Carol to know how much they appreciate her, because others don't understand Carol's importance to their family. Carol agrees. "There's still the idea, 'It's your partner's child.' Emily is Kate's daughter and that is true. I don't want to minimize that, but I have invested just as much as any other parent would, from my heart, my finances, my energy. And yet people say, 'Yes, but she's not your daughter.' I guess the question I dislike the most is, 'Don't you ever want to have children?' Emily *is* my child. This is my family and I am her parent. I feel incredibly blessed and lucky to be a part of her life."

When Emily was about nine years old, she came in after school and announced to Kate, "I'm tired of the secret."

"What do you mean?"

"Well, when people come play with me, they ask whose room is the spare bedroom. I don't know what to say. Sometimes I say it's the spare room, and I have to correct myself and say it's Carol's room. I find it too hard."

"Ok, we'll work out a way for you to tell."

Kate and Carol took Emily to a friend, child psychologist Miriam Jenkins. Kate says, "She was wonderful. She never talked with her about what it was like to have two moms, is it horrible or difficult? She started with Emily's need to tell the secret. At Emily's first session Miriam said, "Ok, Emily, so you want to tell your friends. Let's start with some teasing techniques. Then you can practice using me as your friends, and I will tease you to see how you deal with that." There were no problems. Friends still came to Emily's house. Kate says, "There was just the normal teasing. We hate you one day. We like you the next."

After the counselor had prepared Emily for possible rejection, she said to Kate and Carol, "You two need to come out now. Emily needs to know that you are not ashamed of who you are. She needs to hear the positive stories about coming out and the negative ones." As the counselor suggested, Carol and Kate made their coming out stories casual. They became topics of conversation at the dinner table. In that way, Emily was included in their lives. Kate says, "Emily hasn't really had to struggle much. She has been teased a little, but I think she would have been teased if she had been fat. She's much more open about our life than I am. I'm much more homophobic than my daughter is! At that time, I still couldn't come out to my family and all of the people at work." My struggle in my relationship with Carol has really been about accepting myself and the guilt."

Kate says of their life-style, "We never inundated Emily with 'things gay.' I never put rainbow stickers on my car. We don't live in the gay part of London, mainly because we wanted a bigger house. We live in the suburbs in a two-story home with a large back yard and a pool. We choose our friends because we like them, not necessarily because they are lesbians. Being gay isn't the main focus of our family. Our staying power has been our commitment to Emily. We simply live our lives without hiding."

Their devotion to Emily did not diminish their passion for one another. In fact, it grew. Kate says, "We are strongly connected and still share passion. I think this part of our relationship has gotten better. The comfort level, the honesty, and knowing each other fully have made it so." That comfort level and honesty was won from working through hard times together.

They rented a condominium for a while after living in the apartment, and decided to combine their money and open up one bank account when they lived there. Carol says, "I felt good contributing my half to the family. It gave me a sense of personal power and pride." Kate says, "The joint account was a test of our commitment, which was exciting and scary at the same time." They made a down payment on a house and accumulated other joint debts until they were struggling to pay them off. Neither could afford to live comfortably without the other's contribution. Carol remembers, "Somehow, we began to live with the idea that our collective debt played some role in our staying together. We joked about this, and neither of us took the joke seriously or recognized its potential 'grain of truth,' until we were suddenly faced with a significant opportunity to reduce it."

Kate adds, "We had been together nine years when, in 1999, I received an inheritance from my grandmother. It was a large sum of money, so, suddenly, there was not going to be a debt. It caused a crisis in our relationship. What was going to happen?" Carol worried that the money would be Kate's "ticket out." She felt that her sense of personal power and pride in contributing to the family was undercut. Carol remembers thinking, "It was her inheritance and she could choose to leave me without any concern for financial hardship. Why would she need me now? What did I have to offer? I felt incredibly insecure." Carol began to feel unwarranted anger, as if Kate had already planned to leave.

Kate says, "We went to our own corners of the world and had explosive fights that lasted months and months. Suddenly we didn't like each other, and yet we stayed together. We would blame each other for everything that was wrong in the relationship or that ever went wrong in the relationship, but we couldn't separate. Finally we went to couples counseling which lasted a year."

Carol says, "We worked through very personal childhood issues that were being played out in our relationship."

Kate says, "It was difficult, painful, and a huge learning experience, both as a couple and as individuals. We were hurtful in our actions and words, and we had to learn to communicate appropriately and interact in healthier ways. We healed many wounds."

Many things contributed to their success: They held their commitment to Emily as a sacred trust. They had a willingness to understand each other's fears and needs, and the grace to forgive. Most of all, their love, held hostage for a time by their insecurities, not only prevailed, but grew stronger once it was free.

Kate and Carol knew that twelve-year-old Emily had to be aware of the rift between them. She couldn't help but overhear their arguments. She witnessed their strained attempts at civility in her presence. Both

Kate and Carol tried to comfort her. They explained to Emily that even though they were having a disagreement, the love they had for her was forever. Neither Kate nor Carol felt that their words were enough and knew that their behavior was affecting her. Thankfully, Emily also witnessed their slow but steady progress toward reconciliation, and the power of forgiveness.

Carol looks back at that terrible time with a wry smile, "I'm realizing how faint the memories are, and it seems quite extraordinary that such a chaotic time in our history has faded. It's a nice realization; hard times do shape the future, but they don't have to live on as permanent scars." Kate says, "To this day, both of our paychecks get deposited into one account and bills get paid from there. I think that was an important step to saying, 'I trust you and I trust our relationship will make it.'"

Carol and Kate had been together for 15 years when in 2005, the province of Ontario passed a law making same sex marriage legal. Carol immediately wanted to take advantage of it. Kate was more reluctant. Many of her old fears of being labeled "lesbian" came to the surface with an added one. She didn't want to get married and have it change the way they lived. Kate says, "Our impending marriage created some anxiety in me. I was quite anxious as the date got closer. Kate kept asking Carol, "Are you sure we should do this?"

"I promise you. It is the right thing to do. This is so important to me, Kate"

"We are not married yet, and I'm already worrying about being a divorced woman," Kate responded.

"I'm making this choice after fifteen years, so I'm not blinded by what the future will look like. The best part is, I'll be spending it with you."

"The only thing I know, Carol, is I love you. I will do this for you as a gift of my love."

In the beginning stages of their wedding plans, Kate remained fearful. Carol was joyful. Carol says, "I never thought I would have this option in my life. I'm thrilled that a majority of the population of Ontario have voted to validate our love. I get very emotional thinking about it. I am so thankful that we will be able to join in a public confirmation and celebration."

Kate's respect and love for Carol helped her face her own lingering homophobia, so she could come out to her family and friends and invite them to the wedding. Kate was determined not to allow anything to hurt Carol. She says, "I want our love to last forever."

They set the day for July 14. Carol did not invite her father to the wedding, and her mother and sister declined. Her mother did decorate their home with flowers. There was much planning to do.

In the fifteen years she and Carol had been living together, having her family over for Christmas and other holidays, Kate had never had *the* conversation. She just let them assume what they wanted. She had to come out and talk about it if she was going to invite them to the wedding. Kate says, "What happened for me was, just before our wedding I identified myself as a lesbian and came out to myself!" When Kate told her brother and then mother they were very supportive and loving. Kate says, "I absolutely feel loved. Since we've just gone through this process of talking out loud to friends and family, I realized that I had blocked myself from people, because I was afraid to tell them I'm a lesbian.

Emboldened by her family's loyalty, Kate gave verbal invitations to some of her co-workers who had invited her to their family events over the years. One, whom she had reservations about, yet liked very much, was a Hindu woman named Sarika. Ten years before, Sarika had confronted Kate at work, saying, "I have heard some rumors about you. Is it true that you opted to be a lesbian?" Before she could continue, she began to cry, "In my country, you would be beheaded for such action." Her concern did not prevent her from remaining Kate's friend.

Kate invited Sarika and her husband to the wedding, but she wanted to explain the details to Sarika, so there would be no surprises for her. Kate said, "We will be sealing our vows with a kiss."

"My husband and I would be uncomfortable with that."

Kate told her, "I spend every day of my life worrying about everyone else's feelings about my life style and ensuring that I don't show affection in public. I will *not* take care of other people's feelings on the day of my wedding. That is my day."

"I will speak to my husband Amal to see what he thinks." After stewing about it for a few days, Kate decided to call Sarika and uninvite her. Sarika picked up on the third ring. "Hello?"

"Sarika, I've be--- "

In Spite of Everything....

"Kate, darling, I'm happy you called. I spoke to Amal about your wedding and he said, 'I don't care if Kate marries an elephant, we will be there!'"

"I can't guarantee that I won't kiss Carol at the end or throughout the evening."

"We will be fine. Kate, you should be proud of yourself. You have changed the attitudes of two old Hindu farts like ourselves. Be proud!"

It took them months to prepare. They took the time to make wedding invitations together and little gifts to give each wedding guest. Emily, who still lived at home while attending the university, caught the excitement and made a list of her friends to invite. They decided to keep their wedding casual and have the ceremony and reception at home. Carol says, "We thought it would be fitting to have the ceremony in our music room. This is the place Kate and I often spend singing and having our own personal concerts. It is also a place we have shared with all of our friends and family, singing and dancing, enjoying each other. During family get-togethers we all spend hours jamming and making memories. We would make the best memory on our wedding day." They chose clothes that were casual with a touch of elegance. Carol would wear cream colored, crisp linen pants. She was not used to wearing flowing sleeves, but her open necked white linen tunic fit her perfectly.

Kate would wear a beaded sheer white top which complimented her figure. The spaghetti string straps glistened with a subtle placing of sequins. Her pants matched the blouse, and high heeled open toed sandals would complete her attire.

The wedding day arrived and brought perfect weather. Inside, the caterers set up tables laden with food for the party. A large, colorful fruit arrangement balanced one end of the longest table with the wedding cake at the other. White icing lilies adorned the top and one side of the cake as if they had been casually laid there and turned to icing. A gossamer-looking veil of icing was draped across from the lilies, slipping down the side in a graceful arc. It looked like an alabaster sculpture, a work of art. In the backyard, workers completed setting up tents around the pool for the reception where there would be more food, drinks, music and dancing, toasts and celebration.

Carol remembers, "The last-minute details were coming together, the cake arriving while I was still washing windows. We were busy and I hadn't seen her much during the morning, so when she came down to the kitchen in her outfit, I was mesmerized. She was more beautiful then I have ever seen her. She was radiant, full of joy and excitement." Carol gave Kate a beautiful teardrop pearl necklace and whispered, "You are my love and my life. I am so honored that you will marry me today." Kate kissed her and said, "In spite of all of the worries about who I am, there has never been a moment when I didn't want our love to last forever." Her gift for Carol was a pair of gold earrings to match the gold embroidery on her blouse.

Their wedding was beautiful in its simplicity. Friends and family surrounded them in their music room, many standing, some sitting on the floor or chairs. Carol and Kate stood before Lorene Garrison, who would perform the ceremony. The glow from their faces was enough to light the room. Lorene began by saying, "This love has weathered many obstacles along the way. At times, their love has survived the lack of understanding and even acceptance from the outside world. Their love has grown in spite of these challenges. This ceremony will not create a relationship that does not already exist; however, it does recognize Carol and Kate's existing bond, one that is based on fifteen years of committed love for each other and a deep desire for their love to last forever. What a wondrous experience to be touched by love."

When it was time to complete their vows, Emily, now a poised and beautiful twenty- year old, was ready. She was standing beside them holding the rings. She hugged each one, in turn, as she presented the rings to Kate and Carol. Lorene continued, "In the presence of your family and friends, Kate and Carol, please place the rings on each other's fingers as I say the following: Carol and Kate, with these rings you will announce your intention to continue giving your deepest friendship and love, not only when moments are joyful, but when things get difficult; not only when you remember clearly who you are, but when you forget; not only when you are both acting with love, but when you are not. You will seek always to see the light within each other and to share the light within you, giving all that is good within the both of you."

During the moments the rings were slipped onto their fingers, a cloud drifted past the sun. The glow through the window spread tiny beams of light around their hands. Lorene concluded, "I pronounce you married." A tender kiss sealed their vows.

Before their friends and family could give the married couple their kisses and hugs, Lorene announced, "Kate and Carol would like to share a gift they have for Emily." With eyes sparkling with tears, Kate addressed Emily, "Today provides us with an opportunity to not only acknowledge our love for each other, but the love and commitment we both have shared in parenting you. Our relationship has included you." Carol added, "A thanks to Emily for the gift she has given me, the joy of parenting. We want you to have this gift to remember this day." Emily was surprised and delighted with a handmade gold necklace which Kate couldn't fasten for her, because she was shaking with excitement. Lorene said, "Let us now share in the celebration."

After the cake was cut, the pictures taken, the catered meal enjoyed, the clanging of a spoon on a crystal glass silenced the revelers. Emily asked for the attention of the sixty-five people in attendance. Emily was radiant, taller than Kate now, with her mother's dark brown eyes. She gave the best toast that two mothers could have. "I know how much it means to Kate and Carol to have you here celebrating with us. I have been blessed with not one mother, but two. Some people may say that having two mothers would have made my life hard, but my hardships are nothing against the hardships both of these women have gone through in order to get me where I am today. I absolutely cannot think of two people who show each other more respect admiration, understanding, and commitment. There is no one I would rather see, my mother or my Carolee, standing with today. I love you so much! Let us all raise our glasses and toast these two inspirational women on their day. Sixty-five guests came to their feet, applauding their approval.

Kate says, "The wedding was beautiful. I had no discomfort, not even when it was time for us to seal the marriage with a kiss and hug. I was truly in the moment and present completely. I didn't feel like I owed anything to anyone. I was an equal. Straight people and gay people, even some religious folks, attended the wedding. I would never have thought that marriage would make such a difference, but it truly does. We feel differently. Carol felt it immediately. I feel equal to the rest of the world and have a sense of empowerment. In our case, love did win."

Carol says, "We have shared in the transformation of each of us as individuals, watching and responding to the changes along the way; facing the fear and uncertainty with an intent that somehow remains. We want this: We want to grow old together, and we want the rewards that are earned along the way."

Diane and Samantha

Diane and Samantha have been together for nineteen years, and they still exude the joy of being in love. Seeing and hearing Diane and Sam interacting is a treat and a testimony of their love for one another. There is laughter in their voices and mischief in their eyes. Sam's voice is Maya Angelou-rich, deep but mellow. A slight Texas accent lingers from her childhood. Diane's voice is youthful and full of expression. She is a master of understatement. As they revealed the story of their lives together, there was a gentle inserting and completing of thoughts, like the point and counterpoint of a precisely practiced duet. They have overcome tremendous obstacles with patience and grace, and have settled into that comfortable place where they are secure in one another's love.

Samantha was born in Beaumont, Texas, in 1953 to Barbara Browne, an attractive, chocolate brown woman who wished her new baby had never been born. She lay staring at the ceiling while the cries of her newborn penetrated the darkness. "Love child" — that's what they called babies like Samantha — but there was no love at her conception, and there would be no love in her young life. Her mother had a yearning for a man she couldn't have and lived with a husband she didn't love. By the time Sam was five, her mother had moved to Albuquerque, married and divorced twice, and had born four children by three different men.

One day Samantha would learn that Sam Brightman was her and her baby sister's father. His skin was as dark and smooth as polished mahogany. Sam had a much combed short afro and a smile that could stop traffic. He was a handsome and alluring delivery man who charmed and gave pleasure to the ladies on his route—honey colored to ebony, he didn't care. Samantha was named after him: Samantha Marie Browne.

Sam's mother had four children to raise alone in a poor black neighborhood on the south side of Albuquerque. Samantha remembers, "We were pretty poor, but we didn't know we were that poor, because the people around us were about the same. It wasn't a bad neighborhood." The houses were close together with small yards, so the children played baseball and tag in the street and skipped rope on the sidewalk.

Sometime during her childhood, the other kids started calling Samantha "Sam." She liked it. She didn't feel different from the other kids, except, "I was taller and faster than everybody my age. The boys always wanted me to play on their side, because they would win with me on the team. Everyone just thought I was a tomboy."

Sam was the only one in her family who graduated from high school. She says, "I was always listening to my own beat. I wasn't interested in what my friends were doing." Still, her mother continually accused, "You're going to be just like your friends. You'll end up with a baby and never amount to anything!" She hated her mother for making her tend her little sister and brother without ever saying a kind word and for the beatings she gave all of them. Sam vowed she'd get away as soon as she could.

By the time Sam left home at eighteen, she had learned some things that opened up her world because she had met the Parkers. They were representatives of the University Church of Christ, whose bus rolled through her neighborhood one Sunday stopping for anyone who wanted a ride to church. Her mother didn't seem to care if she got on a bus going to a white church. Sam says, "Mr. Parker was a stay-at-home dad, a lawyer. He took us bowling and skating, things I had never done before." She became a regular worshipper at the church and was baptized when she was seventeen. David Parker saw something special in the tall, lanky girl who wanted something better in her life. He showed her how to apply to the college his children attended and helped her with the loan application to pay for it.

Sam entered Abilene Christian University in September 1973. She says, "It was 99.9% white, but I was accepted there, majored in physical education, and did very well. I also enjoyed playing on the varsity basketball and volleyball teams. To help make ends meet at the end of my sophomore year, I worked for Abilene Parks and Recreation. Two years after I started there, I began to move up." The pay became so good that she dropped out of college with fifteen hours left and continued working as the director of a recreation center.

In 1977 she met Senior Master Sergeant Robert Jeffers, who was stationed in Abilene. He was Michael Jordan-handsome, with military-cropped hair. At six feet, he was barely as tall as Sam. When he asked her to marry him after three months of dating, she said, "Yes," thinking, "He's thirty-five and seems responsible. I am twenty-five. It's the thing to do. At the time, I didn't know anything about gay people or being gay."

When she learned that Robert wasn't responsible with money, and didn't care for her the way she had expected, he didn't seem as attractive. But it was too late to get out of the marriage. She found out she was pregnant and two months after their son was born, Robert was sent to a post in Frankfort, Germany. She followed him because it was a wife's duty.

Her "wife's duty" gave her two more sons. With three little ones, Sam needed all of her boundless energy. She still worked, and then came home to nurture her children. She loved playing with them and cooking for them. She dressed them in freshly laundered clothes. There was little time for anything but work and taking care of her children and the house. Her routine would change dramatically when Robert invited her to join the women's basketball team he had volunteered to coach at the base. You might say it changed everything.

All of the other women on the team were Air Force personnel. They welcomed Sam; not only tall and athletic, she was strikingly attractive and charismatic. Since about ninety percent of the players were lesbians, many of them were interested in more than her athletic prowess. Unaware of their appraising looks, Sam had a good time making friends and enjoying their company. "I didn't see what was going on. It took me a year to get it."

Sam says, "In the locker room one day, someone told me that most of the team was gay. I started hanging around with them to find out what this gay thing was. They took me to the gay clubs in Frankfort." Sam was a magnet to women. No matter their color, they flocked to her. Sam learned quickly, graduating from kissing and petting to having short affairs. She says, "I had never known that there was a group of people out there that in twenty-seven years I'd never heard of. They even had a name for themselves that no one had mentioned." She was through trying to be a good wife. "I was trying to figure myself out and how I felt about things. I wanted to experience what life was out there." Her "sexual duties" to her husband decreased.

Sam knew that Robert suspected that something was wrong, but he never brought up the subject of Sam being gay. Sam says, "Gay, lesbian, homosexual, are not words that the African American community bring into the open." Even so, Sam continued to live the life for which she felt she was meant. She wanted to love all of the attractive women she could, to make up for lost time. "I admit that I was nearly out of control with the ladies."

After two years in Germany she went with Robert to his last post in Seattle, Washington, where some of her girlfriends had also been transferred. They took her to the gay night spots in Seattle. Women were drawn to her there, too. Like addicting, dark chocolate, they couldn't get enough.

When Robert retired, he let Sam choose the place where they would settle. She chose Albuquerque, the only place where she had roots. They moved there in 1981, when Sam was twenty-eight. Robert was a Baptist and a church-going man, so the family joined the Baptist church in the city. The magnetism was still working for Sam, but she was trying to cut down on the affairs. She says, "Settling down in Albuquerque would be permanent, and I needed to make my family my first priority." Volunteering to be the director of the children's program and changing her wardrobe to one befitting a matronly way of life were first steps. With her appearance changed, her charisma quenched, she brought about an end to all affairs. It took great effort to leave the frenetic carefree life of sexual pleasures behind, but she succeeded in becoming a model wife and mother for a while. Then she met Diane, a most unlikely person to win her heart.

Unlike Sam, Diane was born into a family with the education and means to give her a good life. Her birth was anticipated with joy. Diane grew up in Romulus, Michigan, fifty miles from Detroit. Her parents were both educators. She had a sister twelve years older, so by the time she was ten, she was the only child in the house. Diane says, "Until I became a young adult, I thought I was brought up in a typical African

American family. My parents were well traveled, going abroad every spring while I stayed with my aunt or grandmother. There was never a doubt that I would go to college." She lived in a rural area where ranch-style houses were surrounded by acres of beautiful lawns and trees. She considered this a city.

In Romulus, there were two elementary schools. One was predominately white, the other mostly black. Diane's parents, James and Joyce Bryant, sent her to the all-white elementary school, because they thought she would receive a better education there. A cab brought her to school every day. Diane never felt the sting of prejudice there, but her friends were mostly black girls from her own neighborhood.

Diane's mother was the one who discriminated against her. Diane remembers, "My mother grew up in the South and she had a lot of the stereotypical things going on. It was important to have fair skin and good hair. The lighter you were, the better you could get along in the world. My sister had fair skin and good hair. They had tried to have a baby for twelve years after my sister was born. Then here I come, and I didn't have fair skin or the kind of hair my mother wanted me to have." Good hair was fine and straight, easy to comb. Her mother spent a lot of time getting her perms to straighten her hair. She would say, "Oh, I work hard to make you cute," as if that would make Diane grateful. Looking back, though, Diane thinks her mother loved her as well as she was able.

Diane grew up having a rich church life. Both of her grandfathers were ministers and her father was a deacon. It was in church that she met her first openly gay person. "He was the music director. It was typical that in a black church the music director or minister of music was gay. I just remember that he always had the fanciest clothes. The congregation knew it. Those things were just not discussed. People accepted it as, 'that's just the way it is.' Homosexuality was not a topic for the minister's sermons."

It was the spontaneous decision of her mother, whose life was filled with such surprising decisions, which brought them to live in Albuquerque when Diane was ten. She says, "My mother was in a manic phase then, and when she was in a manic phase she had to do something big. We would get a new house, or redecorate, or there was a project of some kind."

In Diane's mother's mind, if she felt well, she didn't need medications for her illness, but not using them caused a cycle of pain for the family. If her mother's crash from the high was severe enough, Diane's father would have her hospitalized. For her sake, he couldn't let the neighbors see when she became vicious, paranoid, psychotic, and suicidal. In the hospital, she would resume the medications she had stopped taking.

At age fourteen Diane was asked to accept more responsibilities around the house. At sixteen she was asked to watch over her mother after school, a job for a skilled psychiatric nurse, not a child who was dealing with all her own upheavals of adolescence. As Diane looks back, she says, "I think I have worked through the anger of being given that responsibility." But at the time, she expressed her anger with rebellion.

She was given access to the family cars so she could drive to school and run errands for her mother, but when her father was home she used the car to get away. Her father was so preoccupied with caring for her mother that he didn't check up on the times his sixteen-year-old daughter got home. "I was going to places where I shouldn't be, like bars and supper clubs. There was a strip of bars and clubs on one block that I loved to visit. My favorite was a club called the Hole in the Wall."

Sheree, an unlikely and probably mentally unstable friend, brought sixteen-year-old Diane there. Diane says, "I babysat for her kids and she hung out down there, and I ended up hanging out with her."

When Diane walked into the Hole in the Wall, for the first time, wave after wave of sensations washed over her. Temporarily blind while her eyes adjusted to the dimly lit room, she felt the darkness. It was as tangible as the smell of the burning cigarettes, the sound of the deep base of rhythm and blues, the laughter and chatter of many voices. When her eyes adjusted, people emerged, every shade of brown. They were sitting at round tables on spindly chairs, upholstered with worn plastic seats. No one looked under thirty-five. Through an entry way at the back she could see a dance floor and part of a bar. Laughing, flirting, dancing—there was an energy here missing in her lonely, middle-class life.

A tall slender man with broad shoulders approached them from the dance floor in the adjoining room. The boys at school never looked at her with the frankness and pleasure that this man did. His black beard and mustache enhanced the white teeth he flashed at them. "Hello, Sheree, who's this you've brought with you?"

"This is the girl who babysits my kids. I thought she might like to have some fun tonight. Diane, this is Rodger." She added, laughing, "Watch out for him, Honey. He's a lady-killer." Rodger had a reputation for dating much younger women. He was thirty-six and didn't want anyone over twenty. It pleased him that Diane was very young and inexperienced. He lowered his voice a little and said, "It's a pleasure to meet you, Diane."

Diane couldn't think of anything to say so she just smiled. "It felt like I was in a movie and I was playing a part," she says. "At sixteen I was naïve and had no common sense. I was dazzled by the fact that he was interested."

Rodger was interested in parading his sixteen-year-old "girlfriend" around and fantasizing about sex. He liked having a virgin on his arm. Diane was a child more interested in fast food, Michael Jackson's music, and driving his car than Rodger's advances. "He took me to any of the places I wanted to go—Burger King, McDonalds. It was way, way fun. There were no limits to what he could purchase. I had all of the Michael Jackson albums, all of the ice cream I could eat. Even with all of the gifts, I was probably a cheap date compared with the women he had dated."

After Diane was seventeen, Rodger wanted more and more of her time and body. She was wise enough to get away from him and live with her aunt in Arizona, where she finished high school and entered Arizona State University. Before she left, because she didn't want to lose him all together, she decided to give him a "parting gift."

The sexual act in itself solidified her plans to leave New Mexico. With understatement that is so natural to her, Diane says, "That was a less than desirable event. It was painful and repulsive and I wanted no part of his body after that." She still enjoyed the shopping, the fast food, and driving his car. Diane's parents and aunt were unaware that Diane was still communicating with Rodger from Arizona and planned to marry him as soon as she was eighteen. "With him, I didn't have to do anything I didn't want to do, and I would never have to go home again." At semester's end, she went back to Albuquerque.

She and Rodger were married in Las Vegas, July 26, 1985, with her mother in attendance and her father pacing the hall outside. He could not be a part of giving his daughter to a "pervert." Diane was looking forward to a life of fun and freedom from responsibility. She forgot that she would have to have sex with Rodger.

Diane considered sex a "chore." She never felt any desire for Rodger and tried to put him off as much as possible. Once a month was about all he could coax or bully her into. The only arguments they had were about sex. When their baby daughter, Courtney, was born, Diane naïvely decided that she had fulfilled her responsibility as a wife and that would be an excuse for not having sex any more.

Diane and Rodger began to live separate lives. Feeling the sexual tension, Rodger went out with friends and women at the bar. The last thread holding them together was Courtney. Rodger had a true affection for his daughter.

Diane had resigned herself to the life she was leading. Her joy was Courtney. She had her daughter, her friends, and she liked her job at the furniture store. She furnished the house with the discounts and money she earned there. She thought that was the way it would always be. She would have laughed if someone told her that the unattractive "fashion challenged" woman she had recently noticed in church would become her one true love.

Diane had noticed Sam, Robert, and their three boys when they started coming to church. Robert was such a handsome man and the children were clean and impeccably dressed. How then, Diane thought, could those children have such an unattractive mother? Her opinion was shared by all of her friends. Diane announced to them, "She is the frumpiest woman I've ever seen! She is tall and lanky, with no sense of style."

Burned into her memory forever was a vision of the first time she saw Sam. Sam was wearing an orange dress that clashed with the honey brown of her skin. "It's horrible," Diane remarked to her friends. "This woman needs to go shopping, like, immediately!" Later, Diane came to see the orange dress, and others just as unfashionable, as a disguise. Diane says, "When Sam is her true self, her magnetism begins."

Sam disagrees, "It wasn't a disguise; I was living a different life. I was working very *hard* to live a different life."

Diane teases, "I think she was trying to win 'Mother of the Year.'"

"I was not!"

Along with being the recreation director of one of the gyms at the Air Force base in Albuquerque, Sam had put her energy into directing the church's youth program. She needed help from time to time. Diane volunteered on one occasion, and they became friends instantly. Neither one of them was thinking beyond that. Sam remembers, "I thought as far as church was concerned she was fine, but as far as a personal relationship was concerned, I didn't think she was up to it. She was young and immature." Sam was thirty-six, Diane, twenty-three.

Diane laughs, remembering, "She told me later that she didn't want to hang out with me, didn't want any part of me." Sam nods in agreement and explains the reason. "Our families had started doing things together. We'd go to the base to hear the old groups like the Temptations or the Drifters, that kind of thing. I liked that, but Diane wasn't into that. She was a youngster. She wanted to go down to the Hole in the Wall where the youngsters hang out. I wasn't comfortable down there. It wasn't my kind of place."

Diane counters, "It was a lot of fun there."

In spite of these differences in age and sensibilities, their friendship grew. When she completed her coursework for graduation from Abilene Christian University, Sam was proud of her accomplishment. "It was a long time coming, so I wanted to go through the graduation ceremony. When you graduate from ACU, you have to have a male escort who also wears a gown. Robert and I would have to spend the night there, so I asked Diane to babysit with our boys."

When they returned from ACU, Diane presented their sons to Sam and Robert just as clean, well-fed, and impeccably dressed as Sam had left them. Sam says, "After that I realized that anyone who would take care of three kids and do the job that well must be all right." The two women began to talk in earnest. They talked on the phone and in person. They talked about everything imaginable and still had more to talk about the next day. Sam remembers, "I knew after we started talking that Diane was my soul mate."

Sam wanted to tell Diane everything, and did. Diane could not believe her own response when Sam revealed her past exploits with her girlfriends in Germany. Diane remembers that she eagerly blurted, "If you ever feel the need to love women again, you should not run rampant like you did there. You should seek me." Sam began to think, "I've never heard anyone say anything like that. What does it mean? Does it mean she's interested in me? Does it mean she's truly a friend and wants to help me?" With all of her thinking, she couldn't understand the meaning of it. Diane didn't exactly know, either.

One afternoon several weeks later, Diane came to visit Sam at her home. Diane wandered into Sam's bedroom. Sam thought, "She must be telling me something." They had not touched or kissed, even as friends, so it was a complete shock to Diane when Sam took her shoulders in strong hands, pinned her to the wall, and kissed her. It was a serious kiss, hard and long. It touched a switch that turned on every nerve in Diane's body. After she stopped trembling she gasped, "What is my mother going to say?" Before Sam had time to finish asking her own question, "What does your mother have to do—?" Diane was gone.

Sam didn't hear from Diane later that day or the next. She thought, "Wow, I think I messed up the best friendship I've ever had." She couldn't call Diane. She felt that what she had done was too appalling for forgiveness. She had never felt anything like the desolation she suffered then. "I couldn't eat. I couldn't sleep or think. I prayed that she would call me." When the phone finally rang, she knew it was Diane. She whispered, "I didn't think you'd ever call again, and I wasn't going to call you, because you ran out."

"No, I'm okay. I was just thinking. Nothing like that has ever happened to me before. There are so many consequences that go with kissing you." Diane was thinking to herself, "This is intriguing and this is going to go further. What's going to happen now?" Later she realized, "That kiss ended my marriage. That was it. There was no one else in my life but Sam."

Among her staff at the gym, Sam was known as a person who avoided phones. Now they noticed she was on the phone every spare moment. After work Diane came out to the base. They talked there. They went out for lunch and talked. Sam remembers a pivotal night, "One night we stayed in the base parking lot in my car and talked until five in the morning. We were really, really connecting then." Sam was learning something about herself: talk is sometimes as important and satisfying as sex.

When Diane realized they had stayed out all night, she was worried about going home. Her husband hadn't been violent, but he was intimidating. Twenty years older than Diane, he definitely set the rules in the house. Sam wasn't worried about her husband. "I figured I could take mine out if I had to. I felt I could hold my own with anybody."

Staying out until five o'clock in the morning was way beyond the limits of their husbands' tolerance. Rodger had been more or less in control until Sam came along. His pride was linked to having a wife half his age, and he treated her like a princess and showed her off to friends. Aside from having sex with him, she complied with his wishes. To Diane, Rodger was a cross between a male authority figure and a sugar daddy. She worked at a minimum wage job and stayed home with their daughter. Almost everything, except the furniture she bought, was provided for her and Courtney. She knew her late night out would not be tolerated.

Sam remembers the morning after. "When *she* got home, her husband was awake. When *I* got home, my husband was awake. They both had called each other, and they both had called Diane's mother. We were in trouble then."

Mrs. Bryant called Sam and said, "I do not want you to sit with Diane's family in church anymore. I do not want you talking to her." Sam was politely quiet until she finished, then forgot about it. It wasn't quite as easy for Diane.

The next night Diane received a visit from her mother and father. Without uttering a word, her father scooped Courtney into his arms and carried her and her stroller out the door. Her mother cornered Diane in the house with Rodger. "I could hear Rodger listing his grievances: 'She doesn't do this. She doesn't do that. She does this with Samantha or that with Samantha.'" Her mother waved her finger in Diane's face and said, "You are seeing way too much of Samantha Jeffers. That's not right, two women sitting in a car all hours of the night. You should be home with your husbands. You need to have sex with your husband. How could you be so disrespectful to God?" Diane couldn't think of anything to say. She never could when her mother got like this. One thing she did know: sex with Rodger was not going to happen. "And another thing," her mother said, breaking into her thoughts, "you are not going to talk with Samantha or sit by her in church any more." When her mother left, Diane had time to think. She *would* see Sam, and she *would* talk with her again. The time was over for her mother to order her around.

A few weeks later, Sam devised a plan for them to see each other alone. She sent their families off to eat Easter Sunday dinner without them under the pretext that she and Diane needed to finish work on the church pageant that evening. Sam smiles, saying, "That's when I kissed her for the second time."

Diane wasn't necessarily looking forward to another kiss. She was in love with the companionship she shared with Sam and was glad to see Sam for any reason. The first kiss had been electrifying, but she treasured more the feeling of completeness she had in Sam's presence. Even so, Diane met Sam's lips willingly, knowing that this kiss would turn her world upside down.

Tensions between Diane and Rodger were tightening. He didn't know if Diane was in love with Sam or a man. His grip on her was loosening and with it, his self respect. His authoritative manner and his money had insured that the women he had known had done what they were told. When he found a note in Diane's dresser signed, "I love you," he was enraged.

Diane was getting ready for bed when Rodger burst into the room with a menacing look in his eyes and the note from Sam in one hand. Diane was not looking at his face. She only saw the hot iron he held in his other hand. He pushed her down on the bed and held the iron over her face. "Who do you love, Diane? Who dares to tell you they love you? Who do you love? Me?" The iron came closer with every question. "Who wrote the note?" Diane couldn't answer. His arm was pressing so hard on her chest that she couldn't. He left as quickly as he had come, throwing the note and the iron onto the bed.

They both divorced their husbands a few months later and everything was settled quickly. The judge awarded Sam the house since she had custody of the children. They arranged for the fathers to have their children every other weekend. In the summers they could have them for six weeks. Sam and Diane never asked for anything from their ex-husbands but child support.

Shortly after his divorce, Rodger went to the Hole in the Wall and found a woman younger than Diane's old age of twenty-four. As time passed, Robert only wanted the boys every other summer and then kept them only three weeks instead of six. Within a year he had married an older white woman who had older children of her own.

In 1991 Diane and Courtney moved in with Samantha, Lavar, Jamal, and Sharrod. The mix was awkward for a while. As Diane puts it, "Four little people were a *lot* of people. The boys were five, seven, and nine. Courtney was two." Sharing was new for Courtney. Unlike the boys who were used to compromising, she was an only child accustomed to all of the attention. Diane and Sam had to resolve the issues of sharing and space, reconfiguring the bedrooms, who was to discipline whom, and what the rules for behavior would be. There were a lot of logistics to figure out. Living with so many bodies was hard for Diane, too. "I came from a small family," she says. "My sister was significantly older, so I don't ever remember a time when there were two kids in the house. I remember thinking that six is a lot of people." Sam says, "Considering everything, there was very little fighting. All of the children got along well. We were going to have a children's bathroom and an adult's bathroom before two-year-old Courtney protested. We ended up with a girl's bathroom and boy's bathroom because Courtney said, 'Boys have cooties!'"

In six months, when the living arrangements were running smoothly, Sam thought it was time for them to have a commitment ceremony in the Metropolitan Community Church in Albuquerque. Diane laughs and says, "It was to be one of many ceremonies." Sam has to agree: "I'm a ceremonial person."

"She'd have a ceremony every year."

"Yeah, just so she knows how much I love her. Anyway, we had our first ceremony in July of '91. We wrote our own vows and exchanged rings."

Inside their rings were the words, "Love Prevails." They didn't know then, just how much they would rely on those words.

Poverty was their major problem. Sam had just finished college a few months before and Diane had not yet gone back to school. Diane says, "We had to get me through an elementary education degree and her through her master's in parks and recreation administration, then me with my master's in administration, and Sam finishing her doctorate." Sam was the major breadwinner at first, but $19,000 a year didn't go very far with four children to feed. After Robert remarried he had pressure from his wife to spend his money on her children instead of his own. Rodger never remarried and helped Courtney consistently.

Since she was Director of Recreation at the base, Sam could hire Diane for one of the many part-time jobs that were available. Diane also worked as a part-time aide at an elementary school. When asked how they got by in those lean years, Sam quickly replied, "By the grace of God. When we were down to our last nickel, a dollar would show up. Sometimes we'd go to the mail box and there would be a letter from someone we didn't remember, or some company would give us a refund because we had overpaid the bill." Sam had a three-year-old Honda Civic and Diane had a new Chevrolet; they sold the cars in order to send the children to a private church school. Sam says, "We bought two raggedy old Volkswagens. The kids were afraid to ride in mine, because you could see the street through the rusted-out floor boards." They drove those cars for eight years.

Diane took on the responsibility of cooking and it was a challenge to have healthy meals. Sam says with a laugh in her voice, "We use to buy potato soup in giant cans from Costco. We served it quite often." One evening at dinner, Sharrod, Sam's oldest son, put down his spoon and looked at his mother. He puffed himself up until he looked like the spokesman for the other children, and pronouncing each word slowly with determination said, "We…don't…want…any…more…potato…soup!" His request was granted, but Diane would not budge on Malt-O-meal, even when at breakfast one day Jamal said, "No more Malt-O-Meal for no reason!" The hot breakfast cereal was part cream of wheat and part chocolate malt — nutritious, inexpensive, and easy to get on the table in a morning crowded with preparations for school or work. Diane would fix eggs once in a while, but Malt-O-Meal was the staple. Diane says, "We also had a lot of chicken and ground beef, rice, and potatoes. The butcher at the grocery was really kind to me. He told me how to cook the cheaper cuts of meat and how to make them go farther by adding carrots and potatoes. We also had a lot of spaghetti."

They dressed their children well, but designer clothes were out. Sam and Diane would search for sales and shop in affordable department stores. The younger boys received some hand-me-downs. If they got name-brand clothes for Christmas or a birthday, it was from Sam's mother. Diane remembers, "We worked very hard to be sure that Christmas was a happy time. The children had multiple resources at Christmas. They would get gifts from us and from their dads and grandparents.

In Spite of Everything....

Christmas and birthdays were never an issue. It was day-to-day life that was hard." Diane says, "We would tell our children that life was going to get better. Things were going to change because Sam and I were going to school." The big question that the boys asked was, "When will we be done with Arizona jeans?" Even though they have more than enough money now, both Sam and Diane are frugal shoppers. Diane says, "I never pay full price for anything."

The boys complained about food and clothing. Courtney had deeper concerns. When she was in second grade, Diane found a note Courtney had written. Printed in capital letters were the words, "I HAT LEZ BEANS." By the time she was in sixth grade, she was having crushes on girls and was worried that she was a "lez bean" herself. Diane explained that she wouldn't be a lesbian just because she and Sam were. It was natural to have very close girlfriends in school and she should enjoy her friendships. By the time she was beginning middle school, Courtney was very interested in boys and had come to accept Diane's and Sam's relationship.

It took eight years of dedication and sacrifice to reach a comfortable living standard. Education was their means to success. They thought taking turns going to school would take too long and only tried that for one semester. Sam began to work in the day time and go to school at night. Diane went to school in the day time and worked at night. Sam says, "Since I was supervisor of activities at the base recreation center, I could take the kids to my job. Being supervisor allowed me to work out our schedules to suit our lives."

Every other Friday the children would go to their fathers. While Courtney would only spend one day with Rodger, the boys would spend the weekend with Robert. Sam adds, "We did what we had to do, and it was long days and short nights. There was little money and little food, but I think we did a good job with what we had." When their friends would ask, "What keeps you going?" Sam's immediate answer was, "Our love for each other, wanting to do the best for our kids, and trying to be the best we can be. When people are gripey and things are stressful, we always look inside our rings and say, 'Love Prevails,' and if we think about that and talk about that, we figure it out."

In 1995, Diane got a job as an elementary teacher. With both of them working, Diane says, "We felt like we had made it." They didn't stop there. After three years, Diane started coursework for her master's degree in administration.

Every day of every year that Diane and Sam were struggling to overcome poverty to give their children a good education and educate themselves, Diane's mother was calling on the phone at five or six in the morning to warn them, "You're going to Hell. God will punish you for living in sin. You'll die in a burning Hell." Diane remembers, "She never could let it go. She thought if she could continue long enough, she would be able to break us up."

In spite of her mother, Diane and Sam continued to bring the children to church. Diane explains, "We always believed that the children needed to have continuity. Robert was there. The grandparents were there. My father had a leadership role in the church. We continued to think that church was the right place, even though my mother was being mean. She would tell people that we were living in sin and asked them to pray for us. Our names would end up on the prayer list, announced to the whole congregation. Through all of this we never had any issues with anybody. They knew us and knew our children. We had a history there. It would be difficult for someone to mistreat us or the children." Sam adds, "Her mother's friends were our friends, too, and they would tell us what she was saying. They would also say, 'We love you for who you are.'"

Finally, Sam and Diane had enough of Mrs. Bryant's harassment and moved to Las Vegas. They were only an hour-and-a-half flight away from Albuquerque, so their children could still have relationships with their fathers. They were both able to get better paying jobs there, with better chances for advancement. Courtney was starting middle school. Lavar and Jamal were in high school. Sharrod, who was twenty, stayed in Albuquerque to be closer to his father.

After teaching for a year in Vegas, Diane secured the job of assistant principal of an elementary school. It wasn't long before she was promoted to principal of another school in Old Las Vegas where the first wealthy entrepreneurs had settled. The children in her school were from families who had lived there for generations, including the mayor's and the governor's children. Besides the old money from the established population, there was new money from the hotels and casinos. Deservedly proud, Diane says, "I am the first minority to be chosen as principal in the school's history. The school turns fifty-one years old this year."

Because she had dropped out of college to live with Rodger, Diane made up for lost time by going to school every summer, earning certifications that far surpassed the candidates in her age range. "I felt that I had wasted five years of the time it would take to be where I wanted to be professionally. We have also tried to set good examples for our children." After fifteen years with Sam, the summer of 2005 was the first that Diane was not taking university classes.

When Diane got the promotion, she was allowed to take some of the teachers from her previous school. Because she was respected and well-liked, many more wanted to go with her than could. "Four or five teachers came with me from my old school where I was assistant principal," Diane says. "Some of them knew that Sam and I are partners." Most people didn't seem to care one way or the other. The exception was Anne Davis, one of Diane's best teachers. Before Diane made her final list, she was torn between taking or leaving Anne. "She was hurt and very dramatic about our being lesbians," Diane says, "Even so, she wanted to come. I was apprehensive at the thought that she was so upset about our relationship." A mutual friend told Diane that Anne had said, "I just don't understand how she can go to church and be in a lesbian relationship."

Diane made her decision on the merits of Anne's teaching ability. She says, "Anne is an excellent teacher, so I sucked it up and picked her, even though there might have been problems. Sam moved all of the teachers' books and equipment. They didn't have to worry about anything. They loved her for that kind of thing. When Sam told Anne, 'I'll take all of your stuff, too,' there was an immediate turn around." Later, after they had all settled into their new surroundings, Anne said to the other teachers, "If everybody had a Sam, they'd all be happy all of the time."

Diane readily acknowledges that her popularity may have been boosted by the fact that many teachers were "in love" with Sam. Sam volunteered her computer and organization skills on Fridays. She still helps the office staff and any teacher who needs help anywhere in the building. Diane says, "It doesn't matter what color. It doesn't matter what age. Women are smitten with her." Then with an impish grin, she adds, "I too, was drawn into the trap."

Diane thinks she knows the reason why even the straight women love Sam: "Sam is a caregiver. She is also androgynous. For straight women she embodies the strength and power of a man but has the sensitivity of a woman. She cares about what's going on with them. If something needs to be fixed, Sam will fix it. She's a whiz on the computer and can help them solve any problem there." Sam meets their problems with a familiar phrase, "I'll take care of it." Diane says, "You can tell when people are having crushes on her, because too many things go wrong with their equipment that *never* go wrong. The more people that give her attention, the happier she is. She establishes relationships with the new teachers and the whole office staff has a collective relationship with her." There are lots of gay people in the Clark County School District. Sam says, "No one would ever guess about Diane unless they saw me hanging around. She is sooo femme." Diane laughs.

Sam has a bachelor's degree in physical education and a master's degree in parks and recreation administration. She had begun her doctorate when her career unexpectedly changed. Sam remembers, "It was after I was working at the gym on the base in Albuquerque in a civil service job that I got my first computer and began to learn a little about it. I was doing some things for the base gym that had never been done. No one knew how to work with a computer. I was making flyers about the programs at the recreation center. The people in the command headquarters saw what I was doing in the Moral Welfare and Recreation Department I worked under." The chief over MWR came to ask, "We need someone to run the network for all of Albuquerque. Would you do that?"

"I'll try."

Her title was Computer Specialist. She says, "The job requirements were listed. All I had to do was find a book and figure it out. I spent a good deal of my time learning how to solve problems with computers. My career has been on the rise since then." By the time they moved to Las Vegas, Sam had become competent in many facets of computer science. She landed a job with the government as head of computer technology for Las Vegas. Diane calls Sam a "geek." Sam counters, "That's because I read a lot of computer books so I can understand what I'm doing." Sam is very modest about her success. "I've done a few things, nothing huge, but some things were noticeable and rewarded."

"When we moved to Las Vegas in 1999, everything changed, because both of our salaries doubled," Diane recalls. "We went off and left everybody we knew in New Mexico behind, professionally, economically, socially.

In Spite of Everything....

We went from making $50,000 a year together to closer to $90,000. Now we almost make that much individually. Sam went up a government grade or two when we moved here. We had a small house in Albuquerque and moved to a house in Las Vegas that had 3,500 square feet. It was a huge change and obvious to the children." Diane and Sam used their rise from poverty to teach their children the importance of a good education. Sam says they told them, "If you are going to be successful, you have to do whatever it takes to get an education." Diane adds, "We have had that conversation with them a number of times. They're all old enough to remember what it was like *before* we graduated and *after* we graduated." Sam says, "Everything in the house is new. We brought nothing from the old place. We earned it. We bought it. We deserve it."

In 1999, Diane's father died. Mrs. Bryant grieved for a long time, but began to adjust. Diane's sister Beverly offered to come and live with her, but Mrs. Bryant said, "No, I don't want you living with me. I have a new life and I don't need anyone." For three years, she stayed on her medicine and enjoyed her friends and a place of prominence in the church. She read, sewed, and enjoyed taking care of her house. In 2002 she stopped taking the medicine because she said she didn't need it. "That was the cycle," Diane says. "Every three to five years psychotic patients tend to go off their medicine. There are a few months of deterioration and then years getting back to normal lives again." This down cycle was a disaster for Mrs. Bryant. She shocked her friends with her paranoia, disrupted church services, and called people on the phone and insulted them. She lost everything.

When she realized what she had done, she would no longer attend church or face her friends. Without her "queen bee" position, Joyce Bryant wanted no part of her old neighborhood. Mrs. Bryant called Diane and asked her if she could come live with them. Diane refused; she felt that her mother would be a disruptive presence in their lives. Courtney was in middle school, and sixteen-year-old Lavar and eighteen-year-old Jamal were still at home. Diane couldn't forgive the hateful words her mother had spewed over her all those years.

When Diane hung up, Mrs. Bryant called Sam's cell phone. Sam says, "For her to call me and ask if she could live with us was a big deal. The only right thing to do was to let her. But it's been hard with her being here."

Mrs. Bryant never called Diane and Sam sinners again, and she did ask them for forgiveness for everything she had said. Even so, Diane says, "Once in a while we see that uppity part of her that says, 'I'm better than you,' but then she looks around and sees that she is in our house. The deal is: she has to take care of herself. We leave the medication out and it's up to her to take it. She has to go to appointments when they're due." Diane told her mother, "You can't stop taking your medicine. If you do, you'll have to live somewhere else."

Mrs. Bryant didn't have any interests in life when she first came in 2002. She still doesn't read or sew like she used to. She does enjoy comparing herself to the other elderly women at church, since she looks ten to twenty years younger. She is still a slender, beautiful woman at eighty, and still proud of her light skin. She likes to live with Diane and Sam because they have fine things.

Even though only six percent of the population is black in Las Vegas, they have experienced no prejudice. Diane says, "We go to an African American church with five thousand members. We and the children are very active in the church. While we don't have conversations with people about it, we don't hide our relationship either. When we go to church, we sit in the pew as a family."

Now Courtney is finishing her senior year of high school. Taller than her mother, she has her grandmother's hourglass figure. She is an outspoken young woman, like her mother, and knows what she wants. She is beautiful and likes fine, expensive things. She doesn't like her grandmother living with them, because she doesn't like another adult in the house telling her what to do.

Sam's youngest, Lavar, is twenty and has begun studies at Alabama A and M where he was offered a full-ride scholarship for his 4.5 high school grade point average. The middle son, Jamal, is very much an introvert and didn't find his niche in high school. Diana laughs and adds, "He's the one who is never going to leave home. It was hard to get him to finish high school. He took a test and got a grade-equivalent diploma, but never finished his courses for a regular diploma. He is more than content to live at home and work twenty-seven hours a week at the neighborhood grocery. He makes enough to make payments on a new little car, pay the insurance for it, and pay rent. He's happy. He's a home kid." Sharrod, now twenty-four, is a computer geek like his mother. "He was the one most hurt by his mother's divorce," Diane says. "He was more cognizant of his mother leaving his father for me. When we went to New Mexico for Thanksgiving, he wouldn't see us. He spent time with the kids, but he wouldn't see his mother and me. He was pretty angry, because his father is unhappy in his new marriage."

Sam and Diane are thinking about moving back to Albuquerque. The housing market in Las Vegas has exploded. Diane says, "The house we paid $225,000 for six years ago is appraised at $600,000 now. We can't afford to stay. We can sell our house and pay off another one in Albuquerque. Our salaries won't be as big in Albuquerque, but we wouldn't have a house payment, the biggest expense. The amount of money we spent in Vegas is amazing." Whatever the future brings for Sam and Diane, they will meet it with the faith and love that has sustained them in the past.

"We have a relationship that I never knew could be," Sam says. "I have a person who accepts me just as I am. I have no desire to go out with other women. That was instantaneous when we started talking twenty years ago. Diane is all I want or need."

Diane adds, "Love prevails."

Vida and Helena

Although Vida's and Helena's experiences in childhood were very different, they were both rooted in the culture of Puerto Rico. Their respective parents faced hardship, prejudice, and poverty, but held on to the values of their native land while striving to fulfill the American dream.

In 1929, three years before Puerto Rico became a Commonwealth of the United States, Vida's mother, Madeline Hernandez, was preparing for her third year in college. This was unheard of for a woman then, but Madeline was no ordinary young woman. When she received a letter from her sister Rita in the United States saying that she was being held as an indentured servant, Madeline postponed her education, summoned her courage, and made the long boat trip to New York City to rescue her sister. The wealthy family offered no resistance when Madeline boldly came to the house and took her sister away.

Because the boat from Puerto Rico wouldn't return for six months, the young women looked for work and a place to live. Sweatshops were the only jobs available. The sisters worked twelve to fourteen hours, six days a week, making enough money to rent a tenement in a barrio. Madeline hoped to continue her education in the U.S., but no college in New York would accept her. Even so, she decided to make a life in New York.

Madeline and Rita valued the Puerto Rican custom of living in close proximity with relatives for support and comfort. When two other sisters came to New York a year later, they lived as close to Madeline as they could and moved into her building when an apartment became available. When Madeline married Antonio Salazar, their families became one. Vida remembers, "We lived in one building with one aunt on the top floor, another on the bottom floor, and one on the middle floor where we were." There were always loving hands to care for the children, generous hearts to help others in need. Vida's relatives were poor by most New Yorkers' standards, but they had the power of family combined with the energy ignited by a vision of the American dream.

Antonio Salazar felt that it would be impossible for him to get more education with a growing family to care for. Vida says, "His culture dictated that in order to maintain pride in his manhood, his wife could not help support him." In 1946, when his fourth child, Vida, was born, he was working as a mechanic in an automobile service center, but the family still lived in poverty. His outstanding work impressed a man named Henry Draper, who offered Antonio enough money to leave the security of their extended family.

Vida says, "In 1950, when I was four years old, we left our amazingly loving, passionate, extended family and moved to Chicago. For me it was very lonely. Everyone in the barrio where we had lived in New York spoke Spanish. I was used to seeing myself and my culture reflected around me, everywhere I went and in everything I did. When I went to Chicago, the Puerto Rican Diaspora, a critical mass of people, hadn't arrived. We lived in an Eastern European neighborhood, so there were few people who looked or spoke like me." She only got to see her family in New York City twice a year and relatives in Puerto Rico every two or three years.

Whenever she met any Latino child in her school, she always felt they were her relatives. Whether they were Mexican, Venezuelan, Central American, she thought they were part of her extended family. She says, "I was completely unaware, until I was much older, that there was animosity among Latino groups." She would see a Mexican child at school and think, "Oh, my brother!" When she was rebuffed by some, she realized that there was a difference. Eventually she would learn that Puerto Ricans are the only Latino people who may enter and leave the United States without documentation. Vida says, "It was a huge benefit, to be United States citizens. That caused hostility between Mexicans and Puerto Ricans; after all, they had once settled in California and Texas."

Vida's family spoke Spanish exclusively at home. So that the children would not forget their native customs, her mother cooked Puerto Rican foods, danced Puerto Rican style, and recognized the island's celebrations and festivals. Even though she loved her heritage and her people, Vida's mother encouraged her children to marry "white" so they would be as American as possible. Vida says, "She had internalized the prejudice of a hierarchy of color. She thought that more opportunities would come with whiter skin." She was glad that Vida was light-skinned, brown-eyed, and had fine, wavy hair.

Vida's older siblings married, lived nearby, and had children. They were building their own extended family in Chicago. Vida remembers, "On Sundays all of my family in Chicago would come to my mother's and father's home. Father would cook Sunday dinner. Then, after the women cleaned up, we would play games, relax, talk, nap, just be together. On Saturdays, my father would make my mother breakfast in bed."

"In our house," she continues, "love was the biggest part of family life, but it was also the era of spankings. Father's law was that children had to be in the house when he got home from work. Sometimes that was 4:30 p.m.. Yelling, screaming, and castigation would ensue if we were late. We got hit for acting out, talking back, or not doing something right. We knew our parents loved us," Vida says. "We would laugh, hug, kiss, and play with each other and tickle and wrestle. We were very physical. Everything was in the extreme — extreme joy, anger, love."

There were definite lines drawn that separated the behavior of the sexes. Father, the macho man with a gruff voice, was the breadwinner and protected the family. Vida says, "The law was what he said. Negotiating and how to get around it were one of my life's goals." Her brothers were conditioned not to cry. Girls couldn't date without a chaperone and they had to live at home until they were married. Women were docile and needy and got their way by manipulation. "I was brought up to be dominated by a man, a subservient, dependent woman."

But Vida didn't quite fit into the niche that was carved out for her. Girls were to wear frilly blouses and crinolines under their skirts. She was a tomboy and liked to wear pants and play softball. She wanted a sled when she was ten, but that was a boy's toy so she was not permitted to have it. She didn't mind toe-dancing lessons, but insisted on wearing black shoes with her pink tutu. She thought black was more passionate.

Vida always had a best girlfriend. One friendship lasted through grade school. When she was thirteen she met a Puerto Rican girl, Rita, who looked so much like Vida that their own mothers mixed them up. Vida says, "When her mother developed diabetes, they moved back to Puerto Rico. I didn't know it then, but she was my first love. I can remember the pain I felt when she left, and the longing, and how I cried. I think she felt that way, too."

It still didn't register that she was weird or different, because she liked boys, too. Vida remembers, "I loved movie stars at the time — Paul Newman, Tab Hunter, Frankie Avalon, and Fabian. I had their pictures plastered all over my bedroom. I definitely was attracted to men and knew it." She attended an all girls' school. She liked the boys she would meet here and there, but didn't have much of an opportunity to get to know them. She lived at home when she went to college.

As she grew up her world became more complicated. Life in her neighborhood was becoming difficult. The Viet Nam War loomed ominously over her family. Two cousins with whom she had played in childhood were killed in Viet Nam within a few months of each other. Vida remembers, "Their deaths were transforming in many ways. They politicized me. When they handed my aunt the folded flag at the first funeral, something snapped in me. I might have been killed, too. My father would say, 'I'm backing my GI's in Viet Nam,' so I felt it would be unpatriotic to question the war." However, when her other cousin was killed seven months later, Vida became an anti-war activist.

Shortly after the deaths of her cousins, she met the man she would marry. Glen Watkins was very political, very aware of what was going on in the world. Vida says, "He was my education that burst the bubble I was raised in." They had little time to settle down after their marriage, because once Glen got his draft notice, their lives centered on avoiding the draft. Vida says, "We were sure that one morning the FBI would come and arrest him. We moved around in Chicago and New York until Glen couldn't run any more. Then we became hippies, with the hair, the VW van, and free love."

Vida began reading about philosophy. "I got much smarter and through the anti-war movement I met women who were active in resisting the draft." On weekends and holidays she traveled to Indiana and Michigan to participate in the ecology movement which was gaining momentum in the Midwest. Unlike the women she met in college, these women were knowledgeable, strong, and driven by purposes beyond finding a man to marry. Vida says, "I remember talking with a group of women and telling them that I wanted a man to lead me around like a cow with a ring in its nose." Vida saw a mixture of emotions on their faces, including horror, pity, compassion, and disbelief. "They gently, compassionately, caringly and firmly set me free." She went home and told Glen, "You don't have to light my cigarette, open the door, or any of that shit any more." Glen was, surprised and relieved. He didn't like doing that "shit" anyway.

Along with the political turmoil, women's liberation, and conservation awareness, it was the time of "free love." Vida remembers, "As far as love and sexuality was concerned, there was the questioning, the exploration, experimentation, and challenging of rigid norms. You didn't have to be patriotic, do-or-die. Maybe there was room to question other things."

In the midst of this turmoil, her good friend, Joan, who had been maid of honor at her wedding, told her without any preparation, "I have always had sexual feelings for you." Vida was shocked; she had never thought about this aspect of life. She toyed with the idea of having sex with her but by the time she made up her mind, Joan had changed hers.

"When I came to the realization that I was even interested in having sex with her, I thought I could be a lesbian. I didn't question it. I put it aside but realized it might be something I would try, although I still thought I was straight." That would change when Vida was twenty-three years old.

Vida was waiting in line at the checkout counter at Woolworth's, idly looking out the two sets of double doors onto the street. "I did something that I had probably done many times in my life but wasn't aware of until then. A very good looking woman walked past the first set of doors, and I positioned myself so that I could get a glimpse of her at the second set of doors. In Woolworth's, I learned that I was a lesbian. I don't remember ever hearing the word 'dyke' before, but that word came to my mind about myself as I enjoyed the slow graceful walk of the woman on the other side of the door." Vida had taken in every move, feeling an elemental stirring. At this realization, Vida's whole body said, "Wow! *I am a lesbian.*"

She didn't act on the inspiration "until I met a woman named Nikki, who was gorgeous. Man, was she gorgeous. I got a crush on her to beat all crushes. She made some moves in my direction." Nikki got to the point: "Why don't we do something?" Vida says, "I was a little afraid. The dyke concept was completely just in my head. I didn't know what to do." They did get together and it was as if Vida had come home. "All I wanted to do was touch her body, the softness. When I touched her, I thought, 'Oh, my God. I've been looking for this my whole life; it's so amazingly luscious, warm, and wonderful. This is where I want to be." Suddenly, she wanted Glen to go away.

On a warm summer evening, Vida's and Glen's lives separated. They were sitting on the curb in front of their apartment with their legs stretched out on the pavement, lazily discussing the issues of the day. Glen had been doing most of the talking, as usual, when she interrupted him. "You know, you have taught me so many things, and because of the things you've taught me, I have been able to learn and access so much more than I would have if I hadn't met you. But now I'm getting smarter and realizing that I know some things you don't. I want to also be able to teach you."

"Oh no, no, I can teach you, but you can't teach me."

They stayed together for a while, but at that moment a huge Detour sign sent Vida on a different route. "There was no way I was going to tuck my knowledge into my back pocket and leave it there to make him comfortable." She became part of the Feminist Movement while remaining a staunch anti-war activist.

Vida was drawn away from Chicago in the course of the next few months. She met Janet, a very serious anti-war activist, and followed her to Boston. Vida says, "In that year in Boston, I realized I would rather be with Janet and live in the company of women." Glen wanted to be with women, too. After he met someone, he and Vida divorced. Vida and Janet lived together for two years before they decided to live as friends. Vida met another woman whom she loved very much and lived with for six-and-a-half years.

Vida did enjoy dancing in the lesbian bars in Boston, but she rarely met women there. She enjoyed interacting with the women at concerts, poetry readings, or bookstores, or by doing political work where women would come together to make a difference in the world, and support one another. Vida says, "I always look back on being a young adult in the late sixties and through the seventies as having had the privilege and opportunity to live and think and grow in an incredible, exciting time." The times would get more exciting as her path led her into the world of music where she would meet her life-long love.

In 1976, a friend who knew of Vida's interest in drumming, told her about a woman in Boston who was an expert percussionist and willing to teach women who were interested in drumming. The instruments, of African and Caribbean origins, were gourds carved or filled with beads or adorned with "skirts" of beads. The gourds were hit with sticks, stroked with picks, or shaken. It took energy and a strong sense of rhythm to become a part of the group. Vida had both.

The group of seventeen women decided to become a band and called themselves La Triba. Vida remembers, "Because we were all women, we feminized the Spanish word *Tribu*, which means tribe. We were wonderfully diverse: Latina, African American, white, Jewish, Asian, Hawaiian, straight, lesbians — an amazing group." The names of the instruments were as exotic and diverse as the women who played them: conga drums, Arguido, shakeries, maracas, ding ballies, bongos. They started performing in a couple of lesbian bars. Vida helped put together an educational program which traced drumming from its roots in Africa to the Caribbean into the southern states, where it influenced jazz. They played in schools and were in demand for concerts. They played for National Women's Day and Take Back the Night events.

A woman wearing dark aviator glasses noticed Vida in one of the first concerts. She loved the exciting sound of hands beating taut leather, coupled with the shaking, stroking, and hitting of the gourds. Vida's full breasts and hips excited her. Vida moved gracefully, rotating her shoulders while she drummed.

Vida noticed the young, skinny woman, but there was no spark because, as Vida explains, "I am a person who needs to look deeply into people's eyes. When I looked in her direction all I could see were the glasses." But Helena didn't have any trouble seeing the enticing Vida through her cool, aviator glasses. It was 1976. Helena was twenty-one, eleven years younger than Vida, and a long way from gaining her attention.

Like Vida, Helena was born of Puerto Rican parents and brought up in poverty in New York City. Her parents, Joseph and Elana Rodriguez, wanted the best for their children and made sacrifices for them, but there the similarities ended. Helena's life was drab; the family was confined to a certain set of rules laid down by their Pentecostal church. It was quiet in her home, with little outward expression of love. There was no dancing and no popular music. The dreariness was compounded by her father's inability to provide for his family. He was fifteen years older than her mother. After losing his job at age fifty, it was very hard to find another. He finally found work with the City of New York as a health liaison officer, but barely earned a subsistence salary. To make matters worse, Joseph was a functioning alcoholic. He drank through the savings he had accumulated before he was married.

Helena's mother kept a tight rein on what there was of the money he currently made. The family was never able to get out of the projects even though Joseph tried his hardest to find other jobs. He was good in math and did some bookkeeping and accounting. Sometimes he would fill out taxes for people on the side. Five-year-old Helena would take the extra forms and pretend she was a bookkeeper, too. She put neat little numbers in the boxes, not knowing what it was all about. It brought a sense of order to her life.

Helena's mother had to get a job in a sweatshop to help pay rent. She worked from eight in the morning to five and went back from seven to eleven, sewing dresses, carefully hurrying, getting paid by the piece. She wouldn't allow herself any rest, sewing even after she got home, ignoring the pain in her fingers as the needle plunged through the cloth. She finished as many more pieces as her tired hands and eyes could manage. She had her own dreams and saved everything she could to attain them. But even with the combined wages of both parents, Helena's family lived in poverty.

After Helena turned nine years old, she came to the garment factory after school and helped her mother until she came home. Helena also took care of the house. She was well behaved in school and at home. If she did something wrong, she would be whipped with a belt, a brush, even with an electrical cord — anything that was handy. Her parents didn't do this in anger; it was the only option they knew to discipline children, as their Pentecostal church encouraged vigorous discipline.

"Spare the rod and spoil the child." Helena says. "I have reconciled the issue of the way my parents raised me and my brothers. They really didn't mean harm. They didn't know better. They did some very good things for us. They knew that the way out of poverty was academics, study, and culture." Even though popular music and dancing were forbidden by the church, Helena's parents believed that classical music would enhance their lives. They sacrificed so that Helena and her brothers could have music lessons and attend classical concerts. They even bought Helena a piano so she could practice her instrument of choice. Helena loved playing and improvising her own tunes.

Helena was a straight A student and valedictorian of her eighth-grade class. Because of this, she was able to attend Spence, an elite private school for the rich and famous which allowed gifted underprivileged students to attend on scholarship. Helena laughs, "We're not talking *little rich*. We're talking *big rich*. It was hard to fit in there." She went to school with Katherine Ford, whose parents owned the Ford Modeling Agency. Victoria Cartier from Cartier Diamonds was in the class behind. On holidays her classmates would go to Europe to ski or shop. Helena went back to keep house for her family on the twenty-first floor of the South Bronx project, where the borough's incinerator coughed its poison into the air. In spite of all the deprivation, Helena was accepted to many universities, including Yale and Harvard. She received one of the first Martin Luther King Jr. scholarships to Brandeis University. It was an opportunity of such magnitude that her parents did not protest her living away from home. In any case, it was time for Helena's mother to fulfill her own dream. She had saved enough money to put a down payment on a house in Florida. Soon after Helena entered college, she and Helena's father moved there.

At Brandeis, Helena majored in chemistry, and then switched to sociology before she graduated in 1978. College was an eye opener. She lived in a dorm her freshman year and began to realize that there were things other than drudgery. "I never got too wild, just missed classes once in a while." She didn't make straight A's because she was taking time to make friends.

In 1977, her junior year, she met Olivia, her first love. "I always knew that I had an attraction for girls and women, but this was the first time I acted on it." Helena had carried the irrational fear, promulgated by the church, that she would be struck dead if she committed the "eighth sin of homosexuality." But even the threatened wrath of God was not going to keep her from touching Olivia — Olivia, whose warmth reassured and thrilled. In her childhood, Helena had rarely been rewarded with a hug or a loving touch, but Olivia made up for that.

Helena became involved in college politics. *Standard Operating Procedure* was one of the books she had checked out of the library when in junior high school, so her political awareness had already been raised. "The book blew my mind, because I realized that the news being reported about the war in Viet Nam was false." During that time she had also come face to face with the politics of race in the ghetto where she lived. "As a Latino person I felt caught in between the African American community and the white community, and even within my own Puerto Rican community, because I had white skin privilege." Ninety-nine per cent of Puerto Ricans are a mix of black, native, and white. Having light skin gave one an advantage. It was considered more attractive and socially acceptable in the world. "My skin was light and I was born in America. But was I an American? I spoke Spanish and was brought up in the Puerto Rican culture. Who was I?"

She met other students of color at Brandeis who energized her. "I got affirmation from associating with a group of African Americans and Latinos who were outspoken. They were in rebellion of the philosophy of the idea that 'white is better.' All of the value put on various colors was just a hierarchy of oppression. You can't live in the South Bronx without seeing bigotry. I have come to believe that there is a fire in all of us and it just takes something to spark it." Her own experiences, along with Martin Luther King's assassination, and having read the Warren Report, contributed to Helena's interest in politics.

Helena graduated in 1978, but even with a degree from an esteemed college, she soon realized that business weren't lining up to snatch sociology majors. Helena wondered how to support herself. When Olivia's parents, Walter and Sylvia Smith, hired Helena to help them in their business, she found her true niche. In about three years she went from being a sales clerk to managing two stores. One time one of the Smiths' customers needed help with their bookkeeping and they paid Helena to assist their customer's CPA. The forms he was teaching her to use looked comfortable and familiar. They were much like the ones she had played with as a child. Helena found she had a gift with numbers and math and enjoyed the work immensely.

Helena and Olivia broke up in 1979. Helena says, "It was a typical break up with feelings of abandonment, but it wasn't a 'hate your guts' parting. I think we both participated in things 'not working.' Most people don't have their first partner for the rest of their lives. You have to practice at it. Part of the problem with coming-out relationships is it's really hard to figure out what you're doing. I was young and inexperienced. Olivia was bisexual and with a guy for a period after our break up."

In the next few years, many important changes occurred. Helena got her own apartment. She began working for the CPA she had been helping. She began to think that she could be an accountant, and she met Vida — energetic, colorful, dynamic, emotional, Vida.

Through the course of several years, Helena had seen Vida at *La Triba's* concerts and other gatherings of women. She had tried to flirt with her, but Vida hadn't responded. Helena was not deterred. Aside from the physical attraction, there was something in Vida's energy and joy of life that she was drawn to.

It was a piano that brought them together. Helena missed having one in her apartment. When she was growing up, practicing would take her to a different world. Now, every time she was near a piano, she couldn't resist playing. At the intermission of an open air performance of *La Triba*, Helena began improvising on the grand piano. Vida was taken by Helena's easy way with the instrument, how she was lost in the music. She still had the aviator glasses on, but they didn't matter so much this time. Vida says, "We began interacting, getting to know each other."

When one of the members encouraged Helena to audition later in the month, she accepted immediately. Although she had never had much practice on the conga drum, her rhythm was perfect. After the successful audition, Vida asked Helena if she wanted to join some of the members of the band at a woman's bar called Somewhere Else. She told Helena that Melanie, the disc-jockey, would play Latin music if enough Latinas came in. Before they had settled themselves in their chairs, the rapid salsa rhythm and beat struck like an electric charge. Before she knew it, Vida was in Helena's arms, whirling around the dance floor to a hot salsa number. Helena was strong and an excellent dancer. She led Vida at breathtaking speed. Vida says, "It was as if we had been dancing together forever. We connected in that dance and began to talk."

Vida excited Helena. Her soft, full breasts and sexy hips generated heat. Helena remembers, "I wanted to keep engaging in conversation, to keep her with me as long as possible." She asked Vida if she could drive her home. Helena confesses, "We were getting close to my apartment. We reached a point where, in all honesty, each of our houses was five minutes away. I gave her the line, 'How about if we stop at my house for coffee? I don't want to fall asleep on the way to your house.'" Vida looked away and rolled her eyes, but she said, "Okay." They talked as people who are attracted to one another do, but the specter of infidelity was lurking in the room, because Helena knew that Vida had a partner. She didn't know that they were in the process of separating.

For her part, because she was in a committed relationship, Vida felt it was wrong to engage in any kind of intimacy, even intense conversation. Even though her partner of six years and she had decided to separate, they were still living in the same house. They didn't start seriously dating until Vida was living alone. In fact, it was 1981, after dating two years, before Helena came to live with Vida in her apartment.

"Opposites attract" is an accepted concept. Often we are drawn to others who complement us. The abstract, free flowing, emotion-driven personality seeks a concrete, ordered, rational partner. With a little compromise, life is fuller and more energizing. Cool, reserved, independent, all-business Helena met hot, passionate, spontaneous Vida. In short, the immovable object met the irresistible force with a collision of nuclear proportions. With the help of a therapist for the next eleven years, they worked on defining themselves in the relationship, finding core elements of their personalities that were essential and shouldn't be given up, while discovering things that were essential to compromise so they could be together. They remember the arguments, the waving of hands, Helena's silences, and Vida's tears. In frustration Helena would say, "Feelings, feelings, feelings, everything is feelings. You can't make judgments on emotions. Emotions hide practicality. You're talking to me in a way that is hard for me to hear."

Vida would counter, "I don't want my expressions stifled."

Vida says, "She's Type A and I'm all over the place." Helena says, "Her feelings are huge and take up a lot of space. I can be too quiet about my feelings until they reach a certain point. We needed help in finding balance. We were doing everything we could to stay together. We made a commitment. For us, it was important to do whatever work was necessary."

Helena says, "Part of the reason for our early dynamics was that I'm a very independent person. We got into the control issues. I love to be able to control my own life. When you're in a marriage, there's a certain amount of control that has to be given up. It's always a work in progress. For me, the eleven-year gap in our age was more significant at ages twenty-three and thirty-four than it is now. She had a certain amount of maturity that I didn't have at that point. I didn't want her to keep me from being my own person, because there were things she wanted to change."

Vida's favorite song at the time began: "Just once can we finally find a way to make it right? Make the magic last more than just one night?" She says, "That's how I felt. We would have these wonderful passionate moments and next day we would have a big fight." After years of counseling and compromise, they found that sacrificing ego was not as painful as the thought of separating. Helena says, "It's always a struggle for us, but you know what? We found out that it's not that important. Being together is important. We love our companionship and the life we have made together."

One of the things that attracted Helena to Vida was Vida's attitude about life. Helena's pessimistic motto was, "Don't expect anything. Don't expect good things to happen. Just plod along." After living with Vida over a period of years, Helena began to see how negative her life mantra was. She says, "Vida helped me change that perspective. I watched how she lived. She's not so tied down. She sees the joy in life. When she smiles, you see the sun. I finally stopped thinking I was doomed to walk on this earth with shit on my shoe. Vida comes from the Spanish word 'vida,' meaning 'life.' She gave me life. She has helped me open up to enjoy myself. Sometimes I still feel like I'm a deadbeat. Part of it is the fact that I work a lot; sometimes it comes at the expense of having fun. Vida brings it to my attention that I need to relax. That's a life-long struggle for me."

One of the things that Vida loves about Helena is her determination and confidence. She says, "Anytime she would say to me, 'You know what

I've decided to do?' I learned that she would do it." Vida first experienced this determination shortly after they were together. Vida had picked Helena up from her work with the accountant, and as soon as she was in the car, Helena had said, "You know what I want to do? I want to be an accountant."

"How are you going to do that?"

"Well, I've got a college degree, so that's all I need as a prerequisite. I'll take two accounting courses while I'm working, then take the CPA exam."

Vida says with pride, "Her business is very successful."

Helena adds, "That was it. I hung up my shingle in 1983 and I've been in practice ever since. I've been going along with what was happening in my life and not fighting it. I've been very happy with the work I do. I try to be very empowering to other women."

Vida was working at a job she loved, teaching high school psychology and counseling. Their relationship was running more smoothly. Helena said, "You know what I'm going to do?" The answer — and result — was a master's degree in taxation from Bentley University.

In 1991, after eleven years together, they had settled into a good life. Having invested in a two-family dwelling with Carmine and Diana, another couple they had known for a long time, they were building equity in a home. Vida was a highly respected educator, now working on her doctoral dissertation, and Helena's accounting and tax firm was lucrative and expanding. Vida loved coming home to a quiet house and dinner with Helena. "I worked on my dissertation without interruption, then put my feet up, forget the stresses of teaching, and indulge myself in the comfort of our home. I loved the life we had made together."

Vida's bliss had a heart attack and fell to the floor when Helena said, "You know what I've decided to do? I'm going to have a baby." Vida knew what this meant, so she kept to herself thoughts which were, "Oh, no, oh no," and "No babies, no babies." Helena began to explore the possibilities. Vida began to articulate her reservations. She remembers, "We had been together for so many years that I knew I wasn't going to break up with her over this. I didn't want this, but knew I couldn't do anything to stop it."

Helena had always wanted children and knew the time was now. She was thirty-seven. She felt she had matured and had a lot to offer a child. She explained to Vida, "It's time. I'm going to have kids and you can be as involved or not involved as you want, but this is something I feel I need to do." Helena knew this decision might impact her relationship with Vida, but she was determined about having children.

Helena chose the sperm donor alone. After visiting several sperm banks, she settled on a small establishment, which outlined in detail the donor's personality profile. She chose a white man who had all of the attributes she wanted in a child.

Helena went to the first inseminations alone. Vida stayed at home, thinking, "No baby, no baby, no baby." The first attempts were unsuccessful, and Vida could see the disappointment in Helena's eyes. Vida says, "I knew I was doing the wrong thing. I came to the realization that I wouldn't be the first or last person to become a parent without wanting to, and I wouldn't be the first or the last to rise to the occasion." They talked with a therapist who validated the feelings of each. The therapist said to Vida, "Let her go with this, and you participate as much as you care to." Vida decided that she couldn't allow Helena to go it alone. Just before Helena went to be inseminated for the third time, Vida said, "Hey, Helena, how about if I go with you tomorrow?"

"You want to come?"

"Yeah, I'm here now. I understand what you need."

"Oh, I'd love it if you came."

For good luck, Vida brought an Akwabaa doll, an African doll that certain African women carried with them when they were pregnant to infuse beauty into their child. After Helena became pregnant that day, they were on their way to motherhood. In bed at night Vida would gently lay her hand on Helena's swelling belly, willing their child to be honest, loving, talented, loyal, and intelligent. "Every night I would add more attributes and adjectives."

In 1992, Vida was in the delivery room helping coach Helena through the delivery. Their friends Carmine and Diana were there, too. Vida was sure that she could see all of the attributes she had hoped for in their son the moment he was born, but there was one that was a big surprise. "Even though we knew the donor was white," Vida says, "We didn't expect the whitest baby we had ever seen and with red hair and freckles everywhere." Helena laughed at a picture that was taken shortly after the delivery. Vida is holding their little redhead, Alberto, with friends looking on. Helena says, "Who's paying attention to me? Afterwards it was like I got to carry the diaper bag and she got to carry the baby." Vida was totally involved. Helena says, "We always treat him as *our* kid. I just happened to birth him, but he is equally ours." Helena stayed at home for two weeks to enjoy their new son. For the next two months she went to work part-time and took him with her. She says, "Since I own my own business. I had the flexibility of bringing him to work." Helena did most of the caregiving at first since she was nursing Alberto. Vida bathed and read to him.

When Helena wanted another baby three years later, Vida was with her all the way. This time when she put her hand on Helena's belly at night, she felt a tingling. Vida said, "This baby does not want to be told what to be. The fetus is rejecting my efforts." She stopped trying to encourage personal characteristics and resigned herself to trying for curly hair. When their baby, Leta, was born, she had dark, curly hair, and she definitely had a mind of her own. Vida says, "She doesn't identify with girls. Before she could speak clearly she would say, 'I a boy.'"

"No, you're a girl."

"I a boy."

"You're a girl, because a girl has a vagina and a boy has a penis. You have a vagina."

"I a boy."

Vida says, "Here I have a boy and a girl and the girl thinks she's a boy. I wear makeup and have my hair styled. I pictured a cute feminine little girl. I bought her dainty little dresses, put ribbons in her hair. From the beginning, Leta wanted nothing to do with these things. She pulled out the ribbons, fussed about the frilly dresses. When she was two years old, we were all leaving the house. Leta had a dress on over a pair of leggings. In the morning, you know how it is, the parents holding the lunchboxes and the kids' hands on the stairway railing in a hurry to get to work and pre-school. Leta stopped midway down the steps. Everyone watched as she took off her coat." Vida wondered what she was doing., and she found out when the dress came off over Leta's head. Vida couldn't believe it. "Why are you doing this?"

"I *not* wearing."

Vida went back into the house and returned with a shirt. Satisfied, Leta raised her arms to be dressed. Vida says, "That was the last dress she ever wore."

Alberto stood up for a wedding one year. They had to rent a tuxedo for Leta, too. Vida says, "The people at the wedding know our family, so all they said was, 'Isn't she cute?'"

They manage a smooth-running household. Helena does the cooking and gets the children ready for school in the morning. Vida is involved with Alberto, now fourteen, who has discovered that he loves acting. He was chosen to be in his school play, a production of *Lord of the Flies*. It gives Vida pleasure to share one of her loves with her son. She is always amazed at his self-assurance. After the play, there was time for the audience to discuss the bullying issues explored in the play. Alberto answered one question with, "It's akin to the way people are dealing with the gay marriage issue."

Helena goes to work at 7:15 a.m. because Alberto needs to be at the city bus stop by 6:45. Since he gets home at 3:30, she tries to be home by 4:00. Helena says, "I don't want to have latch-key kids. Even at his age I think it's nice that they have someone at home." Vida takes Leta to her school bus stop at 9:00 a.m.

Unlike their parents, Vida and Helena don't discipline their children with belts and slaps. Helena says, "We try to reason with them, but at some point in time we might have to say, 'We are not going to discuss this any more. Go to your room. You *will* do as I ask.' Alberto is a very easy person to live with, but there are times when he gets so stressed out or hungry that he can't listen to anything. It's taken me a long time to figure out that need to disengage and talk to him later, when he can listen. If the cause is hunger, I give him a sandwich and come talk in half an hour. An emotional reason may take longer. Maybe once a year I get to the point of fuming, and twice in his lifetime I've had an actual fit. I've said I'd never slap him, but you don't know. If I find him on drugs, I might break his leg!"

Helena says, "Vida is excellent at parenting. She is very clear. I appreciate that because sometimes I'm too lenient. Leta is such an easy child to discipline, but wait 'til she's thirteen. That might change. We try to deal with each one differently, in his or her own style. It's not so much looking at the kid's problem, but looking at the whole dynamic."

Vida says, "It was good to wait fourteen years to have children. We were old enough to learn from our mistakes. We worked so hard on our relationship that by the time our kids came along, Helena was ready to accept and affirm affection. She is amazingly affectionate with our kids; still, when they're feeling sad or have troubling emotions of any kind, they come to me. I'm the one who will listen instead of saying, 'Oh well, that happens.'" Helena is supportive, but as a child she had to deal with her emotions by herself. There was no one to sympathize with her. She uses reason and logic. They get the sympathy and kisses from Vida. One day, Vida was listening to a conversation between Alberto and the adopted daughter of two of Vida's and Helena's friends. They were talking about inherited traits. Alberto said, "I get love of drama from Mommy Vida and love of math from Mom Helena."

"What do you mean you inherited something from Vida? She's not your birth mother. How can you inherit something from her?"

"Well, you know what? I think I got it from all the kissing."

Vida and Helena wanted their children to have the best education possible, so enrolled them in a Montessori school. Helena remembers, "We faced such incredible homophobia there. It was a painful, painful experience. We shared some of it with the kids, because they need to know about it." Since Vida taught multicultural education, she offered to chair the school's diversity committee, and Helena offered to help. At the first meeting a Muslim parent and a Jehovah's Witness parent appreciated Vida's suggestion that they discuss how to get more cultural and religious diversity into the students' books, however, trouble started when the subject changed to family values. Vida and Helena mentioned that they were both Alberto's mothers and it would be a good idea to mention that there were different types of families. The rest of the committee made it very clear that they didn't want any books on same sex parents. When they found out that Vida had volunteered to read at story time in some of the classrooms, they objected. Helena says, "They didn't want Vida in the classroom reading *any* type of book. The books she was reading had nothing to do with same sex parents or anything gay. They treated her like a pedophile."

Vida says, "We took our children out and sent them to a progressive Catholic school, where we found a wonderful teacher, very affirming." When Alberto's class was asked to write a memoir on the significant things in their lives, Alberto talked about Matthew Shepard, the young gay man who was beaten to death in Wyoming. Helena says, "I'm not a very emotional person, but it brings tears to my eyes whenever I think about the part where he said, 'I hope something like this doesn't happen to my moms.' Even now he says, 'You don't know all of the stuff I hear.' In spite of this, he is really clear about who he is. We give him the strength and love, so he can feel comfortable with who he is."

Around Alberto's thirteenth birthday, Vida decided she should have the "You are Getting Older" talk with him. When she approached the subject, Alberto had a mature and wise reply. "Ma, I don't even think about these things right now. I don't know whether I'm straight or gay. I don't know anything, but we'll cross that bridge when we get to it." Vida was surprised and relieved. "All right," she said. "Good enough."

Vida says, "In Leta's class there are five other students who have same-sex parents. At age eleven, she appreciates the fact that she is a girl, but she doesn't identify with the role many girls play." Helena adds, "She doesn't like being mistaken for a boy, though everyone does that when they first see her." Vida says, "I'm not ruling anything out with her. Maybe she will someday say, 'You know, I think I actually am a boy.' If she comes to that, I hope I will be able to be as supportive of her as I am now. We have raised her to be comfortable in the life she chooses. What if in her puberty she grows a beard? What if she is a transgendered person? All I know is Helena and I love this human being with such depth that we will support her no matter what."

Around the time the children were born, Helena came out to her parents. Her mother was receptive to Vida and loved the children, but Helena's father hardly ever came to see them. Helena says, "At Christmas time he sent cards addressed to me and the children and left Vida out. I kept trying to navigate the thing between my parents and Vida."

Finally, on one of Helena's visits with the children to her parents' home in Florida, she had had enough of her father's disrespect for Vida and their lifestyle. She said very pointedly, "You know what? Whether you like it or not, Vida and the children are my family. We've been together a long time. We go through the ups and downs of any relationship. Vida is my partner. If you're going to send a card at Christmastime, either you send it to everybody or don't send it to anybody. If you send it to me and the kids, I'm going to throw it out. When you visit at our house, respect Vida. I will not have our relationship negated in front of the kids. If you don't get to see our kids, it's your own fault."

When her father died a few years later, Helena learned that without his influence, her mother was much more open to them. Shortly after her father died, her mother was diagnosed with colon cancer. She declined Vida's and Helena's offer to join them in Boston, so Helena went to Florida to help her. The doctor was totally unsatisfactory, and Mrs. Rodriguez ended up in the hospital. Helena says, "I had to fight to get her out of the hospital. I got her on a plane so she could complete her treatments at home." Helena found an excellent oncologist who saved her mother's life. In 2003, the year that her mother was with them, Mrs. Rodriguez saw firsthand how congenial and nurturing Helena's family was. Helena even took her to some weddings of her gay friends. Helena says, "She was able to let go of some of the negativity, but every three months when she comes back from Florida for monitoring, you can see the church's influence. She's old school, but I think that there is someplace inside her that is trying to reconcile what the Bible says." One day Helena said to her, "You know what? What the Bible says is not always true." She pointed out a passage which, loosely translated, said, "If your children disobey you, you should kill them." Then she said, "You have to use judgment in what you accept."

God is still a big part of Helena's life, but not in a destructive way. She says, "I certainly believe in God but don't presume to know what God is. I feel it's our combined spirit that created something bigger than all of us. We are all one, and irrespective of what you believe, we should do as much good as we can. We try to follow the precepts of the Golden Rule." She says, "It isn't spirituality when you can't engage in discussions about diverse paths to God. Let us talk about that spirit which brings us all together. Let's talk about the important messages from the Bible, or Torah, or Koran that serve as lessons for living. I want a church that brings us together in spiritual peace. I haven't found a church that does that. We talk about that spirit which binds us all with the children, and at least now I'm able to have that discussion with my mother."

Vida's philosophy about whether to come out to her own mother was, "Why does anyone have to know, anyway?" She and Helena were loved by Vida's family. She had some inkling from her liberal-thinking father before he died, that he knew, but they had never talked about it. Homosexuality was taboo for Puerto Ricans, but not in Vida's childhood home. She remembered that when she was seven years old, her parents would go to dinner at a male relative's house who lived with another man. One would cook while the other entertained the guests. Through the years, Vida did come out to her sisters, brothers, aunts, and nieces, but never to her mother.

When Alberto was born, Vida's mother sent Helena a card congratulating her. In the margin, she wrote, "Hi Vida, you must be very happy to have Alberto come live with you." Vida wrote her mother a ten-page letter telling her that Alberto was her child as well as Helena's, which made Vida's mother Alberto's grandmother. She ended with, "I want you to love him the way you love all of your grandchildren."

Vida waited two weeks, and then began talking to her relatives to find out if her mother had said anything. Vida's sister, with whom her mother lived, related, "She just says she doesn't have any problem with your relationship with Helena, but she doesn't understand how Alberto is her grandson." Her niece told Vida that she tried to explain it to Vida's mother this way, "If Vida had adopted a child, would it be your grandchild?" Vida's mother's response was, "Of course," but she was still confused about Helena's child.

It was a tradition of Vida's mother to give Vida and Helena each a special tree ornament at the family Christmas gathering. Vida says, "She always writes in her worst handwriting with a Magic Marker on the back of the ornament, 'Love, Mommy, Merry Christmas.' Contrary to detracting from the beauty of the ornament, the love her words express make it more beautiful." For Alberto's first Christmas, soon after Vida and Helena arrived at Vida's mother's house, she presented them with a bag containing three ornaments. Vida and Helena unwrapped theirs, grateful for the Magic Marker messages of love on the backs. Then Vida unwrapped Alberto's and saw that his ornament was special. "It was something Mama had sent away for," Vida remembers. "It said, 'Baby's First Christmas.' It had a little plaque on which his name was engraved. On the back, she had written in her worst handwriting with her black Magic Marker, 'Dear Alberto, Merry Christmas. Love, Grandma.'"

Helena and Vida feel grateful that they live in a state as freedom-conscious and visionary as Massachusetts. Helena says, "Massachusetts has a cross adoption law tailored to gay partners with children so that both have equal parental rights. In a marriage it's presumed that the two spouses have custody. Before this, only the birth mother had custody rights in a lesbian relationship. Now, with cross adoption, we shouldn't have any trouble in at least forty-eight states."

Helena says, "Parenting has made both of us much better people. It brought Vida out of herself. I cannot begin to tell you how wonderful motherhood is. You get back so much more than you give. The love our kids have for us, the respect. If you could ever meet them you would see that they are magnificent kids. I call parenting the toughest job I've ever loved."

They both consider it their good fortune that Carmine and Diana are still a part of their lives. They were with them when their children were born and grew attached and committed to their children immediately. When they lived next to one another, Carmine and Diana asked if they could spend quality time with Alberto and Leta on a regular basis. Vida and Helena said, "Of course, we value your influence."

Unfortunately, the relationship between the two couples became strained regarding their joint interest in the house. However, their tension never interfered with Carmine's and Diana's relationship with Alberto and Leta. Carmine and Diana took care of Alberto and Leta every Friday. Their love and concern for Alberto and Leta was evident and the children loved seeing them. Coming from an extended family culture, Vida and Helena had learned that you never hold grudges; consistency is the commitment of the family, and so anger was put behind them. Helena and Vida enjoyed having a night to themselves to go to a bookstore or a movie or mix with other adults. Still, there was a barrier between the couples.

At an education conference in Baltimore, Vida learned something that dissolved that barrier. The keynote speaker said, "The best ratio for raising a child is four to one, because a child needs the stimulation of other adults." She thought. "Oh, my God, I always missed my children having an extended family, which to my mind was my Puerto Rican relatives. I suddenly realized that my children *did* have an extended family with Carmine and Diana, two women who have had such love for them since birth. Since the day they were born, they have been the other parents who have also been responsible for their upbringing." That Friday, when Carmine and Diana came to get the children, Vida said, "I have to thank you so much, because I realize why our kids are so great. Helena and I are good parents, but our kids are greater because they have you two and what you give to them."

In Spite of Everything....

Vida and Helena remain active in state and national politics. When the same sex marriage law was being considered, they attended meetings and wrote letters to state representatives. They allowed their children to become involved, too. When she was eight years old, Leta wanted to write a letter to State Senator Robert Travaglini, President of the Massachusetts Senate. An amendment to ban gay marriage was going to be presented at the constitutional convention. She wrote: "Dear Mr. Travaglini, my moms have been together for twenty-four years, and they have the right to marry each other just like any other person. Anybody should be able to marry anybody they want, because we are all people and should have the same rights. I love my moms and I love my family. Thank you, Leta Salazar Rodriguez, Age 8."

In November 2003, Vida was outside the courthouse when the Supreme Judicial Court of Massachusetts was deciding whether people of the same sex could marry. When the announcement was made, she rushed to a parent-teacher meeting at Alberto's school. She arrived late and slipped into an empty seat beside Helena. Vida took a tablet from Helena and wrote, "The Court came down with their ruling today." Helena read it, tight lipped with disappointment. The news was probably bad. She mouthed, "The answer was no, wasn't it?" Vida took the pad again, wrote a message, and handed it back. "Will you marry me?" Helena's face was radiant, eyes brimming with tears. They sat, eyes locked in wordless communication.

Vida and Helena wanted to be married on May 17th, the very day that it became legal. Time was short. They had to hurry because there was already talk that the law might be changed, maybe even that day after the legislature convened at 9 a.m. In a surprise move, the mayor of Cambridge, who was not gay, announced that the court house doors would be opened at midnight on the 17th so that marriage licenses could be processed and people could marry before the law could be rescinded. There were 10,000 people in the streets in front of the Cambridge Court House that night. The majority came to celebrate with their gay friends, sons, daughters, mothers, and fathers. Vida says, "There was an area across the street for those Looney Tunes from Kansas, or wherever, who pay to get on a plane to stand with their signs and protest. But nobody was paying any attention to them. Two-hundred-fifty couples filed that night."

Vida and Helena decided to go home and get some sleep and then drive to Brookline, Massachusetts, early in the morning, to secure a waiver that would allow them to be married the same day they filed for a marriage license. They thought there would be fewer people filing there than in Boston. On their way home they were listening to the BBC, stationed in the front of Cambridge City Hall where they had just been. Vida says, "You could hear the cheering crowd we had just left. I thought 'Oh, my God, this is a world-wide moment, and we are here.'"

At 5 a.m., Vida, Helena, and their two children stood on the steps of Brookline City Hall, waiting to file intent to marry. Then they went across the street to the courthouse to get their waiver. Every time a couple would emerge with a waiver, the crowd applauded. After they left, Vida stopped at a florist's to get a bouquet. Her straight friend's daughter would be the flower girl. Vida laughs, "I couldn't get my daughter to be the flower girl, so forget that idea." Alberto had already said that he wanted to be the best man, and Leta said she wanted to be the best woman. Alberto had asked if he could say a few words during the ceremony, and Vida had said, "Of course, I will ask Rosario, the woman who will marry us, to let you speak at an appropriate time."

When they took their places in Boston City Hall, Rosario chose to begin with Alberto's words. The four of them were standing up together, one child on either side. Alberto said, "Once upon a time there were two women who loved each other for twenty-four years. Then they passed a law saying they could get married. So they did. Those two women are my moms." In the wedding photographs, all present had glistening eyes.

Vida says, "As it turned out, we were the first women to get married at Boston City Hall. We were all crying, even Rosario, and clerk Felix Arroyo who was straight. The mayor of Boston was very supportive. The city had set up a tent on the plaza where they served wedding cake to romantic, classical music played by a string quartet. Anybody getting married at City Hall would have a place to celebrate."

Helena and Vida both felt that their lives changed that day. Helena says, "Even after twenty-four years, we felt a renewed commitment to each other. We had known we would always be together, but in that moment we were verified." Vida says, "When you're able to marry, it's just phenomenal, life changing. It's a little hard to explain, but I could see the change in Alberto's eyes. The very next morning when I went to wake him up, he put his arms around me and drew me down to him so he could whisper in my ear. 'Mommy, I love you so much, I don't even have words to tell you.' He knew his parents were married, validated. It was one of the most moving days of our lives."

Jan and Xandra

The photo album is cracked along the binding. The pages are curling and yellowing around the edges. Pictures of a young Jan and a young Xandra are faded now, but if you look closely, you can capture the vibrancy of their personalities from across the years. Jan stands relaxed, small and slender, her smooth compact body made for moving gracefully. A strand of shiny, brown hair spills over her forehead. Dark eyes flash and her smile, then as now, reveals her impish sense of humor. Xandra looks straight into the camera, self-assured, aggressive, her stance revealing the controlled energy of the athlete at rest. She is slender yet muscular. Her medium length brown curls frame her face. Thirty-two years have passed since the first pictures of the young lovers were taken, thirty-two years since they first met. Now, as then, you can see the love that flows between them, the easy way they fit together. Thirty-two years. Where have they gone?

"Jerry Lee or Jane Lord, Jerry Lee or Jane Lord," thirteen-year-old Xandra had etched the initials J.L. on the side of her wrist, thinking that Jerry Lee was the boy of her dreams. He was cute and nice and Jerry liked her, but the following summer in 1951, she became confused about the object of the initials. She met a girl named Jane Lord at a summer church camp in southern Indiana. Jane aroused feelings that eventually erased Jerry Lee from her mind. Four girls were housed in small cabins furnished with bunk beds. Xandra was in the top bunk of one, with Jane in the bottom. In the dark of the night Xandra began to feel a compelling urge to slip down into the bottom bunk. With all of the sweet innocence of youth, Xandra and Jane cuddled and found comfort in each other's arms. Xandra climbed back to the top bunk to sleep, but returned every night until the week of camp was over. Xandra decided J.L. definitely stood for Jane Lord. That was in junior high: Xandra's first tangible attraction to another female.

During her high school sophomore year, Xandra progressed beyond the hugging stage. Her first true sexual encounter was with a girl the same age but wiser in the ways of making love. Martha and Xandra ran around together through their sophomore and junior years, but Xandra wasn't attached to any one person. She liked a lot of girls. When she left for camp, there was "the Lord's daughter" and then there was Amy and Mary and, well, others. Xandra never questioned her orientation. "I never gave it a second thought. I never felt strange about it. It all seemed so natural to me." That was all she needed to know. She was enjoying being with the young women she met, but in her senior year, her roving life changed.

She became infatuated with her English teacher, Nell Williamson. Nell had come from Tennessee, following Maggie, the woman she loved. Xandra's home town, Greensburg, Indiana, was the closest place to Maggie where Nell could get a teaching job. By the time Nell's partner left her for another woman, Nell had established friends in Greensburg and decided to stay. It was a small town and she knew most of the people. The townspeople had accepted her as one of their own, Xandra's family included. It wasn't unusual for the residents of the small town to have the teachers over for dinner or to become friends with them. Nell was attractive and friendly with a quick wit and easy smile. Her smooth southern drawl could make a lion purr.

Nell had sensed that Xandra's attentiveness in class went beyond the topic of the lesson. She told Xandra later that she definitely had more than teaching Shakespeare in mind when she saw her in class. A colleague had told Nell that Xandra was a lesbian, but Nell wasn't sure. She wanted to find out. Only in a small town could a plan like the one that she concocted seem reasonable. Tony, one of Nell's gay friends, had taken up the hobby of raising prize cattle. When he asked her to come to a cattle show in a nearby town, she agreed to come. She decided to use the show to have some time with Xandra away from any scrutiny.

Xandra was thrilled when Nell asked her if she would like to spend Saturday and Sunday at the Shorthorn Breeders' Regional Show in a nearby town. Xandra knew it would be an overnight trip. They would stay in a motel near the fairgrounds. "I don't know why my parents didn't think that was weird, but they didn't." There was one double bed in the motel room. Xandra surprised Nell by drawing an imaginary line down the middle of the bed, saying, "This is your side of the bed and this is my side." Nell later told Xandra that she wondered if her information had been wrong and whether she had made the right decision bringing her there. But with the lights out, the imaginary line disappeared along with their student-teacher boundaries.

When they returned from the show, Xandra wanted to be with Nell every day. Even though Xandra graduated from high school that spring, they had to be extremely careful. Eyes in a small town are everywhere. "You can imagine how we had to sneak around. I mowed her landlady's lawn, so that was convenient," says Xandra. "After graduation that summer, I went with Nell to her farm in Tennessee."

At the end of the summer, Xandra began her freshman year at Indiana University. Nell got a job in Indianapolis and rented an apartment. Xandra remembers, "In my sophomore year I transferred to Butler University, located in Indianapolis, so I could live with Nell." There was a thirteen year age difference between the women. Later on in their lives that might not have mattered, but the difference between nineteen and thirty-two strained their relationship. Xandra wanted to experience the college life. She continued her studies for a degree in Physical Education, participated in sports and attended all of the college games. Nell wasn't interested in partying with younger people and had little interest in sports. They argued. Xandra found herself trying to have both the college life and a secure relationship with Nell. She wasn't giving Nell the attention she needed, and Nell couldn't support Xandra in the life she wanted to lead.

"At some point between my sophomore and senior year, Nell and her new friend, Irene, were beginning their relationship," Xandra says, but she didn't know about that for years. "Nell didn't want to interfere with my education. She didn't want to upset me while I was in school." Xandra was so interested in the things she wanted to do that she wasn't even aware of what was going on. She did find out about them after she graduated and accepted it with little regret. They were still friends, and when Nell and Irene built a house in the country, Xandra lived with them, Nell and Irene upstairs, Xandra in the finished basement. It worked out well for Xandra, who was now teaching in college while working on her masters' degree in physical education.

She was also warming up to the single life again. "I had several brief liaisons, one mostly in the back seats of cars." Several of the women she dated married men in later years. She remained friends with Nell, but there was friction between Xandra and Irene. It became clear that Irene didn't want Xandra in the house with them. In the meantime, Xandra continued her fleeting relationships with the women she met in college. She was happy with the arrangements and had no expectations of anything more. The tension between Xandra and Irene was relieved when Xandra left to attend Louisiana State University to begin her doctoral studies. Xandra was too busy at LSU for any romancing. She couldn't have known that soon her life would be changed forever. She would meet, Jan, a woman who would capture her interest and desire for the rest of her life.

"Play ball!" That command always started young Jan's heart thrumming. She loved baseball. She excelled in and participated in all sports, but baseball was her passion. "I played mostly with boys, except for girls' American Athletic Union ball in the summertime. That was fast pitch softball." Other than that, she always played with the neighborhood boys at their games. She got bruised in football scrimmages. She came home covered with mud on spring days, or with torn clothing and an occasional bloody nose. Her family was used to it. No one thought it strange. "She's just a tomboy." She was never told she couldn't compete. It was clear that she was as good, or better, at sports than the boys in the small town of Zionsville, Indiana. It never occurred to her that she shouldn't play varsity baseball for the high school team.

No one knows what Coach Johnson was thinking when the feisty four-feet-eleven-inch freshman stood before him and said she wanted to try out for the team. It is fairly certain, however, that he saw the "don't try to stop me" kind of determination that telegraphed through her body. He let her try out. She made the team and held the position on second base for four years. The boys on the team were the ones she had played with for years and accepted her as a valued member of the team. Jan remembers, "The only person who gave me a rough time was my brother, and it was only because he wasn't as good as I was. Zionsville was a small community. Everybody knew everybody. I don't know why they didn't think anything of it, but they didn't."

The coach was so impressed with her athletic ability that he went to the American Athletic Union to see if she could play on the boys' basketball team. Phil Johnson was a man way ahead of his time, but the rest of the athletic world in 1949 had a long way to go. Jan was denied the opportunity to play basketball, supposedly for lack of a dressing room. The baseball team wore their uniforms to the games, but the basketball team needed to change into uniforms at the game site. Any positive-thinking woman could have devised positive ways around this "big problem," but Jan didn't push the issue. "I became a yell leader for the team."

In the summer Jan played softball on an AAU girls' league which included girls from ages thirteen to thirty. Her team went to the world championships three times. She liked the other girls but didn't notice them much. "I was out to play ball." It occupied all of her attention until a certain overnight trip to Peoria, Illinois, changed things. The team members had to share beds. Fourteen-year-old Jan learned a lot that night from Dee, a twenty-four-year-old member of the team. They began by hugging and kissing; it was thrilling and warm. Jan had never known anything like this. She had never seen the young women on the team in any way but as ball players. Here was a new kind of game — forbidden, exciting, arousing. After that night she knew the way her life would go. Dee and Jan began a relationship that lasted through Jan's high school years, but it was a relationship based more on sexual infatuation than love.

Jan was able to spend many weekends with Dee. The team had to travel to different towns, even different states, to play ball. They traveled on Saturday and played on Sunday. On Saturday night Jan and Dee just played. Jan's life was busy. "I was dating boys, too, just for fun. Three asked me to go steady, so I said, 'Yes,' to all of them. That didn't mean sex in those days. They didn't seem to mind. We were all on the same ball team." Jan loved her life and drank it in deeply. She was like a clockspring coiled in anticipation, ready to leap into the abundance of life.

After Jan graduated from high school in 1942, Dee became Jan's only interest. They lived together for five years, and Jan would have continued to be true to her if Dee hadn't made a fatal mistake in thinking she could control Jan. She was foolish enough to attempt to exercise that control with an arrogant bet. Jan, Dee, and their friend Betsy stopped in a bar to have a drink after a game. Maybe it was the alcohol that made Dee feel reckless. With Jan sitting right beside her she told Betsy, "I have Jan just where I want her. I've got her right under my thumb. Go ahead, Betts, ask her out. She won't go with you." Unfortunately for Dee, Jan had too much self-respect to allow that kind of treatment. When Betsy did ask her out, she accepted. Their break up left Dee bitter for a long time. She learned too late of Jan's unbridled spirit.

Jan had several relationships that lasted six or seven years, all with women she continued to remain friends with after the break-ups. All of her relationships ended with her lovers mistakenly accusing her of infidelity, but it was only Jan's love of people and a good time that made them jealous. She was with women who wanted to keep her all to themselves, a confinement Jan found intolerable. She was a free spirit, feisty and energetic. She had a robust sense of humor and wanted to spend her time enjoying the company of others.

Jan gave up on the idea of having a lasting, trusting relationship and decided she would go back home to her mother's house. "That way I could be free to enjoy life without having to look over my shoulder." She began seeing a married woman, no strings attached. She would go to her house in the afternoon for a secret rendezvous. Jan's friends saw the potential for disaster in this and tried to warn her away from Rae. Her friends also became aware that Jan was drinking too much. She admits, "I got into the habit of carrying a cooler full of iced beer in the back of my car, just in case I wanted to have a party someplace." There were many nights that she didn't remember how she got home. Her mother worried.

Ruth Ann, one of Jan's friends who knew Xandra through Nell, got together with Nell and decided that Xandra should meet Jan. "They thought if they could introduce me to someone who liked to play golf," recalls Jan, "I would feel better about life and spend more time playing golf, less time with Rae, and less time drinking."

Jan loved to play golf but had lost interest in it. Ruth Ann and Nell's strategy was to get a group together to see their favorite female impersonator at Betty Kay's, a popular gay club. Ruth Ann would get Jan to come, and Nell would get Xandra. They knew that neither Jan nor

Xandra would go if either knew it was a "set up," so they kept the plan a secret. Jan was absolutely opposed to meeting anyone. "I wanted to be single and raise hell and never report to anybody." Xandra likewise would have been insulted to have a date set up for her. "I met plenty of women on my own." Each had established her own life. Xandra was twenty-six and Jan was thirty-six.

Xandra worked late as a lifeguard at the Dolphin Club and by the time she arrived at Betty Kay's with Nell and Irene, everyone was seated. The only seat available was next to Jan. They were introduced and the attraction was spontaneous. Was it Jan's smile that was so appealing? Her dancing eyes? The energy and grace in her five-foot frame? Was it Xandra's tan, slender body? Her frank, appraising look? Her easy conversation? Jan says, "I don't know about the easy conversation. I just liked the way she looked." Jan forgot who else was there. They watched the show and talked all evening, enjoying the chemistry that sparked between them. Jan says, "There must have been an instant reaction, because I didn't want to be away from her from then on."

Xandra didn't want the evening to end either. She asked Jan if she would like to come home with her. Without a second thought, Jan said, "Yes," and asked Ruth Ann to take care of her car so she could go home with Xandra. Nell and Irene had brought Xandra to Betty Kay's and were happy to see that Jan was coming along to their home. Jan and Xandra sat in the back seat in the dark, unaware of their surroundings, feeling only the magnetic pull of their bodies. Xandra remembers, "I don't remember any conscious thought. It was so natural to be in each other's arms." Jan laughs and says, "We necked all the way home."

Any plans for them to sleep separately that night ended before they started. Xandra recalls, "I was trying to be the perfect hostess, trying to set Jan up on the couch, so she could sleep upstairs. I hadn't even showed her my sleeping area in the basement."

Jan adds, "It didn't end that way."

"It didn't really start that way."

Their arms touched while tucking the sheets. Their lips touched. The sheets were forgotten. They both wanted more. It isn't clear to either how they got downstairs to Xandra's bed. Hands and lips traced patterns that seemed so familiar. It was as if they had known each other before, as if they had always been together. Without a doubt, Xandra emphasizes,

"It was just like it was meant to be. It was predestined. There was no hesitancy, no fear, only a compelling desire to be close." Xandra realized, "This experience was new. I'd never felt this way before." There was no pretense, no need to impress, just a gentle giving in to what was meant to be. They woke late, tired from long, luxurious loving.

Jan worked in the business office for Stokley VanCamp in Indianapolis. She was supposed to go to a Fourth of July company picnic the next day, but didn't want to leave Xandra. "I didn't ever want to leave Xandra, so I asked her to go." Jan did take time to get her car from Ruth Ann. She barely noticed the smirk on her friend's face when she walked in the door. Her mother noticed a different look about her when she arrived home and was relieved that Jan was sober.

The picnic was in a community park with a swimming pool, picnic shelters, softball fields, and swings and slides for children. The organizers of the event planned a lot of games, with prizes for the winners. Jan and Xandra won practically every activity. They came back to Jan's mother's house with thermos bottles, flashlights, a suitcase, and many gadgets.

Xandra moved most of her clothes in the next day. Jan's mother, Joyce Estridge, was a warm, generous person. She liked having Jan's friends over and didn't find it unusual for Xandra to be there. Because Jan played softball on a semi-pro team, there were always team members staying over, always people in and out. When Xandra spent the night, it was still within the norm, but later, when Xandra moved all of her clothes in for the summer, Joyce knew her daughter felt differently about this woman. She didn't ask questions.

Xandra and Mrs. Estridge had a chemistry of their own from the start. While Jan was at work, they had time to get to know one another. They found that they had one major thing in common, a love of White Castles. They were addicted to the ridiculously thin hamburger laced with greasy onions on a warm soft bun. They would each eat at least three of the stomach boilers and laugh while doing it. Xandra liked doing things for Mrs. Estridge and Mrs. Estridge enjoyed Xandra's company. She really appreciated the fact that Jan stayed around the house with Xandra and didn't come home sick from drinking all night. She not only had her daughter back, she had someone to bring her White Castles. The next four weeks were a congenial time for all.

September of 1962 came all too soon, bringing the reality of a painful separation. Xandra had to return to LSU to complete her course work, then write and defend her doctoral dissertation. Xandra remembers, "It was very traumatic having to go down there for a whole year. I didn't think I could stand it." Everything within her rebelled at the idea, but there was no choice. She couldn't sacrifice her future by staying. Two things made the separation more bearable: She trusted Jan to wait for her, and they would try to meet as often as they could. During that long drive down to Louisiana, Xandra agonized over how she could get back on weekends. Xandra's longing to be with Jan intensified with each mile that separated them. Twelve hundred miles was such a long distance. They didn't think they could see each other more than once a month.

Xandra was only on campus one week before she flew home to spend the weekend with Jan. Xandra remembers, "I think there were only two weekends that whole first semester that we didn't see each other. Either Jan drove down or I drove up, or we met in Tennessee." Eighteen hours, 1,200 miles couldn't stop them. They felt reckless and desperate to be together. They were always in one another's thoughts, dreams, and plans. Thirty-six hours of driving, an awfully long drive for so short a time, but it didn't matter. They had to touch, to hold, to kiss, to love.

They would usually start driving Friday evening and drive all night. It was dark and lonely on the roads and, for Jan, one dark, moonless drive became a nightmare. Somewhere in Tennessee late at night, her total concentration was on the road, pushing the car to the edge of safety, headlights guiding her ever closer to Xandra. Suddenly, blinding lights reflected into her eyes from the rear view mirror. A car was coming up, too close. The dark silhouette of a man was all she could see as the car passed and swerved in front of her. He slowed down, forcing her to brake. Then another car closed in behind her, playing a dangerous game. "I gunned the car to get in front. Both cars chased me until one would get in front and slow down, trying to force me to stop between them." She couldn't outrun them on the curving road.

Jan's heart was pounding. Fear tasted like metal on her tongue; it tightened her neck and shoulders. They were bumper to bumper, racing through the dark. "I knew I'd better not let them force me off the road, but I didn't know how long I could keep up the pace." The pursuit seemed endless. She kept maneuvering around the car in front, escaping from the trap, only to be caught between them again. Finally they sped through a small town where a policeman joined the chase and pulled them all over. While the officer was occupied with the other two cars, Jan pulled out and away. She had a deadline to meet and nothing was going to stop her from getting there on time. "I kept my eyes on the rear view mirror for at least a hundred miles down the road." Jan would have some precious hours with Xandra on Saturday. Then she would drive back Sunday evening. The few hours of love and comfort and warmth would end too soon. The trauma of separation would begin.

"I love you."

"I'll miss you."

"Call me when you get home, no matter how late."

"See you next weekend."

"Don't go. Stay just a little longer."

"Just a little longer."

Xandra laughs, remembering, "We would cry every time we had to leave. We'd call every day and cry on the telephone. I had to figure out how to get out of LSU for my last semester. We couldn't go on like this." After the fall semester, Xandra had only one class left — kinesiology — and then she would begin her dissertation. If there had been awards that year for creativity, Xandra would have won. "I made up this cock-and-bull story about how my dad was sick and my mother needed me at home." She found that kinesiology was being offered as an undergraduate course at a college only thirty miles from Jan's mother's home. She was supposed to be taking a graduate course, but "Somehow I convinced them that the under grad course should count for grad credit."

Xandra finished that first seemingly endless semester and returned to Indiana. She and Jan got a small apartment in Zionsville, not many miles from Jan's mother. Living together was as comfortable as their love. There were no major adjustments, no quarrels about space or how to spend their time. They trusted one another completely and jealousy was never a problem. Jan liked to dance and Xandra did not, so when they went to the bars, Xandra sat and talked with friends while Jan danced. Xandra got so involved with her friends that she lost track of Jan. Her friends would ask, "Where's Jan?"

"I don't know. I guess she is over there dancing someplace."

"Aren't you worried?"

"No, I'm not. If she wants to do something with someone else, she should. Whether I'm watching her tonight won't make any difference. Let her have a good time. What is the point of having a relationship with someone if you don't trust them? Jan doesn't have to be attached to me." Xandra never questioned Jan about what she was doing or whom she was with. She never doubted Jan's word, and Jan never doubted hers. Xandra adds, "From the time I first met Jan, I was never even mildly interested in anyone else." Jan echoes with, "I couldn't love anyone except Xandra."

Jan was grateful for Xandra's trust. She needed someone who would believe in her fidelity. Suspicion is destructive. Jan had been true to the other women she lived with, but they wanted to control how she spent her time. She was open and friendly and enjoyed meeting people. Others wanted to be around her fun-loving, buoyant spirit. The fine qualities that made her so appealing to others made her insecure lovers jealous. They tried to suppress her love of life. She couldn't live with the burden of accusations and distrust. Xandra was just the person Jan wanted: honest and willing to trust others to be just as honest. Jan finally met the one who didn't try to clip her wings. They both gave their love without restraint, without conditions. They each felt free to pursue their own interests, knowing one would receive support from the other. Being together generated the kind of power that made them believe that they could do anything together. Life was good.

Only one small disagreement erupted about once or twice a week, sometimes more often. You could almost predict the sparks when Jan got out the sponge and soap and began to clean the stove.

"You missed a spot."

"I did not."

"I'm not upset with you about it. As long as I don't mind doing it over, don't worry about it."

"I do it just as well as you can."

Xandra never was satisfied with Jan's stove cleaning expertise. "I had a thing about streaks, and always went back to do the job over. I would try to be sneaky about it so as not to hurt Jan's feelings, but Jan always knew." Finally, Jan gave up after twenty years and handed Xandra the dish rag to begin with. "I don't know why it took so long for me to figure that out; just stubborn I guess." They also used to have trouble cleaning the house together until they decided they would start at opposite ends and only see the results of the labor, not the process. Xandra was sure the only way to clean a room was to dust, then vacuum, while Jan was convinced that dusting last was right. As long as they couldn't see one another, house cleaning chores went smoothly.

Other chores were much easier to do. As the years went by, each found the chore that she did best. Xandra pays the bills, but Jan balances the checkbook. Xandra is the planner of parties and trips. She makes the arrangements. Jan is more outgoing with people when they are on the trips. More people respond to Jan. Jan washes dishes and Xandra dries. Jan cooks and Xandra bakes. There aren't many couples, gay or straight, who can list minor disagreements with housekeeping as their only difficulties in getting along.

Their lives were busy. Xandra was commuting to the university to finish the kinesiology course and working in the office at the Dolphin Club for extra money. Jan was working at Stokley in data processing and coaching an American Softball Association women's softball team. It was a fast-pitch game that demanded great skill. There were teams all over the United States. Besides Indiana, their league encompassed Ohio, Illinois, Michigan, Tennessee, and Wisconsin. She enjoyed teaching the skills she excelled in to the mostly college-age young women. Jan's outstanding play in the American Athletic Union had won her the nomination and entry into the Softball Hall of Fame. Her players respected and admired her. "I never let them get by with anything but their best. If they had the ability, I wanted them to make the most of it." Jan's teams made it to the national finals many times.

In 1963, Jan's and Xandra's second year together, Xandra started her dissertation and taught seventh, eighth, and ninth grades in a middle school. It was one of the worst experiences in the classroom she had ever had. She hated every single day. She told Jan, "If I have to teach one more year of this, I will quit teaching. You can't teach this age group anything. You spend all of your time disciplining." While she was facing this turmoil during the day, she was working on her doctoral dissertation in the evenings. She used the girls in her physical education classes to study the effects of various exercises on the development of their cardiovascular systems.

She felt very fortunate to have an excellent advisor. When her dissertation was completed, Xandra paid for his round-trip fare so she could meet with him. She needed to learn how she would be expected to defend her premise. He prepared her to meet the challenges of the LSU faculty. In January 1966, Xandra passed the oral exam. After the interview with the faculty, she had to present at a colloquium, where she would defend her thesis again by answering questions from an audience comprised of graduate students and professors. At the end of January, Jan went with Xandra's parents to her graduation. Jan made the all-too-familiar trip to Louisiana for the last time. Except for family responsibilities, Jan and Xandra would never be separated again.

Both Jan and Xandra loved animals and being outdoors. They saved what money they could and began looking for a house with some acreage. They wanted room for their animals, a garden, and privacy. They looked at properties and thought they had one, but, as Xandra put it, "The realtor sold it out from under us." Jan adds, "Looking back now, we see that it was for the best, but at the time we were heartbroken." They continued to check the real estate ads. Jan saw one that seemed perfect. She felt intuitively that this could be the one. "Let's go look at that."

"Right now?"

"Yes, right now. Somebody is liable to buy it."

They both liked the property. It was in a perfect location, secluded yet close to a small town and within thirty minutes of the city. They could hear birds calling through the trees. The house sat on a rise about one hundred feet off the gravel road. Tall, graceful maple trees shaded the front yard and in the back there was a large grassy area surrounded by woods. There was plenty of room for a garden. The one-story house was small, but there was room to expand. Jan said, "Let's go talk to the realtor." They made an offer which was accepted, but the bank wouldn't give them a loan unless they could come up with one third down. Jan and Xandra felt it was because they were women. They both had good, secure jobs. Jan was now the bookkeeper for an oil refining company, and Xandra was teaching in the women's physical education department at Butler University. There was no logical reason to withhold the money. To make matters more infuriating, the realtor wanted to sell the property to someone else. He didn't think they could come up with the money and told them so. Jan says, "I wasn't about to lose another place that was meant for us. I borrowed money from my mother and from my insurance policy to make the down payment." Xandra says, "We realized it would be a stretch to pay back all of the loans, but we were willing to make the sacrifice." In August, they moved in with their little family: Jan's dachshund, Kelly, and an adopted yellow cat named Gomer.

Soon after they moved in, their little family began to grow, and grow. Xandra seemed to attract stray dogs like a magnet draws iron filings. They stuck to her or she to them, and they collected in her yard. The first was a lost dog that she found wandering around the university. She named him Freckles. The second, she named Trader, after the small town where she picked him up. She took the animals home with the intent of finding permanent homes for them. By the time they had them for three weeks or so, she and Jan had become so attached that they wanted them to stay. They put up a fence in the back yard so the dogs would have room to run. Xandra began to fill that yard. For many other dogs and cats she found other homes. Xandra became well-known among her friends and the community for her relentless efforts to save homeless animals. Jan's coworkers would report, "I saw Xandra on the highway trying to catch a dog," or "I saw Xandra carrying a stray cat toward her car." Jan would shake her head knowingly. She knew these animals would be in their care when she got home. Xandra didn't take animals to the Humane Society. She *was* the Humane Society! She took risks crawling into culverts and under dilapidated houses to rescue dogs too frightened to respond to her call. She spent months coaxing a timid mother with pups to get close enough to be caught and rescued. Many times she forgot her own comfort and safety, and on one desperate morning she was willing to risk going to jail to save a poor starving creature from the hands of a diabolically cruel man.

Some friends of Xandra's had gone to look at a horse offered for sale by their blacksmith. In a stall next to the horse, was a Dalmatian so thin that they could see its every bone. Each vertebra, each rib protruded. There seemed to be no muscle tissue left, only skin on bone. Bob Walker, the blacksmith, said the dog had throat cancer and couldn't eat. Xandra's friends left Bob's place and immediately came to Xandra and said, "We've got to do something about this dog." They needed Xandra's courage to help them take action. They knew she would think of something. They drove up and down the highway past Bob's property, trying to see if they could sneak in and rescue the dog, but there was always a light in the barn

In Spite of Everything....

and he seemed to be inside. They had to give up that night and decided to try to think of another plan.

Xandra was on the road early the next morning. She had taken Jan to work at 4:00 a.m. and was approaching the Walker's place on her way home. When she sighted his barn, she had an impulse to pull in and get the dog. The early, gray light was just beginning to outline the house and outbuildings. Everything was quiet. No one seemed to be up. She stopped on the road and walked into the barn. What she saw was so horrifying that she forgot her own safety and the fact that she was breaking the law. The poor desperate animal was eating the remains of a dead Doberman also left to starve to death in that stall. There was a container full of water placed just out of their reach, as if it had been done intentionally to torture the dogs. She cradled the Dalmatian in her arms and carried her out to the car. She took her home first and as soon as the vet's office opened, she took her there. On the way, she gave the dog some saltine crackers that had been left in the car. This dog with supposed throat cancer devoured them ravenously. Xandra asked the vet to check her over carefully and do anything he could to save her, but put her down if he found she would only suffer by prolonging her life. From the vet's office Xandra went to the sheriff's office to report what she had done. The sheriff called the deputy prosecutor to see if there were grounds for arrest. The deputy prosecutor, a young man just getting into politics, said, "Well, I'm not going to touch this with a ten-foot pole. How would that look? This person rescues a starving dog and I have her arrested?" They sent her home, where she reported the neglect to the Humane Society.

When the Humane Society officials contacted Bob Walker, they foolishly gave him Xandra's name. He started harassing Xandra, calling her on the phone, driving past her house. He wanted to have her arrested, but he couldn't prove it was his dog. There was no collar or papers. Xandra wouldn't have him arrested for the cruel treatment of the dog, because she didn't want to admit it was his dog. The law at that time said that no matter his treatment of the dog, if he said he would change in the future, he could have it back. Xandra was not going to allow the dog to return to him.

When the dog got back from the vet, it needed constant care. Her skin condition was so bad that Xandra had to bathe her in sulfur-based soap. She needed a special diet. Little by little, she regained her health. A bright look returned to her eyes, and she began to run and play with the other dogs. She was a sweet, loving dog and showed Jan and Xandra every day her joy in being with them. They named her Carrie.

A little over a year later, Carrie vanished. When Jan and Xandra returned home one evening, she was gone. They couldn't believe she would run away. They grew hoarse calling, searched the woods and asked the neighbors. She had disappeared without a sign. They were heartsick, but could do nothing more. Months went by. She was still in their thoughts. They would see a Dalmatian in a yard and feel a thrill of hope that it was Carrie. They couldn't stop wondering where she could be.

An odd set of coincidences a year later led them to her. Jan and Xandra were looking for a used lawn mower. They answered an ad in the paper, traveling to a horse farm about five miles from their house. When they turned down the long driveway, a Dalmatian came out to greet them. Xandra exclaimed immediately, "That's Carrie. I know that's our dog." The woman who lived there had horses. Xandra asked her where she had gotten the dog. The woman said her blacksmith, Bob Walker, had given it to her. Xandra told her the story of how she had rescued the dog and literally brought it back to life, only to have her disappear a year later. The woman responded, "Well, I don't know anything about that, but if it's your dog, take her."

"No, if I take her right now he'll just come and steal her again and I'll never find her." Xandra visited Carrie every day for a month to play with her and bring her food. Then one day she just took her. Bob Walker never bothered Xandra again.

Jan and Xandra are still tireless advocates of friendless animals, but have cut back on the number that they keep. Jan expresses her reason for urging Xandra to cut down: "The cost was tremendous and we sacrificed our incomes and vacation times for them for years. We could never take a vacation because it was too much to ask anyone to care for eight dogs and four cats. It was also hard to give them the love and personal attention they needed." They now live happily with three dogs and one cat. Xandra is still the one people call to place a lost or abandoned animal in a caring home.

Even after Jan's baseball and softball playing days were over, she still stayed active and fit. She gave up coaching the women's amateur softball team, but assisted Barb Greenburg in coaching the Butler women's team for two years. She also refereed high school girls' basketball with Xandra. They played tennis and racquet ball and they swam. After ten years of living together, they finally got around to playing golf. It was a good thing that they were both in excellent condition. They needed all of their strength for the blizzard of '78.

The blizzard had been predicted the morning before the snow began to fall. Everyone took the warnings seriously for the weather stations were tracking the snow line as it moved along. It was dropping snow at a rate of an inch an hour with wind gusts up to fifty miles an hour. Schools dismissed early and drivers were urged to stay off the roads. People were buying out supplies of bread and milk at the groceries.

Jan was in Washington D.C. at a computer conference. Xandra was still planning to pick Jan up at the airport at 11:00 p.m. At the time she left for the university to watch the women's basketball team, there were only flurries. The forecasters estimated that the snow would begin early the next morning. "I thought I would have plenty of time to pick Jan up after the game." The fans inside the field house were consumed by a close game. Xandra was unaware that the winds were picking up and the snow was falling early, in earnest. The game went into overtime. She didn't get out until ten o'clock and immediately started for the airport. The snow was blowing horizontally across the headlamps, piling up in drifts across the interstate. By the time she got to the airport, there was such a whiteout that she couldn't tell which one way ramp or which level she was on. She met a car coming straight toward her through the curtain of snow, but managed to swerve around it to finally find the right pick up area. Jan was on the last plane allowed to land that night. She threw her bags in the jeep and they started on the treacherous trip home. Every exit they passed on the way around the city was blocked with cars caught in snowdrifts. They saw the hulking wrecks of jackknifed semis off to the sides of the road. They strained their eyes to search for the edge of the pavement obliterated by blowing snow. Luckily they caught up to a snowplow that exited where they wanted to get off. They had twenty miles to go through a maze of drifts.

Finally, they turned down their county road a mile from home. The five-foot drift that loomed up before them was lost in the glare of the blowing snow. The impact buried the front end of the jeep. They were stuck, alone at 2:00 a.m. in a raging blizzard. Knowing they would freeze in the car, they decided to try and make it to the nearest house somewhere back toward the highway. They knew they would never make it home that last mile in the roaring wind in the dark. They got out of the car, their breath taken away by the raging wind. Tiny needles of snow assaulted their eyes and the gale nearly knocked them over. Jan took a few steps away from the jeep and was immediately lost from Xandra's view. Shouting above the roar was impossible, so the only thing Xandra could do was head for the house, hoping that she would meet Jan there. She didn't see her until she was within a foot of the porch. Jan was waiting.

They pounded on the door, rousing the people inside, and explained what had happened. Their neighbors gave them a place to sleep the rest of the night and breakfast the next morning. Xandra called another neighbor to ask if he could pick them up in his snowmobile. He tried but couldn't make it. The drifts were too deep and soft. Jan and Xandra were determined to get home, because they felt the animals needed care. They didn't know if they were in distress outside or safe in the barn. They wanted to be sure they had food and water. The wind was still whipping the snow along the ground and the snow was still falling, making it nearly impossible to see. Their impromptu hosts tried to convince them that it was too dangerous to walk, but Jan and Xandra wouldn't listen. They couldn't bear the idea of their animals suffering, so with borrowed coats, hats, mufflers, and mittens, they started off. They agreed to stop at every house along the road to check in, rest, and get warm. The drifts were from two to five feet deep and building. The only way they could tell they were on the road was by the tops of the fence posts which stuck about six inches out of the snow. Jan had to walk around the drifts because her legs were too short to walk over them. They would lie flat and crawl over some of the higher ones. They stopped at the first house and called in, warmed up, then started out into the blizzard again. It took them two hours to get the one mile home. They literally crawled much of the way.

Instead of the desolation they had feared, their dogs were in the barn, safe and warm, impatient to be let out, for the drifts had blocked them in. After they had come all that exhausting, harrowing way, Jan and Xandra broke the drifts and made paths so their dogs could get out into the yard. The inside cats and dogs had plenty of water. When they watched the effects of the storm on television that afternoon, they couldn't imagine how their jeep made it as far as it did. Cars and trucks were strewn all along the length of the interstate for miles and miles. Hundreds of people were stranded at the airport, at schools, or at friends' houses. The city was shut down for days. It wasn't until four days later that a snowplow got through to clear their road and free the jeep. Even close friends who knew Jan and Xandra as an unbeatable couple were surprised at their now legendary feat.

Later, without the responsibility of so many animals, Xandra had time to indulge in her love for water. She had always dreamed of having a cottage on a lake. In 1980, Jan and Xandra went in with another couple to buy a cottage on Cataract Lake near Cloverdale, Indiana. In negotiating the closing, Xandra performed her usual magic. Her motto is, "If you don't ask, you won't get it." Since Jan and Xandra were scheduled to leave on vacation in the few days after their offer was accepted, Xandra requested that the closing be in the next two days. She also wanted the furniture in the cottage to be a part of the deal. In three days, they were on a plane to Florida with a furnished cottage to come back to. They had the cottage for ten years, sharing with many friends the enjoyment of water skiing, fishing, and cruising in their pontoon boat.

After twenty years of life together, golf became their major sport due to the wear and tear of other athletics on their joints and feet. Xandra had knee problems and Jan began to develop spurs on her heels, which made it increasingly hard to walk. At the same time, she was diagnosed with carpal tunnel syndrome. She couldn't pick up a glass of water and was in pain much of the time. She decided to have both wrists operated on at the same time and get it over with. Not knowing exactly what "everything" entailed, Xandra said, "I will take care of everything." While recuperating from the operation, Jan was without the use of her hands for the most important personal tasks. "Somehow I could feed myself, but I couldn't do anything else, couldn't wash myself, and going to the bathroom was the hardest part." Xandra remembers, "I passed the test of true love when I helped Jan on and off the toilet and with everything in between."

Jan had her opportunity to be nursemaid when Xandra broke her knee after falling on the cement on the patio. Jan was worried. "Are you all right?"

"I just bruised it."

"That doesn't look good to me."

When the swelling hadn't gone down two days later, Jan said, "We're going to emergency." Xandra was put in a cast from her thigh to her ankle. Jan took good care of her. As with the other trials in their lives, they came through this with good humor and buoyant spirits.

Both Jan and Xandra had been affiliated with churches before they met. In the years they were together, they hadn't been able to find a church that was compatible with their views. They wanted an inclusive church, and they finally decided to actively seek one out. Jan and Xandra had never tried to hide their orientation and wanted to feel comfortable with a congregation that was accepting. They went to many services in different churches and liked some, but didn't quite feel at home. They had heard that there was a lesbian assistant minister named Cindy Bates at St. Luke's Methodist Church in Indianapolis and had thought about trying it out. An acquaintance of theirs told them that Cindy was having a gathering at her house for gays and lesbians interested in getting to know the church.

Jan and Xandra began attending St. Luke's services. They really liked what the senior minister had to say in his sermons, especially emphasizing the concept that love is the most important word in Christianity. In the following years, outreach programs were introduced to invite gays and lesbians to join the church. Jan and Xandra participated in many programs that sponsored dances, hayrides, and picnics for a population which had been shunned by many churches in the past. The couple can be seen most Sundays sitting together in the second pew. They have definitely found a church home.

Jan and Xandra have lived in the same house for thirty years and have entertained hundreds of people through the years. Jan loves people and they are drawn to her robust love of life and abundant energy. Wherever Jan and Xandra travel, Jan picks up new friends. One example is the way they met Clara and Sally at the 1982 World's Fair in Knoxville, Tennessee. Clara and Sally were in front of them in a particularly long line, waiting to see the China exhibit. It was the first time China had been in a World's Fair. Before they reached the entrance to the exhibit, Jan had learned all the essentials of their lives, including the fact that they were lesbians.

The foursome spent the rest of the time at the fair together and promised to see each other again if they could. Since Clara and Sally lived in Jacksonville Florida, it didn't seem likely, but two years later they came to Indiana to attend a friend's doctoral graduation and called Jan and Xandra. Jan invited them to stay at their lake cottage, which was near Bloomington where the graduation would take place. The foursome reunited and began making plans for a cruise to Alaska in 1986.

While Jan gathers the friends, Xandra is the social director. She is an excellent planner and made all of the arrangements for the Alaska cruise and the excursions on land. They were supposed to spend the first half of the trip on the cruise ship, but it had gone aground and was taken to drydock. Xandra says, "We had to take smaller boats to see the calving of the glaciers, the whales, seals, and colonies of puffins. It was really better, because we got to get closer to everything." They traveled to Fairbanks, Skagway, and Ketchikan by train and took a sight-seeing tour by bus.

When they got back, the cruise line refunded half of their fare and gave them vouchers for a free trip to Alaska in the future. True to her philosophy of always seeking the best in everything, Xandra wrote the cruise line. She said, "While I appreciate the offer of a free cruise to Alaska, why would I want to go back there since I've already seen it? Could I use that free trip to go somewhere else?" They told her she could, and that's how the four of them ended up going to the Virgin Islands.

Jan and Xandra have shared many other adventures on the road as well as at home. They are still avid sports fans and use about as much energy supporting their teams as they did coaching and playing. No matter what the weather or how far the distance to travel, they are in the stands cheering. Xandra says, "We go to all of the Zionsville football games and all of the Butler football games. That's two games a week there. In volleyball season we had two or three games a week. It overlapped with football for a few weeks. The basketball season was pretty much on its own. When we watched high school girls' basketball, there would be a game for the varsity and a game for the freshmen on the same night. Add the women's college games and there might be five or six games a week. We try to see the final four in the women's NCAA tournament when we can. We looked forward to watching the softball games in the spring." It may seem that Jan and Xandra wouldn't have time for anything but sports, but they always have room to enjoy their friends or help them in time of need.

More important than the trips or the sports or the other events in their lives, is their sense that living their lives together is an adventure. The joys and sorrows shared are all a part of the abundance of life with the one you love. They have lived their lives without apology for who they are. Xandra says, "We always did whatever we wanted to together. Jan would come to my school functions and athletic events. I would go to the picnics and parties at her work." They wanted to be able to share their lives in every way without hiding. One of their married friends sums up their relationship beautifully: "Xandra and Jan have the best relationship of anyone I have ever known."

Laura and Kathleen

From the time she was born in 1933 near the little town of Bethel, Laura was surrounded by the mountains, lakes, and rivers of Vermont. They, and the harsh-tender change of seasons, shaped her character. She lived through capricious springs where fragile buds were threatened by ice storms. She witnessed the blinding beauty of snow-covered peaks in sunshine, the impossibly red and gold leaves in autumn and clear wild rivers. Such surroundings fostered humility and perseverance. Laura is gentle and soft spoken with a quiet undercurrent of strength, as unstoppable as the current of the rising White River which ran through her town.

When she was in high school, Laura's stomach would churn over the cute boys. She dated many of them and enjoyed their company, kisses, and hugs. "When I went to school, there wasn't such a rush to have sex." Dating was a simple thing in the early '50s, as pristine as the mountains. "We were out for a good time with friends. There weren't any cars available to us, so we would walk to the movie in Bethel when it was open on the weekends or have ice cream at the drugstore."

When Laura graduated from high school, in a class of fifteen, she was able to look forward to college. "All of my family and some of my friends helped me pay for a college education. My mother, stepfather, and my father contributed money. A friend of my mother's worked at Edward Park College in New York and persuaded the board to reduce the tuition so that I could attend." Laura didn't disappoint them. She concentrated on her studies, became a licensed X-ray technician, and got a job in Montpelier, Vermont. Warm and outgoing with engaging laughter, Laura made many friends in the five years she lived there. Jessie and Barbara were two that she has kept in touch with for most of her life.

When her best friends left for better job opportunities in Boston, Massachusetts, Laura left, too. She moved in with several roommates for companionship and economy, and concentrated intensely on her career as a lab and X-ray technician. The mix of women she lived with changed with one exception. Others would come and go, mainly to get married, but Jessie and Laura were constant. "I lived with Jessie for twenty-five years. I respected her and loved her dearly, and I think she loved me, but there was no physical intimacy involved, and we shared the house with one, two, or three other people. We never lived alone as a couple, and Jessie was dating all of this time. I wasn't. I had a great job and a lot of friends. I didn't miss dating." After a time, Jessie and Laura decided it would be wise to invest their money in a house and rent out available space to make money. They chose to return to their roots in Vermont.

Jessie had a degree in business nursing and wanted to start a business of her own. She asked Laura to join her. She needed someone with communication and organizational skills. Laura suggested that she would like to consider helping older people. They explored several possibilities and finally decided on something that would complement each of their strengths. Laura says, "We decided to do something that had not been done yet, build an elegant place where people of means would come to receive living and health care assistance when they needed it. We thought it should have a beautiful setting. They could have three meals a day, would be catered to, and at the same time have someone watch over their health." Jessie would take care of running the business aspects and Laura would interview the families and oversee the care of the residents. She had a gift for knowing how to improve her clients' quality of life.

Her mountain roots and her family's *can-do* attitude prepared Laura for the long arduous path they traveled before there were even glimmers of success. They searched for months for a building in a beautiful setting, and, at last, found the perfect place. Skeptical at first, the banker refused them a loan. He said, "Nothing like that has ever been done before." Laura's and Jessie's persistence overcame his conservative approach. He had three daughters and admitted he could never say, "No," to them,

In Spite of Everything....

either. He approved the loan saying, "I just want to see what two women will do with this opportunity."

They bought an elegant old mansion on a hill overlooking Lake Champlain. It had a wide stone veranda in front with stately pillars supporting the roof. It was an extraordinary property, one they could only afford because it needed major renovation. They risked all they had in money, time, and energy to make their dream a reality. When the first two years failed to attract residents, they advertised as a bed and breakfast. The two women cooked all of the meals and changed the bedding. They were still losing money, so they sold their house and moved into the mansion, living in the two smallest rooms near the kitchen.

After five years of endless days and sleepless nights, their sacrifices began to pay dividends. One of the wealthiest, most respected matrons of the town came to live at "The Pillars," her residency having the effect of a seal of approval for their facility. People began to believe in the work they were doing. The residence was soon filled to capacity and they added staff. In the next five years they added space to double their accommodations. In the course of twenty years, they built or bought three other facilities, one of which Laura designed to care exclusively for Alzheimer's patients. One of their homes was created to help those who could not afford good health care. Their reputations and fortunes grew.

In spite of the great success she and Laura had achieved, Jessie felt that there was something missing in her life. That "thing" turned out to be an intimate relationship with a woman. She confessed this to Laura and said that she wanted to buy a place of her own and pursue this new life. Laura and Jessie had become comfortable living together, but Laura didn't know how she felt about her life-long friend being a lesbian. She didn't reject her, but there was tension between them. Laura felt threatened. She says, "In all of my life, I had never lived alone. That was a very hard time for both of us." They were able to salvage their friendship and business relationship, but it was awkward for some time.

After Jessie left, Laura was alone for only a short time. Barbara, her other best friend from college was looking for a job in Shelburne. She became Laura's new housemate. That arrangement would only last until Barbara got a place of her own. Alone again, Laura had time to take stock of her life. She had accomplished most of her goals, college, a fulfilling profession, a dream to help aging people have comfortable lives. She had become independently wealthy and was rich with friends. It was now 1983, time had flown by. She was now fifty.

"I reached the conclusion that I couldn't go on sharing a house with women who would leave when they married. I always wanted a family. My business was calming down so I said, 'So what, I'm still young enough. I can still have a family.' Dating was a little scary after so long, and I was afraid to go out with strangers. I looked around and found a singles' club and decided to join. It cost $500, so I thought that amount of money would insure my meeting professional people."

She was pleasantly surprised. She had a good time going out with several men and enjoyed their company. Then she met Doug, a man who met all of the criteria she had listed when she joined the club. He was handsome, had a good job, didn't smoke, and said he only drank socially. He was divorced and had a son, Brad, and a daughter, Sara, whom Laura was ready to accept as her ready-made family. Doug only saw Brad and Sara on weekends anyway. Laura's friend Barbara had reservations; she counseled caution. She watched Laura become more and more attached to this charming, considerate man in spite of the times he carried his "social drinking" too far. Barbara would have been completely shocked when a year after Laura married Doug, she divorced him for the love of her life, Kathleen Shepherd.

At the time she met Laura, Kathleen had been married to Carl for twenty-four years. Kathleen and Carl went to the same college and had become good friends. Kathleen was dating other men, but there was something about Carl that was special. By the end of her first year, she had fallen in love. They both enjoyed the usual college pastimes, parties, and drinking with friends. They also had an admiration and respect for one another. He was majoring in theology and she in Spanish and education. They married just after Kathleen's second year.

Kathleen was very much in love with her husband in the first years of their marriage. She was proud of him and the work he was doing. His drinking wasn't a problem then. Their first son, David, was born in Tennessee, where Carl worked for the YMCA. His job was connected with inner-city ministries. Their second son, Christian, was born in North Carolina, where they had moved to be closer to their families.

Kathleen remembers, "As Carl's drinking began escalating after we moved to North Carolina, our quality of life began shrinking. When he was offered a church in Vermont, I suggested that when we settled down there, it would be a good time for him to stop drinking." By then their sons were two and four years old. "He'd be all right for a while after I'd blow up; then he'd get drunk again and I'd blow up again. I was a slow learner."

Increasingly, Kathleen was losing her companion and the children their father. "I began to realize that any conversation we had in the evening was meaningless the next morning. The alcohol clouded his reason." Carl was short tempered with Kathleen and though so patient when counseling his parishioners, he railed at his own sons. "He managed to be sober enough on Saturday night to prepare a sermon which he would deliver Sunday morning without a flaw. Only a few members of the congregation knew. He could always find a parishioner who would offer him a drink and then another."

During the day, Kathleen had other things to occupy her mind. Being a minister's wife isn't easy, but Kathleen fit quite well into that role. Intelligent and efficient, she headed committees, entertained guests, saw that her husband's life went smoothly, and made special time for their energetic sons.

Kathleen loved to quilt and was quite expert at it. She bought into a quilt shop and became partners with two other women. They sold supplies, provided a place for quilters to meet, helped people with designs, and solved quilting problems.

Laura had become a regular customer of the Quiltsmith, but she had never come when Kathleen was working. The day they met was memorable, because it was Kathleen's first time at running the shop alone. Her partners had tried to let her know what she could expect. They told her, "Someone is bound to come in and want to know how much material they will need and you're going to have to figure it out. The other thing is, Laura Pierson will be coming in because she's in here every other day, getting something or doing something, and you're going to have to solve a problem."

They were right about the problem. A complicated pattern was giving Laura fits. Not being one to give up easily, Laura had worked intensely, sewing and removing stitches and re-sewing the pieces of cloth. She worked while the clock ticked into the early morning hours. Still, it didn't suit her. She hated to quit and have the problem to face when she woke up. At three in the morning, she finally admitted that she couldn't figure out what was wrong. The next day, she headed for the Quiltsmith.

Kathleen was wondering when the person named Laura would come in. She felt that she was prepared to help her. She *wasn't* prepared for the whirlwind who stormed through the door, slapped her quilt on the counter, and shouted, "Fix it!" Although she was almost completely intimidated, Kathleen did fix it.

Laura was in a more amiable state when Kathleen met her in a different setting. Kathleen and her husband, Carl, had a cottage on the New York side of Lake Champlain. Vermonters called wooded property with a seasonal cottage a "camp." Carl had become acquainted with the owner of another camp close to his. It was Doug, who happened to be Laura's boyfriend. Carl suggested that Doug and Laura join them for cocktails one weekend. The men formed a sporadic relationship, but the women became fast friends. Since Laura and Kathleen shared a love for quilt making, they decided to meet and quilt together every Wednesday. Later, Kathleen and Laura went on picnics, visited museums, and planned other outings with their respective children and stepchildren to be.

They went over to Doug's camp one time. Kathleen remembers, "That was the time we found Doug with somebody else. Another time Doug was out in the woods drunk while she had the kids." Because of Doug's excessive drinking, Kathleen began to feel strong empathy for Laura. She knew what it was like to live with a man who drank. She wasn't ready to believe that Carl was an alcoholic, but she could recognize alcoholism in another woman's husband. She knew what Laura must be experiencing.

Regardless of her reservations about Doug, Kathleen made time to help her dear friend have a memorable wedding. She enlisted Laura's friends to make a quilt of memories for Laura. Since few of Laura's friends knew much about quilting, most of the work was done by Kathleen. She worked many hours into the night, thinking how happy Laura would be. The quilt was a great success. Laura was overwhelmed by her friends' gesture.

Jessie was Laura's lady-in-waiting and saw the way Kathleen looked at Laura at the wedding rehearsal. Not a person to concern herself with social indiscretions, Jessie announced to Kathleen, "You're in love with Laura." Kathleen sputtered, "I certainly dearly love Laura, but just as a friend." When Jessie told Laura what had transpired, Laura only laughed.

Laura's first sexual experience was with Doug on their honeymoon. He had spent weekends with Laura but had slept on the couch. She worried what it would be like for the first time at her age. Doug was very patient and gentle and Laura enjoyed sex with him, but she had a little twinge of apprehension when she realized the amount of alcohol Doug was consuming. Barbara's earlier warning was an echo in the back of her mind. She had dismissed it before the marriage, because the drinking didn't seem to affect their relationship.

The interaction between Laura and Doug's son, Brad, was more disturbing. Laura was ready to open her heart to twelve-year-old Brad and ten-year-old Sara, but her illusions of a pleasant time with her stepchildren were soon shattered. Brad entertained himself by tormenting Laura with annoying pranks. It was soon evident that he had as little respect for his father as he did for her and her home. His poor manners and manic energy turned her against him and only her sense of duty prodded her to allow Brad and Sara to return.

Why, four years later, Laura agreed to take Brad in on a full-time basis is still a mystery to her. At sixteen, Brad was tall and muscular, quick tempered, and unpredictable. Mark, his stepfather, was afraid of him and didn't want him there. During the worst of a series of fights with his mother and Mark, he put his fist through a heavy wooden door and ran away. His mother called Laura. "You have to take this child. I'm not keeping him any more." As Laura took in the import of these words, her thoughts remained unspoken. The words she did speak were produced unaided by reason: "Okay, I'll take him, but if he comes to live with us, he will stay here. He will not be bouncing back and forth between us." Laura reflects, "That was the strangest experience of my life. I found that I thought of saying one thing, but something different came out of my mouth! All I could hear was my mother talking. She always took in strays." Laura called Kathleen before she and Doug traveled to retrieve Brad. "Brad's going to be living with us now."

"What?"

"Yes, we're on our way. He's moving in with us."

"Are you sure? You don't even like this kid. Why are you doing this?"

"I don't know, except that it needs to be done."

They set Brad up in a little bedroom upstairs. That night marked the beginning of a slow metamorphosis for all of them: Laura, Brad, Doug... and Kathleen.

Laura had suspected before that Brad wasn't getting the dental and health care he needed. When he was twelve, she had called his mother to ask about Brad's swollen jaw. "Oh, he's always getting something. He's all right." Laura took him to her own dentist to treat a badly neglected abscessed tooth.

In the first weeks that Brad was living with them, she found that there were many reasons for Brad's anger. He had been left on his own many times. He was never hugged or praised by a mother who placed too many restrictions on a young boy. Worse, she learned his early childhood had been damaged by Doug and his former wife who drank, and fought, and verbally abused him. Now he had been thrown out of his stepfather's home. She began to see the loneliness hidden behind his fierce eyes. Laura became determined to make a safe haven for him in her home. That was no easy task.

Laura says, "For the first three weeks that he was there, every sentence he uttered was filled with anger. He hit things. He refused to do what I said. I was at my wit's end." To make things worse, Laura realized that she would have to protect him from his own father. Doug didn't mistreat Brad when he was only staying on weekends, but now he took every opportunity to tell Brad what a "no good nothing" he was. The yelling would go on and on, with Brad standing rigid and pale, anger seething within him.

Laura's only relief was to confess all of these things to Kathleen. She knew Kathleen would understand, because she was raising her own troubled teenaged son. Neither of them could confide in their husbands, who thought verbal abuse was good discipline. Just being together gave them a sense of peace and the strength to keep trying. The respect for their husbands disintegrated, and the bond between Laura and Kathleen grew. It was so comforting to know that there was someone to count on, always. They were both determined to approach their children with firmness and unconditional love.

Laura doesn't know exactly when Brad became "her son," but it was brought about by two factors. First, she told him not to listen to his father when he started yelling at him. "I told him to walk away and come to me." Secondly, she decided to "punish" him with hugs. "I knew I couldn't yell at him. He had had enough yelling, so I went to him and said, 'Every time you act this way, I'm going to hug you, because I know how you will hate that.' That was the turning point." When she started hugging him, he tried to push her away saying, "No, no, no, no!" Laura was firm, "This is what you get, so be quiet." After a week or so, she could see the beginnings of a smile on his face. "He had never smiled." There were troubles after. Doug was jealous of Laura's attention to Brad. He seemed more determined than ever to show the *boy* who the *man* was in the family, but the connection had been made between that boy and the only person who had shown him love. He would hold on to this new, wonderful relationship and be changed by it.

Laura could rejoice with Kathleen about the progress she and Brad were making and also share her disappointment in her husband. She told her friend that she didn't want to live with a man who said such terrible things to his son. It was for her children that Kathleen was staying with Carl. Now she wondered if she should leave for her children.

Kathleen's and Laura's lives seemed complicated enough without further problems, but Kathleen's efficiency as a good wife and mother was beginning to diminish due to a herniated disc in her lower back. When it threatened to cripple her, she had an operation to have two vertebrae fused. It laid her up for weeks. She couldn't climb the stairs, so she slept in the downstairs bedroom. Carl did sleep on the floor beside her and she appreciated that, but the alcohol kept him from any meaningful conversation and smoke from his cigarettes made her sick. "I didn't realize that his smoking was bothering me so much," she says now. Carl didn't seem to understand why Kathleen couldn't get up and take care of herself. "I got a breakfast and a change of underwear out of him," She says wryly. Even though he worked across the street, he didn't come to help her during the day.

It was Laura who came several times a day to see that she had enough to eat and to make her comfortable. It was Laura who moved a TV and a telephone into Kathleen's room, brought books, and fluffed her pillow. Kathleen came to feel that Laura was the kindest, most compassionate person she had ever known.

Kathleen and Laura knew little of the emotions that had quietly been building beneath the surface of their friendship. A parting hug brought forth warmth, not passion, and the need to be near one another wasn't based on desire. Kathleen *did* feel that something "wasn't quite right" when she stretched the phone cord as far away from her family as it would go to keep her daily call from Laura private.

An innocent trip to New York City brought their emotions to the surface. Laura's stepdaughter, Sara, wanted to go to New York City to check out a fashion studio. Doug didn't have time to take her, and Doug's ex-wife didn't *want* to take her, so Laura volunteered. "I asked Kathleen if she wanted to come and bring Chris and David along. Kathleen could help me drive and we could all stay with a friend of mine in New York." David decided to stay home, so the foursome started out early in the morning.

Laura's friend, Barbara, was very gracious. They were given a choice of guest bedrooms. There was a double bed in a small room downstairs, twin beds in one of the two upstairs guest rooms, and a double bed in the other. Sara quickly spoke up for the bed downstairs. Kathleen hadn't quite finished saying that she and Chris would take the twin beds when Laura interjected, "No, I think we should take the double bed so Chris can have a room to himself." This announcement wasn't as much of a surprise to Kathleen as was the feeling in her stomach. Things had become effervescent down there.

Once in bed that night, neither could sleep. They sat in the middle of the bed and talked as if they had never talked to one another before. Sometime before dawn, Laura reached over and took Kathleen's hand. Kathleen caught her breath but tried not to telegraph her excitement. Laura was a person who touched to communicate friendship. Was it that, or more? Was Kathleen hoping for more? She was beginning to feel differently and it worried her. "I thought something wasn't right. I shouldn't be feeling that way." Only Laura knew that she had never held hands with any of her friends in high school or college. Only Laura knew it wasn't just communicating friendship.

Another friend of Laura's put them up the next night. Kathleen says, "The kids slept on the floor in the living room. There was only one extra bedroom and it had a double bed. Laura and I insisted to our hostess that sleeping in the same bed would not be an inconvenience." They held hands all that night. After they got home, Laura would take Kathleen's hand every time they rode in a car together, though nothing was said. Kathleen remembers, "It was as if we didn't want to acknowledge what we were doing."

A year passed before they had an opportunity to take a trip again. Kathleen's eldest son, David, was going to New York City. They would take him as far as Albany to join some of his friends. They had planned to stay again with Laura's friend, Barbara, for four nights until David got back. Instead, they spent two nights with Barbara and two incredible, life-changing nights in a motel.

Laura suggested that they go to the motel so Barbara wouldn't be bothered for all four days. Kathleen made Laura go into the office to register, because she was too embarrassed to ask for a room with one bed. "I never would have asked for a king-sized bed. I was mortified. I wouldn't go in the office. They'd *know* if I did. It would be written all over my face." So far, they really hadn't done anything "wrong"; a little hugging and hand holding wasn't so bad, but getting a motel room? They now had a hard time denying their expectations for their third night in a bed together. Embarrassment gave way to anticipation and fear was overpowered by a sense of abandon. When Laura came out of the bathroom ready for bed, she knew by the look on Kathleen's face that this night in bed would be different. Before she could think, she said, "Don't start something you can't finish." By the next morning they both knew with certainty that they were no longer "just friends." Full realization dawned of the physical and emotional need they had for one another. Every touch, every kiss produced a new sensation. Neither had felt such passion before. If only they could stay in that motel forever.

The abrasive ring of the alarm clock was an unsympathetic reminder of reality. It was time to pick up David and go home to husbands and a life that seemed appallingly unnatural now. They were weak, their eyelids heavy, their movements slow. Kathleen says, "We didn't want to go back into the world." Laura adds, "We were sick to our stomachs; we were so tired by then." There was a wrenching sense of loss on the drive home. They were going home to alcoholic husbands who had become strangers in the last few years. They had children whom they loved and would not abandon. Still, their thoughts focused on how they could be together.

They knew they could at least see each other on Wednesdays, because quilting time had already been set up. Laura laughs, "We just didn't do much quilting after that. Before that we accomplished great things." But Wednesdays weren't enough. Two days or three days weren't enough. There was an aching need to be together. Their pleasures weren't only physical. They truly were friends and enjoyed every facet of their friendship.

They were given the gift of more time together from an unlikely source — Carl's church. Carl was offered a position on the board of the Global Church, a part of the Methodist Church's ministry. Since the last person on the board had lived in New Jersey, Carl thought that the family should move there. Kathleen had followed Carl each time he wanted to make a move, but this time, "I put my foot down. I said I didn't want to move." They hashed it over for a while. Kathleen pointed out that the children shouldn't be expected to move away from their schools. "I was involved in the church, and my shop. I was on the school board." Foremost in her mind was the impossibility of leaving Laura. "Would I go with him and just come back to Laura for visits? That would be unbearable."

Carl discovered that the church didn't care where they lived, just so there was an airport near by. He would be traveling much of the time. It was decided that they would stay in Shelburne, but they still had to move out of the parsonage because a new minister would be taking Carl's place. They found a small house a few miles from the parsonage.

"The move was good," Kathleen says. "It got us out of the fishbowl of the parsonage in the center of town." In addition, Carl was gone fifty percent of the time. It was a revelation to Kathleen that his absence was such a relief. "I was glad that he was gone so much of the time, and I felt deflated when I would come home and see his car in the driveway."

Kathleen and Laura were happy every minute they were together. It was when they were apart that doubts began to creep in. On the one hand, they were happier than they had ever been, but on the other, they were experiencing a growing uneasiness about the price they would have to pay to be together. They were torn by a sense of duty to their marriages and an overwhelming devotion to their children. Questions and doubts swirled around them: Would they ruin their children's lives if they continued to indulge themselves in a relationship that might fail when they came to their senses? They knew they were in love now, but would it last? Was this love wrong?

Laura was afraid that if she divorced Doug, and if Kathleen's love would fade, she would be alone again. The idea that she was a lesbian was not only foreign to her, it was frightening. "Did I really want this change after fifty-odd years of living that was completely opposite of my beliefs before? Would Kathleen still love me after the initial thrill was over? What would it do to Brad, whose newfound stability might be shattered? This child had been through so much. I was the only stable thing in his life. How could I ruin that?"

Kathleen had similar thoughts. "Was this a phase I was going through because I was unhappy in my marriage? Would I lose my children? As old as they were with lives of their own, would they accept this startling, radical change in my life?" She had loved Carl so much when they were building a life and a family together. When she asked herself where it went wrong, she knew that even if she hadn't met Laura, she would have ended the marriage. "It may have taken longer, but I couldn't stand to live with a man who cared so little for me or our children." Even so, "divorce" was a word that caught in Kathleen's throat. She was from a family of long marriages. "My grandparents had celebrated their sixty-seventh." Then there was her work in the church; she had established a reputation as a leader. She pictured herself being shunned by the congregation, rejected by her children. Laura remembers Kathleen's fears: "I think she thought she would be tied at the stake and burned!"

Laura was desperate to do the right thing. It was hard to accept that love had ended, when it had begun so well. Memory of sweet beginnings fed the illusion that love still remained. She decided to go away with Doug for a week to see if that would rekindle her feelings for him. They both loved the ocean and a week on the coast of Maine might be just the thing. She didn't want the burden of guilt if she didn't try everything possible to make her marriage work. She made him promise not to drink on this trip. She wanted it to be just the two of them without any alcohol.

Doug promised, and for the first two days everything went well. Doug loved deep sea fishing, and Laura encouraged him to go ahead and reserve a place on the next charter. She planned to do some reading and relaxing and would pick him up at the boat later. Public fishing boats weren't allowed to sell liquor, but customers could bring their own on board. Doug assured Laura that he would keep his promise. As it turned out, Laura spent her time missing Kathleen, and Doug spent his time finishing off a fifth of bourbon. Laura says, "He was so drunk by the time the boat docked that he could hardly manage to get down the gangplank." Laura got him back to the hotel and pushed him into a chair. She packed up all of her clothes, put them in the car, and drove away. She thought, "Doug can find his own way home."

Kathleen's father was visiting her at that time, and they were having an amiable conversation when they were interrupted by the ringing phone. When Kathleen hung up the phone, she was laughing. Her father asked, "What's going on?"

"Laura just left Doug." Her elation was short-lived because her next thought, however irrational, was, "Now I can't leave Carl. I'll have to wait a respectable length of time before I can live with Laura." She divorced Carl two weeks later. The most uncomfortable task after her decision to get a divorce was telling her sons that she was leaving their father. David's reaction was reassuring. "I don't know how you stayed with him as long as you did. I had you divorced in my own mind many years ago." David was quite aware of his father's shortcomings. Chris, a junior in high school, was hurt that his mother wanted a divorce. "He thought his parents' break-up was his fault and thought I should fix it," Kathleen says. He also blamed Kathleen when his father moved out. Carl stayed in Shelburne for two more years, and then moved to Philadelphia and remarried. Kathleen moved into Laura's house with Chris and David.

Kathleen's anticipated turmoil in the wake of their divorces didn't materialize. They weren't tied to the stake and burned. The reaction of Kathleen's church family was an anticlimax. Kathleen remembers, "I found out that my life isn't as important to other people as I thought." Besides, Kathleen's contributions to the church were solid. Carl had not been a part of the church community since his appointment to the Global Church, so the congregation didn't miss his move to another state. No one took much notice of Kathleen's and Laura's new living arrangements. Laura had decided to tell Brad about her relationship with Kathleen after they all had moved in together. Brad said, "I was wondering when you were going to tell me." Nothing else needed to be said.

Kathleen's eldest, David, and Laura's son, Brad, lived in the dorms of their respective colleges. There was room for everyone when school was out for vacations and holidays. Brad and his school classmate stayed in a room above the garage. David and Chris had their own rooms, as did Kathleen and Laura. "Just to be proper," Kathleen says.

For many years, Chris didn't approve of his mother's close friendship with Laura. "He didn't know what was going on with us, but he didn't like it." He wasn't ready to believe that his father's alcoholism was the cause of the divorce. On his weekly visits to his father, he heard a distorted version of his parents' marriage, one that fed his misconception that his father could do no wrong. His father made sure that Chris learned the divorce was his mother's fault. When he graduated from high school, he went to live with his father and his new wife. Without his mother to shield him from his father's "indiscretions," he discovered reality. With a new wife, Carl had little time for his son. He was short tempered and unsympathetic. Feeling rebuffed and disillusioned, Chris moved back with Laura and Kathleen until he went to college in the fall. Time away from everyone helped him become more tolerant.

Laura and Kathleen slept in separate bedrooms until all of the boys moved out on their own. It was a night for celebration when hers and hers became theirs. They have never slept separately since then, even when Kathleen's father became ill and stayed with them for two months. Kathleen says, "Of course, I put my bed in the sunroom for him and I 'had' to sleep with Laura, but he knew. We didn't discuss it. He didn't want to. If we did, he would have had to judge. He had a way of putting things that would brush conflict aside. It would have been different if my mother had lived." She was both judgmental and outspoken. Laura says, "I don't know if we would have gotten together if she had known."

Laura's and Kathleen's lives now center on children, their volunteer work, their friends and the many interests they have in common. Their "children" are grown men now with wives who are also part of Laura's and Kathleen's family. Kathleen is still active in her church, and she and Laura deliver food with the Meals on Wheels program. They both enjoy meeting new people and trying new things; consequently, they have many friends, straight and gay. They are known for their extraordinary hospitality. Although they both used to enjoy winter sports in Vermont, they now head for Florida before the snow flies and come back when the ground is thawed enough to start their garden. Instead of skiing or snow shoeing in the mountains, they have taken up kayaking as a new "winter" sport. Laura was 70 when she bought her first kayak.

Kathleen says, "Our living together is a breeze. We operate differently, but generally speaking, I just do everything that Laura wants."

Laura counters, "I was just going to say the same thing. We've never had the problems that we've heard from others. We *can* be partners at cards. We *can* spend months together without getting tired of one another. *I* just do everything that Kathleen wants."

Kathleen says, "Some people covet their 'space.' We've spent so much energy trying to be together that we appreciate the time we have now. How many other couples have one car to a household? I never had help with the housekeeping before, certainly not the shopping."

Laura says, "Everyday, we're thankful to have each other. We're both strong women, but we really have little conflict."

Kathleen says, "We work in the kitchen the same way. We work in the garden the same way. We have predominately the same interests."

There were differences, of course. Kathleen had an intimation of their most prominent difference when Laura said to her, "There's an open house over at Mekleson's camper place. Let's go over and have a look." They looked at some second hand RVs and got into a truck camper. Before Kathleen had time to think, Laura was signing a contract for a fifth wheel truck and a 30-foot trailer.

"We don't approach some things the same way. Laura's a lot more, 'let's,' and I'm a lot more, 'let's think about this and study it.' We end up in the same place, but Laura's there a heck of a lot faster than I am." By the time they had lived together several years, they had worked out their differences and made them advantages. The experience of building their new home is an example. There were a lot of things about their old house that they wanted to change. While Kathleen was thinking about upgrading, Laura was thinking about building a new house. Laura began looking at developments. Kathleen wasn't aware that they had *started* looking at developments. Laura found a building site that she loved. Kathleen said it wasn't going to work. She pointed out, "Look at the water standing at the back of the lot. There will be water problems here." Laura says, "Kathleen can be very optimistic where I'm pessimistic. Or she can be pessimistic where I am optimistic."

In the case of the drainage, Kathleen saw the yard full of water and Laura saw the yard empty.

Kathleen says "I remember thinking that that neighborhood was going to be a flood zone before I had any idea that we would be looking at it! At the time the builders constructed the houses, they would take care of the drainage on those lots. The drainage on the remaining empty lots got worse, and worse, and worse. The last lot was a flood plain, and that's the lot Laura liked! Laura was driving out to that lot two and three times a day." Laura defends herself: "I loved it. See, this is what happens. I figure out what we're going to get. We get it, and Kathleen has to make it work. Of course, she has to like it or we couldn't do it." Kathleen saw to it that the builder made a plan to drain the lot. She kept after him every day until the lot was dry.

Kathleen and Laura were warned by their friends that people get divorced over the stress of building a house. Kathleen says, "We had a wonderful time building it, even though we approached it 100 per cent differently." Laura was better at coming up with creative ideas about the design of the house. She says, "I'd say to Kathleen, this is what I would like for the kitchen, and Kathleen would make the blueprint." Kathleen says, "I can look at blueprints, close my eyes, visualize a walk through the house and know exactly what it will look like." Laura is fire, while Kathleen is earth. Laura sets out to do something, and by evening it's accomplished. Kathleen's way is to think about it a few days, study all aspects of the situation, then make a decision. Laura has learned to give Kathleen the time to work out the details of the big picture. Their home is grand without ostentation, pleasing to the eye with its symmetry. It is spacious without losing a cozy atmosphere, and every bank of windows brings nature into the rooms. They love living there. They appreciate being fortunate enough to live there together.

Living with Laura is so splendid that when asked what her favorite recreation is, Kathleen says, "Life with Laura." Laura adds, "One reason we are blessed with such a good relationship is that we had a strong friendship first. We had a complete understanding of each other. I never want to be without her."

Ellen and Jo

Jo at eighty-two and Ellen at seventy-six have spent most of their lives in South Carolina, and their faces are tanned and wrinkled from the hot southern sun. Ellen still has traces of red in her graying hair. Her strong, rich voice belies her age. Jo's broad smile and expressive brown eyes are inviting, and if you sit with her a while, you will be treated to lighthearted tales of their lives together. A Northerner will need some translation, for their accents are thick and idioms abound. Neither Jo nor Ellen had lived with any other woman until they met each other, because neither of them had ever met anyone who radiated that special sense of warmth and joy. From the first moment they looked at one another that summer day in 1955, they were captivated. Nothing could stop them from being together.

Ellen's feelings of attachment for women before she met Jo were tentative and fleeting. There was no sexual desire, only the sweet yearnings of a young girl awakening to her womanhood. In sixth grade she had loved a little girl. They wrote love letters, pledging their devotion. Later, she had crushes on a few high school teachers. The adoration she felt for one pretty teacher was shared by the entire football team. Ellen says, "All those burly boys and I longed for her attention. I brought her chocolate covered cherries once but never received any encouragement from the woman. She must have thought I was crazy."

When in nurse's training at the University of South Carolina in 1949, she dated a man she liked, but he wanted much more than the friendship that contented her. "I went home tired from fighting him off every night that I saw him. Finally I had to tell him, 'That's enough, I can't deal with this any more.'" She dated very little after that, disappointed that sex seemed to be the main thing on men's minds.

Ellen had much more on her mind. Upon graduating from the nursing program in Columbus, she did private duty care at night. After a year, she got homesick for Charleston, where many of her friends lived, and as soon as the Medical University Hospital opened in Charleston, she got a job there. With just a year of experience, the administrators made her supervisor of a ward. She did everything from filling prescriptions when the pharmacist was off on weekends to releasing the bodies to the undertaker.

Ellen shrugs off compliments for her accomplishments, except for one. She freed the nursing staff from wearing intern jackets with white skirts and white hose. Those uniforms had to go to the laundry and be starched and pressed. She paved the way by being the first person to wear a pantsuit at Medical University. "It was a polyester beauty, white pants with a colored top. I had to get the approval of the hospital administration, but I thought, 'Dammit if I can wear a pantsuit, I'm going to do it!'"

Ellen was particular about her appearance, especially about her beautiful strawberry blond hair. Although exhausted after a week of twelve-hour days, she still made the trip to Columbus to get her hair done. It was a 100-mile round trip, but she hadn't found anyone in Charleston who could fix her hair the way she wanted. It's funny how a small thing like fastidiousness can change the course of your life. Ellen learned some surprising things about herself after her search for a more conveniently-located hairdresser.

As the daughter of sharecroppers in the mountains of southeastern Tennessee, Jo's life was hard. Growing up in the late 1920s and 30s, she took care of the animals, carried water, weeded the garden, gathered in the crops, and helped her mother in the house. They were very poor. They heated bath water on the stove. Jo wore many a petticoat made out of flour sacks, but never went without food. Her family raised vegetables and had a smokehouse full of cured meat. Jo was the only girl in the neighborhood of fifteen boys, including her two brothers. Jo says, "I would try to outdo all of them. My mother thought that my oldest brother, Dan, was the best thing ever created, so I did everything I could to beat him, to prove to Mama that I was as good as he was." She was aggressive with all of the boys, challenging their strength and skill and winning much of the time. Still, she was lonely, spending her young womanhood waiting for something.

Jo's parents were wise and knew that education was the key to opportunity for their children. Jo was told that if she wanted to be independent in her life, she would need a profession. If girls had been allowed to take science instead of home education in eastern Tennessee in the late thirties and early forties, her options might have been broader. Her mother was a beautician, so Jo chose to attend a beauty college.

First she had to earn enough money. She got a job in a department store called the Charles Store in Knoxville and put aside most of her earnings. The owner noticed how quickly Jo became knowledgeable about the merchandise and that she had a natural ability to connect with customers. With a little instruction, she learned to keep the books and got a raise. In six months she had saved enough money to enroll in a reputable beauty college. There, she excelled and went far beyond haircuts, washes, and sets.

She was an artist with hair, a designer. She took a job with a permanent wave company, representing their products at conventions by doing "platform work." Following a strict set of rules, Jo would compete on stage against other hairdressers, some famous and most of them male. They had forty-five minutes to design a hair-do that would be innovative and spectacular. Jo was cool under pressure and worked her magic deftly. She traveled all around the South, winning a room full of trophies. She is proudest of a trophy for taking third place over competitors from six states. When she tired of traveling, she settled in Charleston to work in a salon, called All About You, where she made as lucrative an income as most professionals.

In Charleston, in 1955, hairdressers wore white, starched uniforms, and white shoes and stockings. Jo's dark eyes and hair made a dramatic contrast with the uniform. Her warm smile melted the effect of the cool clothing and her laugh was light and airy, but she would not tolerate broken appointments or whining customers. She was sought after and could be choosey about her clients. If she had known which one of her customers were spreading rumors that she was queer, she would have made sure that she was always too busy for her.

Jo says, "I knew I was gay all along; it was called queer then. I just didn't know how to go about accepting it. When you grow up being different, you're afraid everyone is lookin at ya. I just wasn't comfortable with it. One of my customers was a psychiatrist, and she told me if I ever wanted to talk about anything, I could come to her office free. She helped me see that I wasn't bad to be the way I was and helped me accept it."

A bright summer day in 1955 would do much to ease her mind by stirring her heart. Her choice of profession, and the skills she had developed to perfection, put her in the exact place at the right time to see a new customer — a nurse — sitting in the waiting area ready for a wash and set.

Ellen remembers, "I was getting too tired driving the long distances from Charleston to Columbus every week. I was working night duty at the hospital in Charleston and kept going to sleep on the road." She told her hairdresser, "I can't keep this up. I'm going to kill myself for a good hair-do." She finally asked her beautician if there was any one in Charleston.

Her beautician replied, "Well, you're kind of hard to please. The only person I know who can please you is someone who went to the same school I did, and that's Jo Graham down there in Charleston."

While she was in Columbia, Ellen called All About You, in Charleston, and asked for Jo. Then she went out to lunch with some of her old classmates and told them about changing beauticians. One said, "Oh, I don't think you want to go *there*. I heard she was queer."

Not knowing what fate had in mind for her, Ellen snapped, "I'm not going to bed with her. I'm going to get my hair fixed!"

On the day of her appointment, Ellen chose a *Life* magazine to read and sat down in the comfortable waiting area. Jo's station was in the last booth from the door, and when she arrived in the waiting area to tell her new customer that she would be a few minutes late, she couldn't speak. Sitting there in a pink dress was the sweetest, most precious woman she had ever seen, an angel with fair skin and red gold hair, with the cutest sprinkle of freckles over her nose. Jo waited, gathering her scattered thoughts. She had only seconds more to speak or look like a fool. Her brain realized that this was the woman she had been waiting for all these lonesome years. She thought, "I've fallen hook, line and sinker." What she said was, "Sorry, I'm running a little late, but I'll be with you soon."

It took Ellen time to assimilate and comprehend the momentous thing that happened to her when she looked at Jo for the first time. She, too, knew, somehow, that this was a woman she wanted to be near. At twenty-three years old, she had never experienced anything quite like this. When she sat in the chair in Jo's booth, she felt a warm sensation flooding her chest, a prickling of excitement as Jo's strong hands shampooed her hair. Jo was so close, working quickly and expertly around her. Ellen couldn't seem to get enough air, but she didn't want the session to end.

Jo, who never associated with her clients, heard herself asking Ellen to go to a movie. She couldn't bear the thought of letting Ellen walk out that door. She wanted to see more of her today, tomorrow, forever. Since Ellen didn't seem to understand, she had to repeat the request. "Would you like to go to a movie tonight?"

"No, I'm going to go home and look at TV."

"Okay, I get off today at 1:00. I have a Scout Troop that I sponsor. I'll be with them this afternoon. If you change your mind, call before 1:00."

Ellen left the beauty shop feeling confused. She was so captivated by this slender dark haired woman but felt awkward about going out with her. After all, she *had* been warned. Ellen didn't call by 1:00. She wanted to, but Fear laid its cold hand on her shoulder that afternoon and delayed the call until it was too late to reach Jo that day. The telephone rang, but there was no answer. Jo's booth was empty.

After one o'clock, Jo had no time to think about Ellen. For the next few hours, she would be surrounded by a group of twenty-one little girls. She was off to the Lutheran church to meet with her charges, all between the ages of eight and ten. They were going to work on a badge project that she had devised. She was the sole leader and undaunted with taking on the task alone. They loved her. She could match their energy and exuberance and was as fun loving as they were. She was in the center of a whirlpool of noise and activity, giving each one her attention, helping, encouraging, scolding, making sure they felt the pride of accomplishment. Exhausted but happy, she would go home and think about the "little doll" that sat in her chair that day and wonder why she hadn't called.

Ellen did look at the television that night. She looked and saw nothing. More surprising to her, she couldn't eat. "I never lost my appetite, even when I was sick. What was wrong with me?" Ellen began to understand just how powerful her feelings were for Jo. Ellen says, "I knew I had to take the chance. I was living with an aunt and uncle until I could find my own place. They would not approve of my getting involved with a woman, and I didn't know if I could keep my feelings a secret. My uncle was chief of detectives on the police force and watched over me." Her feelings for Jo were so strong, in spite of the brief time in the beauty parlor, that she was willing to risk reputation and her family's rejection to see Jo again.

While Ellen was still trying to summon the courage, Jo called. They talked as long as Ellen dared and made the first of many arrangements to see each other. As the summer progressed, they went to the drive-in movies, down to the beach for picnics, and for long walks along the shore. They watched the sandpipers poking their long bills into the sand, waded in the frothy surf, and sat looking out over the wide expanse of the Atlantic. The sun was hot. The ocean breeze was refreshing and carried the sounds of the pounding surf and crying gulls. They had long intense talks as new lovers do, not wanting the days to end, lingering on together, wanting to touch, to walk arm in arm — simple but impossible things for lesbian lovers in 1955. There were many on the beach who would be watching. No one must know.

Jo invited Ellen to a Fourth of July party sponsored by her church. One of the members with a home on the beach hosted the party. Jo was an active member of the Lutheran church and was respected by the clergy and congregation. She was warm and friendly and her buoyant sense of humor often bubbled over into laughter. Just being near Jo made people happy, as her smile was full of mischief and her eyes merry. There was a musical lilt to her voice that rose to a high pitch when she wanted to accent a humorous word. Her voice rose and fell like the swells in the ocean or the rolling hills of her childhood home. She would be a prominent figure at this party, because she was often the center of attention. She also invited Larry, a gay friend, and a woman named Clair, so that Ellen would not be her only guest.

When Ellen saw Clair, she was immediately jealous. They joined the gathering and were introduced around. There was lots of laughter, food, and good cheer. Soon, Jo was swallowed up in the festivities. They begged her to play the guitar and lead some songs. She lost track of Ellen for a while, not knowing that she was feeling left out and jealous.

Ellen left the noisy revelry and walked down to the beach. She was barefoot, not caring whether the oyster shells cut her feet or not. She walked and walked, feeling nothing but jealous anger and fear. The feelings that Ellen had for Jo were strong and frightening. She was so insecure in her brand new love; she couldn't bear to think that it might not be real, so she sat on the beach digging holes in the sand. She held a piece of driftwood dagger-like, punching it into the sand and dragging it backwards, carrying the sand up and out of the hole — agitated punches, punctuating her loneliness. Stab, pull. Stab, pull. Many holes later, the shadows on the beach began to lengthen. The sun was setting.

At a lull in the singing, Jo looked around for Ellen. She wondered where she could have gone. "Larry," she asked, "have you seen Ellen?"

"The last time I saw her she was heading for the beach."

Jo went down to the beach. She knew the currents could be treacherous here and hoped that Ellen hadn't gone out for a swim and been swept away on a riptide. She walked faster and faster, checking the little outbuildings along the way, beginning to worry now that it was getting darker. Finally, she saw Ellen sitting in the sand, still digging her holes. Jo was so relieved that even Ellen's anger couldn't dampen her spirits. She said, "I was worried about you. I missed you."

"Well, it didn't seem like it. You had time for everybody else, and you brought that other woman along and I didn't think you cared."

"I wasn't interested in her. You know I wasn't interested in her."

"Yes, I know that. I was just worried."

"Come on. Let's go. Let's take Larry and Clair home and go someplace where we can be together. I don't want you diggin' any more *holes* in the *sand!*"

Jo drove Ellen to her rented room in the house of a good friend, an elderly woman she had known for years. The house was located in the country, about thirty miles from Charleston. Her landlady had gone to visit her son for a week. She invited Ellen to stay the night. Alone for the first time, it didn't take long before they were in each other's arms. Tentative, uncertain caresses became more natural as they lost all awareness of everything around them. Jo could finally stroke that soft golden hair. Ellen, who had carried such awkward and strange feelings, relaxed and realized the exquisite tenderness of love in Jo's arms.

After that night, they desperately wanted to get a place where they could live together, but they had to work it out so Ellen's uncle would not suspect. He didn't approve of Jo, even though he had only seen her once. Ellen told him that she was going to get a place of her own. He still wanted to control where she lived, saying, "It's too dangerous for a woman to live alone. You need to live with someone else."

They sublet Billy Joe's apartment. He was one of Jo's best friends who was moving back in with his lover. To keep her uncle from finding out that she was living with Jo, Ellen told him that she was moving into an apartment with another woman who would be getting married next year. Luckily, Jo knew a young woman who had emigrated from Germany and needed money. They paid her ten dollars a month for letting Ellen hang her uniforms and some of her clothes in one of her closets. Ellen says, "The first time I took my mother over there, I was sweatin' blood. That lasted for two years. It was hard."

They lived only a short time in their first apartment because the neighbors complained about the window air conditioner they had installed. It was in the stairwell leading to the neighbor's upstairs apartment, making it inconvenient to climb the stairs. Jo and Ellen began looking for another place that would still allow them to put away money for better cars and a home of their own someday. They were both used to making the most of hard times and didn't need space or luxury to be happy. The Sunday classifieds listed an apartment above a two-car garage. Jo said, "If we could get this, it would be private. We wouldn't be in a building with other people."

When they got to the site, the owner was driving out the driveway with his daughter. He showed them the apartment and watched as Jo looked down through the floorboards to the garage below and Ellen surveyed the small rooms and tiny kitchen. But the price was right. They decided that the privacy and the money they could save on rent would be worth the sacrifice of space.

The living room was about fifteen by fifteen feet, and when they pulled down the table that was attached to a wall in the kitchen, it took up most of the kitchen space. When they sat down to eat, one was in the kitchen and the other was in the bedroom! One thing good about the small space was that they didn't need much furniture. They covered the floorboards with rugs but that didn't stop the floor from shaking when they walked on it. Whoever built the apartment had done a quick, careless job. Jo surprised the landlord by reinforcing the floor herself. She bought four by fours and, with the help of Ellen and a friend, built sturdy supports for the second story. The owner would never have to worry about maintenance with Ellen and Jo there. She also made some furniture for the apartment.

Ellen and Jo were both paying for cars and a little furniture, but also saving money for a place of their own. After all of this plus the rent, there was very little money left for luxuries. Jo remembers, "There was many a time that we looked through the drawers for coins until we had money in a big enough pile to buy a steak. We'd get tired of just eating the regular old thing. Two dollars in those days would buy steak enough for two." Ellen says, "Jo could have been making more money, because she was an award winning stylist, but she felt sorry for her customers who had a hard time paying forty or fifty dollars for a perm. She charged thirty and that was that."

Some of Ellen's and Jo's special pleasures were the dogs they had through the years. The first one they shared was a big surprise to Ellen. Ellen remembers with a laugh, "I was takin' a shower on a quiet Sunday morning, and Jo came in and stuck this little black and white Boston terrier inside the shower curtain. I didn't know Jo'd even gone lookin' for a dog. It just about scared me to death havin' that pup appear out of nowhere! We named her Dumplin. She had one black eye, like the RCA Victor dog." Jo adds, "We bred her to one of my customer's champion males and raised puppies for a while. That's how we made the down payment on Ellen's new 1961 Volkswagen." They kept a puppy from Dumplin's last litter and named her Lady.

Ellen's expertise and managerial skills elevated her position to assistant director of the hospital. Her salary was better, but she had to spend more money on clothes. Gone was the pantsuit she had fought to wear. Instead, she wore suit jackets and skirts with silk blouses. Jo, who still made more money than Ellen, helped out. She remembers, "I wanted her to look her very, very best so I bought her expensive suits and shoes to match, jackets to match, gloves and all that sort of stuff."

They didn't have anything in common with the other lesbians they knew, but they entertained each other and had a rich relationship with many gay male friends. As Jo says, "We ran with the boys. Pete and Chet were two of the best. One time Pete and Chet had a big party. They were over three hundred boys there, and Ellen and I were the only women in the whole place. We used to have the most fun. One time Pete brought in this whole crew and they were in costume and did the Can Can, and Fiddler on the Roof. Those boys were hard to beat."

Ellen and Jo were extremely closeted because Ellen still felt her job could be in jeopardy. When the staff at the hospital would tell interesting stories about their spouses, Ellen would have liked to have joined in. She had lots of stories about Jo, but didn't feel free to mention her. She resented it, even though Jo was always invited to hospital social gatherings. Ellen remembers a time when they entertained a nursing consultant from California. The director was there with some of the other administrators. "I had had a little bit to drink, and I almost said, 'my wife.' It almost fell out of my mouth. I thought to myself, 'You fool. You want to blow it right now don't you?'" That was the closest she came to making a blunder.

So that they didn't have to worry about letting a pet name slip in front of unsympathetic people, they called each other Sookie, a word they made up for each other. No one would know it was a term of endearment rather than a name. Jo laughed and added, "I call her Sookie Junior and she calls me Sookie Senior." Now a lot of people call Ellen Sookie, not knowing why or how it originated.

There were two gay bars in Charleston, but Ellen and Jo never went to them, afraid someone might see them going in. They met at friends' houses or had their friends over to their small quarters. Besides, they spent most of their spare time enjoying the many recreational opportunities on the lakes, rivers, and ocean beaches of South Carolina.

In 1959 they went looking for a piece of the landscape they could call their own. Even though they enjoyed their life together in the garage apartment, Jo felt they should invest in some property for a future home. She heard that there were lots for sale on Marion Lake, a huge 110,000 acre lake outside of Charleston. She got a map from the developer so she and Ellen could explore the area. Jo says, "I figured it wouldn't cost us anything to look, and we might just find a way to buy something if we liked it." They took Lady with them, thinking she would enjoy a walk in the woods, and drove sixty miles to the lakefront property.

When they pulled up to the area where they would find the lots, they realized no development had begun. There were flags to mark the lots, but that was all. The humid summer day was threatening rain. Lush undergrowth covered the ground and the dark trunks of pines rose to the cloudy sky. Ellen spied what looked like a small island near the shore. She wanted to explore, so Jo said, "Go right down there and look and then come back here. I'm stayin' in the car." About twenty minutes after Ellen left, it began to rain. Jo waited for quite a while, worrying. She finally stepped out of the car into the warm summer rain, unfurling a purple umbrella that contrasted with her bright blue britches and the black and white Boston terrier on a leash at her side. She began to call for Ellen, but choked back the last word when a huge man stood up out of the bushes not five feet away. Why was he hiding there? She didn't like the look in his eye. Her heart started to pound when she thought of Ellen out in the woods alone. Was she lost or…? Jo hurried back to the car and got an ax out of the trunk. It was the only thing there that could serve as a weapon. So armed, she went, umbrella and leash in one hand, ax in the other. She walked along calling and searching. She came upon another man who asked, "What's the trouble?"

"My friend is down there and I'm trying to call her. If you see her, please direct her back."

The dog was no help. Boston terriers have no patience with fools who trudge out into the rain. Lady was sensibly trying to get back to the car. Yelling at Lady to come, Jo went on, with the rain pouring down in sheets making the ground slippery. She was trying to keep her balance and not get lost in the brush, watching her feet as much as the way ahead. When she looked up, she blinked her eyes in disbelief. Four trees were moving toward her! "Ain't no way I can see four trees move. I can't be *that* hysterical." She looked again and four men were standing there carrying machetes. Jo said, "Did you see a girl coming along here?" No answer. They were probably speechless in their own disbelief at encountering Jo with her dog, ax, and purple umbrella. She began shaking the ax, shouting, "Did you see a girl coming this way?"

"Shh…shh…shhh…ure. She went thata way."

Jo decided to get out of there. She was nearly frantic with worry now, running and crying, calling for Ellen. Finally, she heard Ellen answer. By this time, tears were rolling down Jo's cheeks and she needed to blow her nose, impossible with the ax in one hand and the leash and umbrella in the other. She spied a nearby stump and swung the ax in a high arc to set the ax in it. "Of course, the dang thing went clear to the ground." She had underestimated the strength the surge of adrenaline had given her. She started to blow her nose and felt the eyes of others boring into her. Jo looked up and saw the machete-toting men watching her from the bushes. She reached back to get the ax and couldn't pull it out of the stump!

Ellen came up then; she too, had been crying. She explains, "That's when I smoked, and I didn't have a cigarette. I was upset." She had been lost for two hours. Together they ran back to the car, and later discovered that the men were guarding a still that was hidden in the woods.

The story of their lake-lot adventure has been told around many a campfire and coffee table. Ellen always protests, saying, "I'm not gonna listen to that one more time," but she always stays to hear it again and laughs with the telling of it.

They weren't able to buy any of the lots they looked at that day because there were eighteen hundred people before them. A realtor called a few weeks later, however, to see if they would be interested in leasing a lot on the other side of the lake for one hundred dollars a year. They signed up for a property one hundred yards from Lake Marion and began to go out on weekends to clear brush and plant trees. They bought a used eight by forty-foot house trailer as a temporary weekend get-away.

In 1967, Jo noticed a slight secretion from her nipples. It was greenish colored and had a strong odor. It stained her clothes. She couldn't wash it out or bleach it out. The doctor said it was an abnormal secretion from her mammary glands and should be monitored with regular check ups. A year later the test from the discharge indicated precancerous cells.

Ellen, who had seen much disease and suffering in her career as a nurse, knew the best and worst scenarios. She had been calm and efficient in the hospital treating the worst cases with compassion and confidence, but finding out that Jo had precancerous cells in her mammary glands brought her close to panic. She needed all of her strength to remain positive. During the operation to remove the ducts, she paced the waiting room and prayed. She was at Jo's side when Jo woke up and smiled at her. "The doctor says he took out your ducts and you don't have to worry how you look. He got everything out through the nipple and then put the nipple back!" The surgeon told them that if the discharge didn't come back in two years, Jo would be fine.

Two years later, in the spring of 1969, the civil rights movement marched its way into Charleston. Segregation had been abolished in 1959, but there were other ways to keep people oppressed, such as discrimination in salaries and in who received promotions, and respect. When 400 staff members didn't show up for work at the University Medical Hospital in March, all of Charleston became enveloped in the conflict.

As assistant director, Ellen had the job of managing personnel, hearing grievances from the staff and traveling from Charleston to Columbus for hearings with the state grievance committee. She knew of the dissent well before the strike, because she had become very close to some of the staff. She says, "I really sympathized with the strikers. The strike was horrible, but the black employees didn't get the respect and recognition they needed. They couldn't eat in the same cafeteria we ate in or use the same restrooms. The hospital was built on a segregated basis to begin with, and it wasn't until 1959 that they integrated the hospital. When they came to me with a problem, I told them that I'd never make a promise I couldn't keep. I told them I'd do everything I could, but many times there was nothing I could do." What she did do was treat each person with respect. The employees were finally granted their demands, and long after the strike was over, former employees would greet Ellen in the grocery or on the street and thank her for caring.

Just as the anger began to build with the strike, Jo noticed the telltale stain on her blouse. When she pressed her left breast, the thick greenish discharge oozed out, and she knew she would have to have a mastectomy. She wondered how Ellen would feel toward her with a big scar across her chest. Ellen made it clear: "I love you, Sookie. I love you. The only thing that matters to me is that you are with me and free of this cancer. I don't care about a scar or any missing boobs. I love you."

Ellen was caught between her loyalty to the welfare of the patients and her love and concern for Jo, who was recovering from her mastectomy in Rowland Hospital across town from University Medical. Ellen's director refused her request to work nights, so she couldn't visit Jo during the day. She rushed across town on any break she could in her twelve-hour workday. Then she spent the night with Jo, unless she needed to stay at

University Medical all night. Thankfully, Jo was recovering rapidly and came home after five days. By the time the disturbance had reached its peak, she was well enough to go back to work and help Ellen with things at home.

The strikers persevered for months and months. Their cause was just, but the atmosphere became uglier as time passed. The National Guard was called in and stationed around the hospital. Coretta Scott King led a march with over a thousand protestors. Angry workers marched and chanted, trying to keep nurses from coming into work. When the hospital was critically understaffed, Ellen spent the night there.

One night, Ellen and Jo heard noises below their garage apartment. Other places had been firebombed. Jo decided that they needed to move up to the lake. She remembers, "It wouldn't have taken much to set that old building on fire. We brought pictures and anything else of importance up to the lake." Jo took Ellen to work, let the dogs off at the apartment, and at 7:00 a.m. got to the beauty salon, where she usually had a customer waiting. When she got off work, she waited with the dogs until Ellen got off at six in the evening. Then they made the trip back to the lake. Since Ellen was a salaried employee, she wasn't receiving overtime. Months after the strike, the hospital board finally decided to compensate her. Ellen says, "We took that money and built a chain link fence around the lake property so no one could drive a car in there."

As the strike was becoming a memory, Jo became fully healed. Ellen was so loving and supportive that Jo didn't suffer any trauma from worrying about disfigurement. She says, "All these people that have to go to all these get-togethers and clinics to discuss all of it....I ain't got time for that. I've got other things I want to do. It makes a big difference to have someone who loves you no matter what." Ellen suggested that Jo get a bra with prostheses if she wanted. Jo says, "I got some that I can stick in, and if I want to be a B size I can be a B size and if I want to be a D size I can be a D size."

"She doesn't wear them that often."

"Only when I get dressed up."

"Which ain't often!"

During the sixteen years that they lived in the garage apartment, Ellen's family and friends became adjusted to the idea that Jo and Ellen lived together. No one brought up the subject of their relationship, and

Ellen and Jo were not going to announce it to anyone. Even Ellen's uncle came to visit from time to time. Ellen thinks he even got to like Jo, but Jo says, "I don't think so." Jo's mother and father loved Ellen from the beginning. Occasionally they came to visit for a week. They were all so congenial that the small space didn't seem cramped.

In 1971 Ellen and Jo bought a double-wide manufactured home and moved to the lake. They had a 120-mile round trip to work, but that didn't matter. They were living in paradise. They made good use of their beautiful state, the rivers, Lake Marion, and the ever changing Atlantic beaches. Pete and Chet bought a home seven miles across Lake Marion, to be closer. They would all meet on the island near Pete's and Chet's place and cook the fish they caught, lounge on the sand, and water ski. Ellen and Jo would pitch a tent and spend the night. Ellen named their camping island Arrowhead because of the Indian arrowheads they found there.

They had several boats through the years, but the one they enjoyed most was a seventeen-foot Seafarer Sunliner with a seventy-five-hp engine. Jo says, "It would take anything the lake would give it. It had a windshield and a top you could zip up in the weather or at night for camping. We had a little TV that connected to the battery in the boat, so we could watch it from seats, which made into beds. We had mosquito netting around the windows, so we could have them open. We were snug."

They trailered the boat to the Cooper River, which had water gates at intervals to control the level of water released over acres of unused rice paddies along its banks. They camped on the riverbank or on the boat. When the rice paddies were flooded, the water reached a depth of fifteen feet. Jo caught a seven-and-a-half pound bass there, which was mounted and still has a prominent place on their front porch.

From the first day they lived together, they had not been separated except for Jo's time in the hospital. Ellen had no idea what it would be like for her when she consented to go to a hospital convention in Florida. She felt that the trip was necessary in order to keep her job secure or she would not even have considered it. She drove down and stayed in a motel with a friend of theirs who also worked in the hospital. Ellen says, "I have never been so damned lonely. I was so upset. I was so worried about Jo that I called her as soon as I got there to make sure she was all right. Before I left she told me she was going to go fishing and I thought, 'My God she could go out there and drown!' Not that she hadn't been fishing for the last thirty years and knew everything about a boat. I'm a worrier. I worry all the time, and when she didn't answer the phone the first time I called, I thought I'd die." Ellen survived that separation and swore that she and Jo would never be separated again. She says, "I have never been on a plane because I am afraid to fly, but if it was a matter of life and death for Jo, I would get on a plane right now to get to her."

Twenty-six years have passed since Jo's mastectomy and there has been no recurrence of cancer. But Ellen has paced and prayed in hospital waiting rooms other times for Jo, who had a hysterectomy ten years after her mastectomy. More recently she had a heart catheterization. Ellen says, "I know a catheterization is not a big deal any more, but I worried about her. I don't know what I'd do without her. I can't stand the thought of anything being wrong. Jo had some blockage in her coronary artery and some in the collaterals which take the blood from the heart, but a person can live a full lifetime with that condition."

The operations did not take any of the sense of adventure out of Jo, who came home one day all excited about the "cutest little mini van" she had seen in a parking lot. She had stopped and talked with the people who had rented it. She related their conversation to Ellen. "They said it was a mini version of all of the comforts of home. It had a camper on a Toyota frame." Jo's enthusiasm was catching and soon she and Ellen were "just looking" at small motor homes. When they inspected one like the Toyota, they felt it might be a little too small; however, their interest was kindled and they began to look at others. Jo felt a motor home would solve her problem. She needed to keep her legs elevated when they went on long trips in the car, and Ellen's Mustang would not accommodate Jo's long legs. They bought a never-used 1986 model in 1987: an over-the-cab camper on a Toyota chassis, a little larger than the first one they saw.

They went to the mountains in North and South Carolina and to Florida, but couldn't be gone for more than two weeks at a time because of work schedules. While in route to Canada, they had many impromptu adventures which made them forget about time. Near Princeton, New Jersey, they pulled into a state park where they expected to find slots for RVs and were wearily disappointed. Jo says, "It showed on the map that there was camping." Ellen says, "We didn't know what we were going to do, because we'd never been on a long trip before. Then we see this fellow coming across the field walking his dog. He stopped and told us he lived close, and we could come and stay in his yard. He and his wife taught at Princeton University." Ellen and Jo barely had time to level the motor home before Mr. Phillips came over to socialize. Ellen remembers, "The fellow came out and was talkin' to us. I invited him in even though we were so tired, and I had to go to the bathroom so damned bad I thought I would die. That was a little Toyota, not more than twenty feet long. It wasn't like you could just close off doors or anything. There wasn't any privacy, so I managed to wait three hours until he left. He was really nice, though."

Another stop was Newport, Rhode Island, a picturesque town with houses perched on the hillsides leading down to the Atlantic. There were lobster fishermen pulling up their catches and sailboats farther out, skimming over the water. They went down to the wharf to look over the lobster catch. Ellen remembers, "A man picked out a live one and steamed it for us. We took it back to the RV and ate the best lobster we had ever eaten."

They stayed three nights at a campground in Montreal and went to the National Art Museum to see a special Picasso exhibit that had been organized by the artist's daughter. There was a King Tut exhibit in Quebec. Jo says, "Anytime we saw something cultural, we just jumped in on it." They were having such a good time that they forgot they needed to be back at work in four days. They were nearly 2,000 miles from home. Jo laughs as she recalls, "We got so far away that we had to drive 500 miles a day to get home so we could go back to work. That's not easy when you're driving an over-loaded mini camper."

After four years of travel in their little camper, it seemed to have shrunk in size. Ellen remembers, "We had to crawl up into the bed above the cab, and, of course, we couldn't sit straight up in the bed. You'd bash your brains out if you did."

"It just wasn't that comfortable," Jo adds, "and it was overloaded before it ever got off the rack. The bearings were worn out. I didn't want to make any more trips, 'cause, I thought, 'If this thing stops on the side of the road, what are we gonna to do?'" They bought a thirty-two foot Winnebago in 1991, which was much more comfortable, but it still had a small bathroom.

Ellen remembers the day when their whole concept of camping changed. "This woman came in a van with three dogs. She was small or they wouldn't all have fit. Her name was Jeanie and she gave us some information about an organization that was for women who traveled in motor homes. We finally decided to join in 1992 and went to our first rally in Charleston." RVs driven by women, mostly lesbian couples, occupied half of the campground. Around the crackling campfire, they shared the camaraderie with many who would become life-long friends. It was easy to keep in touch, because at the next rally they would meet new people and become reacquainted with those they had met before. With the directory of names and addresses of members, they could call their new friends and plan together which rallies to attend. Now Jo and Ellen know many of the people in the campgrounds from the Atlantic to the Pacific.

One of their favorite places to camp was on Edisto Beach in South Carolina, where they looked for fossils, sharks' teeth, and mastodon bones. Ellen says, "I found a rib from either a wooly mammoth or a mastodon." There they met Harold and Becky. Harold asked Jo and Ellen — and all of their friends who were camping with them — over for a drink. Jo says, "There were about ten of us, all lesbians, sittin' around in their trailer havin' a great time. Becky up and said, 'I feel like a minority here.' We all laughed. After we got to know them, Ellen and I traveled with Harold and Becky to Pekin, Illinois, to visit Sharon and Carla." Ellen adds, "We all went on the gambling boat and had a good time together. We had a lot of straight friends down at Edisto. We liked sitting around the campfire telling tales." Jo built a liars' bench for fish stories.

In 1998, the refrigerator gave out on the Winnebago. A new one had a thousand-dollar price tag, so Jo suggested that they go to the RV show that had just opened in Columbia. Jo says, "We'd been there about thirty minutes looking at a thirty-two foot diesel-powered beauty, and I told the man, 'Put the key in the door.' That's when we got our diesel pusher with an engine in the back." The thirty-two foot dream home on wheels was spacious and luxurious — a fitting accommodation for queens of the road. Ellen likes the spacious, *private* bathroom. Ellen and Jo have been RVing for twenty-one years and never tire of one another's company or of meeting new friends.

As much as they love the excitement of exploring new places, they love their home and property on the lake more. They have spent many years creating a place that is as comforting as southern hospitality. Ellen says she's the gofer, but Jo says she couldn't do without her. Together they built an outbuilding to use as a work shed. Later, when they wanted to move it, Jo says, "It took four men to tear it down after a hurricane couldn't even budge it!" Jo's most ambitious project as an amateur landscape artist was a patio that wrapped around the side of the house and continued on toward the lake. She had imagined it with used bricks, but the land sloped down to the lake and they couldn't afford to haul in dirt to level it. Typical of Ellen's and Jo's resourcefulness, they found a way to have a beautiful, decorative patio with little expense.

Their neighbor, noticing that they had some leftover PVC pipe from a drainage job, asked if he could buy it. Jo's mind immediately leapt to his front-loading, dirt-moving machine. "We won't charge a thing if you will haul us two scoops of fill dirt so we can have a level patio base." He brought his huge machine over the next day and dumped a mountainous pile of dirt about fifty feet from the house.

Then the heavy work began for Ellen and Jo. They used a wheelbarrow to carry the dirt to the sloping hill so that it could be leveled with rakes and hose later. After the dirt was level, they put a layer of sand over it to make a base for the 900 used bricks from various places that would be laid on top. Jo took real pride in the bricks made in England 200 years earlier that had come from one of her customer's houses. A ninety-eight-year-old customer donated a wrought iron fence railing from her home in Charleston. Their biggest expense was $380 for five big volcanic rocks. Jo brought them home in her pickup truck and pushed them out with a hydraulic jack, and then Ellen and two other friends helped lever them into place with two-by-fours. (This was all done before Jo took a brick laying course later.) For a final touch of elegance, they got permission to go onto some land the developers were clearing and moved thirty three dogwood trees into the yard. The whole effect was one of genteel southern charm...but the crowning glory of the yard was yet to come.

Forty-nine years of life together whirled by like scenery from a fast-moving train. Jo and Ellen lived simply, laughed often, and loved each other and their friends deeply. Dear friends Pete and Chet died at ages seventy-two and seventy-nine, respectively. The time for boating and tent camping passed. Ellen and Jo missed those days, and still miss them, but they haven't stopped living. With their abundance of new friends from their RV travels, they have made a tradition of celebrating Jo's and Ellen's anniversaries at Lenoir Campground near Boone, North Carolina.

Their forty-ninth year brought a delightful surprise. Jo had always been eager to learn if there were antique shops near the campgrounds, so Ann, a very special friend from Charleston, took them to an antique/junk store along the highway. There was a statue in the front and Jo had to see it. When she and Ellen came closer, they saw it was not the usual backyard statuary. This was a work of art, not just a statue, but a bronze fountain of two five foot tall mermaids. There was fine detail in the hair and faces, and the scales from the hips down were covered with a blue-green patina. Their graceful arms were reaching to touch lily pads that seemed to float above them, and their hair seemed to be gently lifting as in a slight current. The sculpture emanated total serenity. Jo and Ellen stood quietly in admiration, each thinking, "They belong with us," as if the mermaids were living beings. The storeowner, a congenial but businesslike woman, broke their reverie saying, "It's not for sale. I've turned down $6,000 for it. It brings people in and I'm attached to it myself."

Over the next three years, they came back to the campground and visited the statue, becoming more and more friendly with Mrs. Farmer — Mary. During the summer of their forty-ninth anniversary, the statue was not in its place of prominence in front of the store. For Jo and Ellen, the hot summer day suddenly turned cold. When Mary came out to greet them, Jo found her voice first. "Mary, what happened to the statue?"

"I moved it to the back, behind the fence. Some antiques have been stolen."

Ellen took a deep breath. "We were afraid you had sold it."

"No, but I've been thinking. I believe I'm going to sell it to you."

Ellen said, "It's our anniversary. It was meant to be."

"I think you're right." Then the business side of Mary took over. "I want $3,000 cash today."

It took them awhile to find a bank in order to retrieve some of their money, and they still had no way of getting the 800-pound statue to their lake home. Joyce and Sharon, a couple from Charleston they'd just met at the campground, came to the rescue. Joyce, a teacher, and Sharon, a school principal, said that they would pick up the statue and deliver it to them. They had an extended-bed truck, which they used to pull the trailer they camped in. Sharon said, "If I can get the tailgate up with the statue in the truck, we can haul the statue and still bring the trailer home."

The next day, Ann, Sharon, and Joyce followed Ellen and Jo to the antique shop. Mary had asked her nephew to come and help. Sharon got the truck positioned so all could help tip the statue onto a carpet on the truck bed, then shove and maneuver it in diagonally so the tailgate would close. The mermaids rested peacefully on the ride to Charleston, but may have wondered in their bronze brains how in the world they would get out! Jo dreaded the thought of having to make small adjustments if they didn't place it just right. That would have to wait until the next weekend because it was too late by the time they got home. Sharon had to drive the truck to school all week with the mermaids — covered snugly up in a blanket, of course. One of Sharon's students, who had been in much trouble himself, suspected foul play. He whispered, "What's that body doing in your truck?"

It was hot the afternoon the fountain was delivered. "Hotter than the hinges of Hell," Ellen said. She kept the lemonade and beer flowing. Ann had come to help Jo dig a small pond for the statue to rest in. They lined it with rubber sheeting and finished surrounding it with flat bluestone just in time for the grand entrance of Sharon, Joyce, and the mermaids. Sharon backed the truck up to the pool and the five friends began pulling the carpet with the statue. Slowly, they pulled it half-way until it started tipping. Jo said triumphantly, "It came down into the exact, perfect spot." She attached the hose from the pump to the tube that carried the water up through the statue, and then turned the pump on. The water began to flow and cascade onto the tiers of lily pads that rose between the mermaids, then onto their bodies, their entwined tails, and down to the water below. It was music and magic at once, a crowning masterpiece to celebrate all of the work they had done to make their dream come true.

Jo and Ellen celebrated their fiftieth anniversary at home on July 4, 2005. Their RVing friends, gay and straight, from all over the United States, sent flowers. Jo says, "Every time we looked out the door on the third of July, there was a florist." Ellen says, "I knew it was our fiftieth anniversary, but I didn't expect people to send flowers. Four of our very good friends got together and sent a beautiful arrangement of yellow roses. Jo's brother, Clarence and his wife, Beverly, sent an arrangement. Joe and Susan sent us one in a basket." Jo adds, "Kathy and Gloria sent us one, and Marie; it looked like a florist shop around here."

They wanted to be home to celebrate with a few friends, people who lived within reasonable driving distance. Most of them stayed the whole weekend. "Ann churned ice cream. We cooked out. Some went down to the water to fish. They had a big cake for us. It went on for two or three days."

It seemed as if they had just finished drinking the champagne for their fiftieth when another three years flew by. Fifty-three Fourth of July's, fifty-three years, at eighty-two and seventy-five they remember a life well lived and look forward to many more years together. Ellen says, "The years have gone so fast. Where have they gone to? I could live with her another fifty-three. I could live with her forever."

Jo nods her head and smiles.

Faith and Ann

Dare she say, "I love you?" Ann had never remotely considered telling a woman that until she met Faith. Now, thoughts of Faith flooded her mind, threatening to drown reason. Faith was so petite and energetic. Her eyes actually twinkled when she smiled. But Ann had been in the Navy long enough to know what happened to lesbians or those even remotely suspected of being lesbians. She wouldn't even have a trial. "The Navy would only have to state cause and I would be dishonorably discharged." Her public humiliation would reverberate through her family and friends. All hope of a job in public service would be gone. In the 1950s, in all of the armed forces, homosexuality was an abomination to be eradicated. Listeners and watchers were everywhere, assigned to pursue the suspicious. Lives were shattered with a whisper, long service ended with an accusation.

Knowing all of this, Ann struggled with the idea of revealing emotions that were foreign to her. More terribly, they were threatening to swell out of control. Joy and fear mingled in a chaos that left her weak. She certainly hadn't expected this. She had never felt this way about a woman, about anyone.

In high school, she knew she was different but didn't know why. She dated men in college and liked some of them, but she couldn't feel the spark of sexual attraction she knew she was supposed to feel, though her dates certainly became aroused. "In those days they used the word 'frigid' for women who were not interested in sex, and I just thought I was one of those." Only some intense friendships with female classmates in high school and college came close to what she was feeling now. She had heard the word "lesbian" in high school when she witnessed a girl named Sharon being taunted. Ann thought it was cruel, but it didn't occur to her that she had anything in common with Sharon.

After serving in the Navy for two years, she witnessed the beginning of the witch hunts. All the branches of the military assigned personnel to spy on those suspected of being homosexuals. Recruits who signed up had to answer the question, "Are you a homosexual?" This means of screening would continue until the "Don't ask, Don't tell" shift in 1993. Homosexuals were considered mentally and emotionally dysfunctional and would therefore weaken the armed services. Inductees were encouraged to report unnatural behavior. Some under suspicion were followed or interrogated. Gay bars were off limits and monitored. Some of the accused were pushed into making up a list of names of people they thought might be gay in order to escape a dishonorable discharge. It was such a terrible thing to be accused that one young woman Ann knew from her early training got pregnant to get out with an honorable discharge.

Ann didn't know that lesbians don't "fit" into a specific physical or personality profile, that lesbians are all races, body types, nationalities and, yes, even hairstyles. Like so many raised in the late '40s, she had no idea that she was a lesbian herself. "It was quite a while until I finally figured it out."

In boot camp there had been communal showers and toilet facilities without doors. She had slept in a barracks with other women, dressed with them, and brushed her teeth beside them. Ann remembers marching everywhere. Even eating was extremely regimented. As the daughter of a naval officer, she knew of the rigors in the military and she accepted the treatment for what it was, a program designed to create a strong, disciplined, fast-acting force to protect her country. Still, she was not accustomed to such close living conditions, and sharing every private act or noise with a room full of others, was embarrassing. Trying to pee quietly was like trying to hush Niagara Falls. The women were stripped of all softness in their lives, and the harshness of the environment matched that of the discipline. Many did not make it through basic training.

While in the Navy, Ann became acquainted with Shirley. They got an apartment off post, an option open to those who finished basic training. The move wasn't unusual for women tired of barracks living. They formed a close, loving friendship. Ann says, "I wondered if other women felt as strongly about their best friends as I did about Shirley. During the time I lived with her, the thought became planted that maybe there was something 'different' about me." The women were separated when they received orders for different places.

Ann was assigned to Pensacola, Florida, and had to move back on base for photography school, but her living quarters had improved. After years in the Navy, she had finally gotten some privacy on the post, a room to herself in the barracks with a door she could actually close — not lock, but close. The open barracks now became a thing of the past. Ann luxuriated in her huge assigned room with a bunk on each side and big closets all to herself. She spread her belongings everywhere.

She didn't know that it was her great, good fortune that the Navy would soon disrupt her solitude. Another photographer third class would soon be assigned to her room. When Ann returned from school one evening, there were suitcases, trunks, and miscellaneous "stuff" cluttering her sanctuary. Her space had been invaded! She built up a stockpile of indignation and was ready to ambush the enemy who dared invade "her" room.

Faith, the enemy, one photographer third class, entered. Ann launched a verbal attack. A generous smile that disarmed most of the people she met faded from Faith's lips. She sat heavily on her bed, too tired to respond, but she was thinking, "Oh, my God, what have they put me into? This woman is a witch!" Ann softened when she saw how Faith's shoulders sagged and how tired her eyes looked. Faith was clearly weary from travel. She had arrived too late to get to the mess hall for dinner. Compassion overcame anger and Ann took a grateful Faith off the post for pizza. Over pizza, without the cloud of anger to blind her, she saw that Faith was cute.

As the weeks went by, their friendship grew. Faith's luminescent smile returned. Ann welcomed her into the room and into her heart. Ann remembers, "I found that sharing was easy." Faith brought a lightness to her life she had never known. They began spending more time together, mostly with other people, but sometimes alone, because they felt so comfortable together. They were both quick to grasp the humor in their lives and laughed often. Still, Ann had no premonition that her affection for Faith would grow into anything more than she had experienced with Shirley. She had never been awakened to sexual desire. She would touch Faith affectionately or playfully but not seductively, not knowing why it was so important to be close, to touch.

Faith soon felt a familiar chemistry between them. Ann was tall, slender, and had a quiet confidence and serenity about her. Faith wasn't feeling particularly serene herself. She was having trouble with her eyes. They kept wandering over Ann's body. Faith liked the way Ann moved, and sat, and laughed, the way Ann's eyes would look directly into hers. "I couldn't stop looking at her," Faith says, "I didn't want her to catch me staring, but I had a hard time keeping myself from looking at her."

Faith began thinking dangerous thoughts. "How would Ann's body feel close to mine? Should I tell her how I feel?" What should have been the best thing ever to have happened became a nightmare of longing, for she knew what it was like to love a woman passionately, with abandon, to feel the soft contours of a lover's body, and be electrified by the response. She wanted to touch Ann like that. She wanted everything.

She knew by the look in her friend's eyes that Ann loved her, but love takes many forms, and Ann seemed more friend than shy lover. One misplaced touch and Faith knew she would be out of the Navy with a dishonorable discharge that would follow her to every job interview the rest of her life. She felt fairly certain that Ann wouldn't turn her in, but as important as her career was, it was more important not to do anything that would hurt Ann. She didn't want to see a look of shock or dismay — or worse, repulsion — if she tried to kiss her. She definitely didn't want to be the one to awaken Ann to the frightening world of homosexual life in the Navy. She valued their friendship too much to take a chance on losing it. Thin walls, a door with no lock: insanity.

From the time she could reason, Faith thought she was gay. In 1952, at age twenty-two, she felt pressure from her mother and friends to marry, so she joined the Navy. In the Navy, she experienced an intensely loving, physical relationship. After basic training and attending Advanced Photography School in Pensacola, she was sent to Moffett Field in Santa Clara County in California and served there for three years. Moffett was labeled "the country club of the Navy." In their time off, she and her many friends went to the beaches and bars and generally enjoyed everything southern California had to offer. During that time she met a photographer third class, Shana MacIntosh. Mack seduced her, and Faith felt the excitement of romance and sex for the first time. Mack moved on when the thrill was over and left Faith with the cutting pain of betrayal and loneliness, unable to share her feelings with anyone. She recalls that months later, when she got over the sting of rejection, "I knew, really knew who I was."

A year later, she met Karen, a good-time girl, who ran up bills in Faith's name, then left her devastated and deeply in debt. "If this is what loving a woman means, I don't want it," she thought. She also came to believe that she could not fulfill her need for love and still have a career in the Navy. She was willing to suppress her need for love to keep that career. Meeting Ann made her resolve harder to keep. She must never let Ann, or anyone, know of the desire that was erupting inside her.

Faith was petite, fun-loving and so feminine looking in her uniform even in coveralls and hard hat that you would wonder why she was concerned about being under suspicion. It didn't take much, though, to make Navy personnel the target of an investigation. She knew of women who were accused who didn't know themselves if they were gay, but the incessant, interrogation they endured brainwashed some of them and they confessed out of confusion and weariness. Others left the service out of anger against such unfair treatment. Faith didn't feel that she could hold up under a brutal inquisition. She'd been traumatized enough in boot camp.

While Ann took the attitude that the rigid rules and harsh discipline were a part of the game, Faith's reaction to boot camp was different for several reasons. Although her stepfather was also a military man, a colonel in the army, Faith remained a free spirit. She couldn't stand the regimen. "I thought it was bad. They treated you like dirt." She dreaded standing in rank at attention waiting for inspection. The Commander would pinch their collars to try to make a dent. If there was a dent left by her thumb, they received demerits. "I starched mine so stiffly that I had a permanent red mark around my neck the whole time I was in boot camp." Faith was softer than Ann, her feelings closer to the surface. Another reason for her difficulty was that she couldn't see the point in having the bed covers pulled so tightly that the inspecting officer could bounce a quarter off them. She learned very quickly to make her bed tightly enough to pass inspection. Having her sheets and blanket ripped apart while she stood at attention made her a perfect bed maker.

Overcoming her desire for sweets was another matter. No one was allowed to keep cookies, candy, or any other snack in her locker after lights out at ten o'clock. Any package which contained sweets had to be eaten before then or be confiscated, and if the box was a big one, there was very little time to finish it all. Mail was distributed after all the classes and dinner were over. Faith's mother often sent homemade cookies or candy. Thinking it a shame to let the drill instructor take her candy, Faith invented original places to hide it, willing to risk getting demerits for having the comfort of a chocolate bar after lights out. "I emptied a Kotex box and stuffed it with candy bars," she remembers. But Faith soon found that it was impossible to hide anything from the drill instructor because she had seen it all before. Faith thought the woman must have had the nose of a bloodhound. "I got demerits out the kazoo in boot camp." Faith ended up scrubbing floors or cleaning up the kitchen for punishment. "Yeah, oh yeah, they don't fool around with you."

With boot camp over and the crimes and misdemeanors behind her, Faith took on the challenges of learning as much as she could in the many courses the Navy offered. She loved associating with the disciplined, loyal, men and women willing to give up their lives, if necessary, in defense of their country. She, as Ann had done, qualified to take the more difficult courses of Air Controlman School. WAVES were not allowed to fly but could take the training anyway. "Up to the end of my service in the Navy, none of the services allowed women to be involved with the flying of an airplane."

She wanted to make Air Controlman her career, but didn't pass the eye examination. She chose photography school instead. If her eyes had been a little better, she would have been an Air Controlman and not have met Ann. "My lack of 20/20 vision was a little nudge from fate to bring us together." As an expert in photography, after security clearance, she was assigned to the team that would photograph military functions at the White House. With more security clearance, she would be assigned to photograph aerial views of cities and installations important to United States security. She hung out of helicopters later in her career as a civilian hired by the Army, taking pictures of army installations.

Faith and Ann were rooming together, were in the same class at school together, and were taking every opportunity to be together in their free time, neither knowing the other's feelings, neither able to risk that first move. Ann says, "We call what happened the night after three months had passed since we met, 'The night of spontaneous combustion.'" The tension of separation became more than Ann could tolerate. They had gone out to dinner that night and had a couple of drinks, enough to bring the barriers down. They readied for bed as usual, said, "Good night," and lay down in their bunks. In the dark, Ann lay wide awake, reliving the sound of Faith's laughter, the warmth of her smile, her petite body smelling of soap and cologne. Ann recalls, "It was like there was a heavy weight on my chest. I knew I had to do something."

Guided by belief in Faith's love and made bolder by the alcohol, Ann crossed that twelve-foot barrier between them to sit on Faith's bed. The look in Faith's eyes was calm and inviting, and Ann knew if she didn't act upon the love she felt for Faith now, she would lose the chance. Ann leaned over and kissed Faith tentatively at first until the kiss was returned, softly and full of promise. That kiss released all the longing and need that had been suppressed so long.

Faith says, "I couldn't believe that this woman I had wanted for so long was here in my bed and kissing me." Nothing seemed more natural than Ann's touch. Floods of passion engulfed them and carried them away on a tide of released desire. They forgot the unlocked door, the thin walls, and the threat of ruined careers. Two bodies entwined, two souls finally joined. They lay all night gently touching, savoring every sensation, all questions answered. They marveled at how the fates had designed their meeting, and they willed the night to go on and on.

Before the morning light touched the windows of the barracks, they came back to the reality of how dangerous their love was to their lives, how careful they would have to be. They could only speak of love in private moments. They had to make sure they were not alone together too often. They couldn't touch and had to avoid eye contact. These restrictions were a small price to pay, for their nights were filled with love.

Faith had moved into Ann's room in October. It was January when Ann finally slipped into Faith's bed. Their love was still so new and intense when, in late February, Ann received orders for Newport, Rhode Island, for Officers' Candidate School. It was a separation they both knew was inevitable. Faith stayed in Pensacola, working toward becoming an expert in photography. After having had two devastating break ups, Faith didn't have the blind confidence that comforted Ann. Faith confesses, "I just knew that I would lose Ann now. I thought I would never see her again. We couldn't keep our love alive with miles and years between us." Even so, Ann was all she thought about.

Ann says, "I had an advantage. In OCS they kept you so occupied every waking moment that you couldn't think about anything else. It was easier for me to deal with the separation." Ann was there four months and in that time, Faith was able to visit only one weekend. They had been so careful in writing letters that might be intercepted, with phone conversations that might be overheard, that they couldn't speak the words they ached to say. That one visit was their only chance. As Faith drove toward the Naval Base in Rhode Island, she could feel the electricity but could not allow the sparks to show in her eyes. She longed to hold Ann's body against hers, but there could be no long embraces. She would allow herself a quick greeting, a friendly hug. She tried to prepare herself for the utmost reserve.

Faith showed her military pass to the guard at the gate and was waved through. As was prearranged, she met Ann at the Bachelor Officers' Quarters. Faith was in civvies. If she were in uniform, she would not be allowed to keep the company of an officer. For Faith in particular, who was still in the enlisted ranks, fraternizing with an officer was forbidden, male or female. She wasn't even supposed to be in the BOQ, let alone see Ann. They were both taking a chance.

The impact of that first sighting nearly broke down their intentions to pass as friends. Faith stopped breathing and Ann's legs nearly buckled. Only a moment passed, which seemed forever to them, before they moved toward one another, hugged and began walking through the hall where Ann was quartered. They were keeping an innocent distance, just two friends; one a Navy officer, the other a civilian, walking easily together when, behind them, a voice surprised them: "Little Tiger!" It was the nickname given to Faith in her party days at Moffett Field. One of Ann's instructors, Lieutenant Virginia Franklin, had been Faith's WAVE officer in California. In those seconds before Faith turned to respond to the greeting, both she and Ann came close to a near-death experience. Their whole Navy careers flashed before their eyes, ending in dishonorable discharges. Knowing it could be the last thing she did in the Navy, Faith turned around and greeted Lieutenant Franklin with her most genuine smile. After a brief conversation, they parted and nothing ever came of their encounter. "Did she know?" Faith and Ann never knew for sure, but they did know they were lucky.

According to Ann, the chance that Officer Franklin was a lesbian was in their favor. "There were twelve candidates in my class, and as far as I know for sure, eleven of them were lesbians. By the end of officer candidate training, we all knew each other very well." They all led double lives, camouflaging their identities any way they could.

Although Faith and Ann couldn't spend the night together, they could at least leave the base and go to a restaurant, lingering as long as they dared, drinking in the love that poured out of them, as healing and nurturing as water in the desert, but they both knew that they had a long life in the Navy ahead. Their duty stations could be thousands of miles away.

Ann's orders sent her to Dahlgren, Virginia, which was still in the military district of Washington DC. Dahlgren was only fifty miles from Fort Mead where Faith's parents lived. Dahlgren was the last station her stepfather, an army officer, would serve in before his retirement. It was only a short commute to the photographic center, so Faith chose to live at home. Her parents were happy and it was great being around them. Just as importantly, Ann could come up from Virginia on the weekends.

Since Ann was now living in the Bachelor Officers' Quarters in Dahlgren, her life was less regimented. She had every Friday afternoon and the weekend off. It took her little time to pack a few things and head for Fort Mead. "Come noon, I was out of there. I'd hang around with her mother 'til Faith came home. I made good friends with her." In order to spend three nights with Faith, Ann would get up early Monday morning and drive the hour and a half to work. Ann laughs, "Her mom, bless her heart, never thought a thing about us sleeping in the same bed, just girlfriends hanging out." Faith's parents welcomed Ann into their home, glad that Faith had such a wonderful friend.

Completely unrelated to Ann's visits, Faith was accused of being a threat to national security and to Navy solidarity. Someone had reported that Faith was a lesbian.

Since Faith worked at the Naval Photographic School, she had security clearance to go into the White House and photograph state functions. She even met President Eisenhower when she assisted in photographing him. She was completely taken off guard when a WAVE officer came down to her office and said, "I got a call from Office of Naval Intelligence to escort you over there. Have you got any idea what it's about?"

"No, I can't imagine what the ONI would want with me."

"Come on, I'll drive you over."

They entered a stark, brightly lit hallway with wooden benches placed before each closed door. At the end of the hallway was the ONI office with a window in the door. Faith was told to sit down and wait in the empty hall. She was too numb to feel anything. "I didn't know what I was doing there to start with, because I had been investigated when I received security clearance." No one came to tell her what it was all about, but several times she saw someone staring out the door's window at her. "What the hell's going on?" she wondered. If it was meant to make her uneasy, it succeeded. The whole atmosphere was sinister, and she began to feel a sense of foreboding. After twenty minutes, a man, not in uniform, told her to come in and have a seat in front of a desk. The WAVE officer joined her in the room. "Before I sat down I took a second to look around and there was this man staring from a corner in back of me."

The interrogator seated himself behind the desk and said evenly, "You know why you are here."

"I have no idea."

He looked at the WAVE officer and asked, "Do you know why she is here?"

"No, I got a phone call that I was supposed to bring her here and we have no idea what it's all about."

Looking directly at Faith he said, "We understand from a friend of yours that you are a lesbian."

Faith thought she was going to fall off the chair, but she managed to say, "Well, I don't understand why I'm here."

"I just told you. You were reported to be a lesbian."

"That's not true."

"Do you know Karen Majors?"

"Yes, she was down in Pensacola when I was going through B school."

"Did you know she's a lesbian?"

"No, I had no idea."

"Well, we caught her and in order to save her commission, she gave us a list of twenty-five people, and you are on the list." He started reading the list. In a moment of levity before all of the ramifications set in, Faith thought, when a familiar name came up, "Holy shit, I didn't know *she* was gay." He droned on and on. When he got to the end of the list, he began to accuse Faith of participating in group sex, sadomasochistic relationships, and pornography of all types. Faith felt as if he was pouring putrid filth over her. Faith later told Ann, "He told me stuff I was supposed to have done that I didn't even know what the hell he was talking about, dirty things. I kept thinking, 'What am I doing here, what's going to happen to Ann and me?' That's all I could think of while he went on and on."

Then the man asked, "Who is your best friend?"

"Well, I guess I would have to say Ann Michaels is."

"Who's that?"

"She's a Lieutenant JG."

"Is she stationed here in Washington?"

"No, she's stationed down in Dahlgren, Virginia. She comes up and visits my parents every once in a while."

"You live in the barracks, don't you?"

"Oh no, I live with my parents."

"You live at home?"

"Oh, yeah, my father is stationed up at Fort Mead and I live at home with them."

A slightly disappointed "Oh" issued from his mouth.

Faith couldn't imagine that they didn't know that.

"We can clear this whole thing up," the man said. "All you have to do is take a lie detector test."

As shaken as Faith was, she needed to get out of there. "Okay, fine."

They took her to another room and seated her in a straight backed chair. Another man attached a blood pressure cuff to her arm, then sensors to her fingers and chest. When they finished, they left her alone with the interrogator. With very little time to catch her breath, Faith began answering questions. She was in a daze, hardly hearing what he was saying. All she could think of the whole time was, "Oh, my God, Ann, what are we going to do if I get kicked out of the Navy? What's going to happen to us?" She completed the test and was sent back in the office to wait. She heard them talking in the background. The tester came in and whispered something to the man behind the desk. He then turned to Faith and said, "There must have been something wrong with the machine. You'll have to take the test again." The WAVE officer said, "Go ahead, Faith, do what they ask." Faith endured the inquisition a second time. By now, it was getting dark outside and work hours were long over. Again, the tester came in and said, "We have no conclusive evidence, because the machine is still not adjusted right for some reason. You'll need to take another one."

"No, I've had enough of this."

"It's the only way you're going to prove you're not a lesbian."

Faith was ready to say, "Two lie detector tests and you still don't know if I'm a lesbian? I'll make it easy for you and just say I am a lesbian to get out of here." She held back, though, realizing that wearing a person down with these tactics probably got them many confessions. The WAVE officer broke into her thoughts. "Faith, take this last one, but after this don't take any more." She looked at the man in charge. "No more. This is it. No more."

Faith must have passed the last test also, because when the man came back the third time he said, "You're free to go."

Faith says that Ann was the reason she passed the tests. Her love for Ann made her strong. She knew Ann was there with her. "All I thought about was Ann the whole time they were asking me these questions." When she was released, she rushed home. Ann would already be there, and she needed to be in her arms.

The summons had interrupted Faith in the photography lab on Friday afternoon. About the time Faith was taking the lie detector test, Ann was driving up from Dahlgren to spend the weekend. Ann said, "This was the only time in my life that I experienced a premonition. I knew all the way up that something bad was happening to Faith. I sensed it. I just kept sending her positive thoughts. It will be all right. I will be there soon. We'll be together. Nothing will happen to us." As soon as they were alone, she asked Faith, "What's wrong? I know that something has happened." It was very difficult for Faith to revisit the experience. She felt betrayed by the Navy she had loved and served so well. They had tried to degrade her, and the stench of their foul words was left in her memory. Faith did tell every detail of her experience to Ann, but never told her parents anything.

Faith's enlistment was up in the few months after she was accused of being a lesbian. The routine procedure was to call the enlistee down to encourage them to reenlist for the next four years. Faith's loyalty was erased by the interrogation. She didn't even give them a chance to finish the spiel. "No way. I'm out. When my time's up, I'm leaving." Faith had served nine years. In 1961 she was given an honorable discharge.

In the months when Faith was completing her Navy career, Faith's father retired from the Army and her parents moved to Pennsylvania. Ann was assigned to the Pentagon. She and Faith moved into a duplex with another lesbian couple, because they needed to save money for a home of their own someday. They finally had their own space where they were free to indulge in the luxury of touching, kissing, and hugging anytime they wanted. They thought there would be no barriers to keep them apart. Clair and Peg were compatible and everything went smoothly for a time. Clair was also in the Navy and worked in the Photographic Center with Faith. It was convenient to drive to work together. It seemed like the ideal set up. They all had privacy and yet had friends near at hand.

Unfortunately, the pressures of Ann's position at the Pentagon reached into their private lives, threatening to wrench them apart. It was April 1961, during the time of the Bay of Pigs invasion, when President Kennedy was making plans to invade Cuba. Ann was in communications and served as the liaison officer between the War Room and Communications Room. She was investigated over and over again to reach top security clearance and to be privy to secret codes.

Ann worked twelve hours a day and then was off twelve. The stress of the job was driving her toward a nervous breakdown. She began to feel the eyes of the Government watching. "I was afraid to say, 'Good morning,' in case I'd give away some code." She couldn't talk about her job and was too tired and wary to socialize. Faith tried to support Ann, but Ann was often remote and withdrawn. With too much mental and emotional stimulation on the job and never enough sleep, Ann just needed to be left alone. Faith thought that getting Ann out to a movie or dinner would help her forget the job, but Ann was afraid to be seen in public with Faith. Ann's response to Faith's plans was usually, "Go on out with Clair and Peg. I'm fine by myself." Ann, who was always so strong and caring, shut Faith out and left her feeling inadequate and lonely.

Experience had taught Faith what "needing space" meant. It meant that a relationship was over. She felt sick. She felt that Ann was slipping away and didn't know what to do. "I'll stay at home with you, Ann," she'd say.

"I just need to be left alone."

Faith rode to work with Clair and began to share some of her feelings. Clair listened intently and sympathized. Faith hadn't known that Clair was lonely and anxious for a loving touch, and that she and Peg hadn't been getting along for quite a while. As time went on, Faith confessed that she didn't think Ann loved her any more and that's when a very short-lived, unfulfilling affair began, even though Ann was always in Faith's thoughts. She knew that she would never care for anyone else as much as she cared for Ann and didn't want to live without her. It wasn't Faith's love for Ann that failed; it was her inability to trust in Ann's love for her. She grew more and more uncomfortable with this new arrangement with Clair. Instinctively, Faith realized that she must have confidence in the love that joined Ann and her together. She broke away from Clair. Peg and Clair moved out soon after that.

Ann suspected that something was going on between Clair and Faith, but chose to ignore it. She didn't want to know the details. "Deep inside, I knew that nothing was going to happen to separate us." Months passed before either could talk about it. They never had an angry confrontation; they just gently grew together again. Faith knew that "It was the intense pressure of the job that made Ann turn away," and Ann says, "I had no trouble accepting Faith's need for physical contact." Ann's generous heart, coupled with Faith's realization that she couldn't love anyone but Ann, brought them back together. Their love became a safe harbor that kept them together for fifty-one years in spite of many storms that might have destroyed it. A year after Peg and Clair moved away, Ann decided to resign. She had served in the Navy for eleven years.

"I was a basket case after working for the Pentagon, and just wanted a place to go hide out with Faith," Ann says. They found a little farm house down a lonely mile-long driveway in Pennsylvania. They were looking for something "remote," and they got it.

"We were totally involved with each other and could devote time to each other without any outside intrusion. Faith's parents would visit from time to time, but not on a regular basis." Ann helped the farmer fix fences, put up hay, feed animals just for the sheer pleasure of the physical exercise. She needed to flex her muscles after being cloistered in the War Room for so long. They needed very little to be happy. They stayed there for six months, solidifying their relationship, but with winter coming, they knew they would have to leave. The house was built in the 1700s and had very little chinking between the stones. Ann says, "There were more air leaks than we could stop up before winter." They found a small house closer to town and began looking for jobs in the civilian world.

A friend of Faith's, who worked in Bainbridge, Maryland, called and said, "There are lots of jobs down here." Faith said, "What the heck, working for the government, good pensions, job security, chance to advance." They were both accepted. Faith's job was in photography but Ann took a temporary job until the management position in supply became available. "The next thing you know, I go to work where Faith's working." Faith adds with a devilish grin, "Of course, you know photographers work in darkrooms."

Soon after they got their jobs in 1966, they found a house in Rising Sun, Maryland. It was a small house but very comfortable. They liked the floor plan and the yard but were still isolated from the lesbian community and made no real effort to make friends. Ann says, "It wasn't a conscious thing. It was just a continuation of the way we had been living." The Navy had drilled an underlying fear into its gay personnel that sometimes bordered on paranoia. Unfortunately for Faith and Ann, they had reason to fear. Ann says, "We moved right into the heart of KKK country."

Still, they stayed there, holding out little hope that the rest of the world was any different. Faith says, "We didn't have any gay friends, didn't see anyone that even looked like they might be gay. We assumed they were out there, but weren't certain. But we did all right." They had very special neighbors and got along with the people around them very well. No one in the neighborhood suspected the two single women living together of being lesbians. Of course, they must be sisters.

It was Ann's interest in gems and minerals that helped open the door into gay society. Faith found a gem store in town called The Treasure Chest, where they both signed up for a stone cutting class. They met Donna and Gerry, who asked them to dinner one night. At dinner, they discovered their first lesbian friends since they had resigned from the Navy.

They also met Ginny and Susan at the Treasure Chest. After seeing each other many times in the shop, they all decided to go to a gem show together. While Ann and Ginny were in the car waiting for Susan and Faith to return from an errand, Ginny said, "You two aren't really sisters, are you?"

"No, people think we are, because we live together and are seen together most of the time. We just let them think that because it's easier. We're just good friends."

"How good?"

Old fears surfaced for a moment and Ann hesitated. "By then we were pretty sure they 'were,' and they were pretty sure of us, but in those days, you could pay a high price for trust, especially in our neighborhood." Ann decided it was safe to be honest, so she told her the truth. That began a solid friendship which has lasted thirty years.

Ann met another couple through her work. "Judy looked like a big bad butch to me. If she wasn't gay, I wasn't gay, but how do you approach someone?" They had a chance to meet Judy's partner Jo, when by chance they ate at the same restaurant. "We stopped by their table to talk a few minutes." Judy invited them to come to their house for coffee. They thought, "Why not? It may be a chance to open that next door."

The next doors became harder to open and their love challenged when Faith's mother came to live with them while recovering from a badly broken leg. Although she improved enough to get around with a walker and go out with her friends, she was never capable of living alone again. She was with them for twenty years.

They didn't want her to go to a nursing home, so they got help for her when they were at work. Faith and Ann took care of her in the evenings. That's when they felt the stress. Their caregiving ended the freedom they had just started to enjoy. Ann's motto is, "You can't just leave someone who needs help. You just have to tighten your belt and carry on."

About fifteen years into her twenty-year stay with Faith and Ann, Mrs. Bradford became increasingly demanding of their time. If she thought they had taken too long getting the groceries, she would complain that they were never there. They ate breakfast and dinner with her and sometimes spent evenings with her, watching TV or talking. They had lost the freedom to touch, to kiss, to talk freely. When they wanted to get away, they would go down to their finished basement, start a fire in the fireplace, and watch television together, but it was stolen time. They felt the burden of Mrs. Bradford's presence even when they were alone. Their freedom to be themselves became more and more restricted, but their nights in the master bedroom sustained their love. They dealt with the complaints, knowing that they could never put her in a nursing home, but their lives were becoming as they were in the Navy, watchful and guarded. They were seeing less of their new friends and going on trips to gem shows stopped. They thought they were dealing with their constricted lives pretty well, and they never imagined that things would soon become nearly unbearable.

One Saturday afternoon a friend of her mother's, Mary Cavanaugh, came to visit. Faith and Ann took the opportunity to go shopping. When they returned, Mrs. Cavanaugh was gone. Faith's mother called to them from the den, "I want to talk to you. I must talk to you." The sound in her voice chilled the atmosphere. They looked at each other, wondering. They sat down on the couch and could see by the fierce look in Faith's mother's eyes that she was disturbed. She held Faith with a piercing stare and said, "Are you a lesbian?" It took a moment for Faith to get a breath, but she answered clearly, "Yes, Mother, I am."

"What have I done wrong to make you like this? Your sister isn't a lesbian."

"You haven't done anything wrong. This is just the way I am."

Mrs. Bradford turned on Ann, forgetting the years she had lived in Ann's home. "This is your fault. You made her like this. My husband and I never should have let you in our house."

After that initial outburst, Mrs. Bradford refused to speak to Ann and made it a point to show her revulsion, but she had plenty of words for Faith, "You do everything Ann says. You pay no attention to me. Ann cares nothing about me and you want to be with her all of the time."

Looking back on those years, Faith says, "I don't know how we stayed together. I guess it's because we love each other so much that nothing else matters."

After living a semi-covert life in Rising Sun, Faith and Ann, with Mrs. Bradford, moved to Havre de Grace, a small town across the Susquehanna River, only thirteen miles. But Ann says, it was like moving from Russia to France. "They were two totally different places. There was so much to do in Havre de Grace after so little to do in Rising Sun. There was progress there, people cared. You wouldn't believe we were in the same state." What made the move even better was their location on the edge of town. They had two acres adjoining a big horse farm. They didn't mind the eight mile drive to the nearest store. They were close to the northern-most lighthouse of Chesapeake Bay at the confluence where the Susquehanna River empties into Chesapeake Bay, thirty miles from the water. Ann says, "There were twenty or thirty gay folks living in the Havre de Grace area. Most were doctors and nurses from the hospital staff in Baltimore." Living there was like a breath of fresh air, literally and figuratively.

Even though life was better in Havre de Grace, Faith and Ann were still living in a pressure cooker at home. They needed a long vacation to be together, alone. Faith asked her sister, Katherine, to watch over their mother's health while they were gone. She was glad to do it. She had known Faith and Ann were a couple years before Faith told her. Katherine's children were brought up knowing about their "aunts'" relationship. Faith says, "My niece calls Ann 'Aunt Ann.' She and her husband teach in Annapolis and call us all of the time. They say, 'Can we come over to visit? We need to be with you and Aunt Ann.' My niece is like a daughter to me."

Faith found an assisted living facility and explained to her mother that she need only stay there for six weeks. They would not leave her there against her will. Mrs. Bradford resisted but finally realized that she could not take care of herself, and that Faith and Ann were going away, no arguments. Faith's mother enjoyed the attention she got in the assisted living apartment. She met some women she liked and felt safe in a place where she would have immediate help if she needed it. By the time Faith and Ann returned, she was not only willing, but content to stay.

Within a month after she got into an assisted living apartment, her malice toward Ann melted away. However, after the verbal punishment Ann had taken from Mrs. Bradford, she told Faith, "I'm not going over there. You'll have to go see her yourself." Mrs. Bradford began asking, "Where's Ann?" Faith says, "When mother and I would talk on the phone, she didn't want to hang up before she talked with Ann." Later she called Ann and asked her to come and visit. After many visits, Ann couldn't contain her curiosity about this reversal in attitude. "You were so angry with me," she said "What changed your mind?"

"I was never angry with you. You have always been a daughter to me." Mrs. Bradford did not exhibit a memory loss in any other area. Ann shrugs when asked how she not only tolerated but took care of Faith's mother all those years, "She was Faith's mother. You have to be willing to give something extra."

With her mother safe, Faith and Ann could fully enjoy the abundance of nature around them, go to Chincoteague, and travel in their new RV. They liked Chincoteague so much that they invested in a house to rent out until they could retire there, but their plans were again changed. The fates had decided to present them with a precious gift.

Ann saw an ad in a gay publication that offered lots at a gated community in Florida, a place conceived especially for gay women. They made several trips to inspect the property before deciding to buy. The complex had two lakes, a wildlife preserve, and a well-equipped clubhouse with a swimming pool, but it was the atmosphere in the place that made them decide to buy. It offered freedom to be themselves. After they had made the decision, they could not get down there fast enough. They drove down in their RV, a forty-foot Admiral in which they intended to live until their house was built. They came back to put their homes in Havre de Grace and Chincoteague Island on the market. Faith's sister took on the responsibility of their mother. Their friend, Donna, who was in real estate, took care of the marketing and closing of their two homes.

The Florida sun burns bright and clear, but the warmth of the women who welcomed them to the community excelled the sun's. Faith and Ann are now living in their new home and at ages seventy-eight and eighty are more in love than ever, having the best, time of their lives. Out of that dark, confining closet at last!

Miriam and Rachael

The story of Miriam and Rachael is one of the triumphs of the human spirit. Their love for one another was not suppressed by threats of physical violence, exposure to scorn from their families, the horrors of childhood rape, or by a society which disenfranchised women. In most of the U.S. through the sixties, the husband was the breadwinner, especially in Jewish society. The woman's place was to take care of the home and to serve her husband's and children's needs. Higher education was out of the question for most. Many Jewish women were lavished with material things but had no freedom. They were like brightly colored birds trapped in a gilded cage. In spite of these conventions, Miriam and Rachael fell in love and followed their dream to make a life together.

Miriam came from a financially comfortable family, but there was an undertone of discomfort in the house. Miriam remembers, "At the beginning of his marriage, my father fell in love with another woman. He lived a double life, not leaving his family, but spending much of his time with his mistress." Her father was cruel to her mother, forbidding her to celebrate holidays or to keep kosher. Miriam and her brother wanted to leave home as soon as possible.

In the spring of 1959, when Miriam was nineteen, she went to a resort with her girlfriends. She met a young man named Mel who asked her to dinner and made her feel that they were the only people in the room. She was flattered by his attention and charmed by his manners. Her own father was a man of means and gave her *things* instead of attention.

Mel asked her to marry him after two months. She thought she could provide the home he never had, and that she could heal the wounds of his childhood; besides, marriage would be a way to leave home. Even though she wasn't in love with him, Miriam said, "Yes." Her father's rage, when he found out that Mel had no money and no steady job to support a wife and children, only fueled her desire to leave home.

In June 1959, she married Mel. In 1960 she had her first child. She felt the joy of holding her precious son in her arms, unaware that his birth closed the door on any chance for liberation. Another son and daughter followed in the next four years. The illusion that she would make a happy home with Mel soon evaporated. Miriam says, "He never held a job for very long. He had affairs with many women." Mel's idea of lovemaking was centered on his own gratification, the sooner the better. There was no tenderness for Miriam or an awareness of her feelings. She began to dread the grotesque ritual of Sunday night sex after their bowling league. She found that the way to endure it was smoking a joint first.

Miriam's outlet was still her girlfriends. She knew a lot of the other wives in Brooklyn and enjoyed their company. Miriam's father provided her with another release. He gave her and her family the gift of a summer stay in Upstate New York. Miriam says, "Five years into our marriage, our family began going to a bungalow colony in Monticello, New York. Instead of sending children to day camp by themselves, Jewish people would rent a bungalow up in the mountains where it was cool. The kids went to day camp there and we all had a vacation. There was a clubhouse with an indoor and outdoor pool, nightclub with entertainment on weekends, and a lake where people could fish or boat. We called it 'going to the country.'" The wives and children would stay during the week and their husbands would join them on weekends. About twelve couples from Brooklyn got to know one another and became very friendly.

There were many bungalow colonies throughout the Catskills and Adirondacks. In the years between 1920 and 1970, one million members of the New York City Jewish population went to the Catskills for the summer. Jews were not welcome in fine hotels and nightclubs before the early sixties, and they were refused memberships in social clubs. There were restrictive clauses in housing developments and anti-Semitic college quotas. Although the discrimination is not rampant now, many Jews still maintain the custom of going to "the country." Miriam loved the bungalow colony even before she got to know Rachael there.

Miriam had met Rachael earlier in Brooklyn, but avoided contact at first. "To meet Rachael is never to forget her for anybody. She's unusual." They met in 1962 through mutual friends at the local bowling alley where they both played in leagues. Rachael could make the pins fly; she took it as a personal insult if she missed a spare. Miriam thought she was a maniac. "Rachael was a perfectionist. If she didn't get a perfect ball, she would rant and rave." Miriam didn't like swearing, so she shied away from Rachael.

The vicious way Rachael bowled and the flood of expletives that poured from her mouth were symptoms of an emotional wound of which Rachael was not aware. In the depths of her subconscious lurked the shadow of a man coming to her bed at night, a molester, not a father, a rapist, not the protector of his seven-year-old daughter. The things he did to her and her twin sister stayed in the darkness. It was not safe to remember then. Six years of horror stayed hidden from the light.

There were other reasons Rachael was rough around the edges. She was brought up on Manhattan's Lower East Side in a tenement. "I was a very, very tough kid in those years. You had to be. All of my friends were tough, too. I remember liking the way the guys wore their pants. I have a picture of me with jeans and a bowtie trying to look like them."

The toughness softened a little when she attended a summer camp at age fourteen, her expenses paid by the Educational Alliance, and the Jewish Federation, organizations that helped underprivileged children. "I absolutely fell in love with my counselor, Marilyn, absolutely. I didn't know what that feeling was, but, in retrospect, I can see I had always been a lesbian." Rachael wasn't about to let a little soft feeling take her off guard. Emotions were her enemy; she moved through life not allowing herself to feel anything. Even though her mother did nothing to stop the raping, Rachael didn't hate her. She felt pity for her mother, protective of her. To keep her mother safe, Rachael kept quiet. "I thought that telling my mother might have forced her to act. My father would have killed her if she protested." The child who was without care became the caregiver. She feared her father, hated being at home to watch the destruction of her mother, felt no emotional connection with her twin sister. Life was something "out there" for Rachael. Killing all feelings was the only way she could stay alive.

She knew a few things about her future. She would marry and probably have children. She would obey her husband, and she would find a way to kill herself if nothing could relieve the indefinable agony in her soul. She had already attempted suicide at age ten. What Rachael did not foresee was that something good could happen. When she was sixteen, life did get better. She met Adam, a young man who treated her with kindness and respect. They dated for two years. Rachael's fear subsided and she let herself love him. He was very much in love with her. However, Rachael's fragile hope for a better life was shattered when they married.

Rachael married Adam at age eighteen and had her first child at twenty. Before Steven was born, she began stealing tranquilizers from her mother. Adam, so gentle in the day, was brutal in bed. Without realizing it, he was physically abusing her in his relentless effort to climax. Sometimes he continued for an hour, sometimes more. "I'd never been with a man before. I just thought this was the way it was done." She didn't know it then, but with every thrust, the monster in her memory stirred. "I took myself away from it with drugs." By the time her second child was born, Rachael was addicted.

Adam provided very well for Rachael and their family. "He gave me money for everything I wanted except an education." He would tease her with little putdowns when she answered the questions on the TV game show, *The $64,000 Question*. "Now you're going to think you have all of the answers. A woman isn't supposed to worry her pretty little head about things like that." Even so, Rachael says, "Aside from the sex, he was very good to me." They lived in a fine home in New Jersey.

Adam became an alcoholic and encouraged Rachael to drink with him. She refused for many years, because by age twenty-five she had her own addiction. "Maybe he didn't want to know that I was addicted, because the evidence was plain. In my medicine cabinet there were three bottles of Valium and another three of Librium, ninety pills in each bottle. I was addicted to the point of stealing prescription papers and writing my own prescriptions." With no computers in pharmacies then, all she had to do was drive to different drugstores and collect the drugs.

"I finally took my first drink with Adam to please him." One Piña Colada was enough to hook Rachael. "I'd have blackouts while I was in the car driving the kids. They didn't know, but I did. I'd get home and not remember where I'd been. I was a functioning addict and alcoholic for most of my marriage."

Rachael had no expectations; she wasn't conscious of what was missing in her life. "But there must have been something, because I was drugging and drinking." She stayed away from people, driving her expensive car around to shop. She took her children to school and to other activities. She cleaned house, cooked, got her hair and nails done, and took enough pills and liquor to keep the memory of incest buried. She thought she had control of her life until she met Miriam.

When Miriam went to the country in 1971, all of the bungalows near her friends were occupied, so she rented one on the other side of the lake. It was inconvenient for her friends to visit, and Miriam's shyness kept her from going out to meet the strangers around her. She was lonely for a time until Rachael reintroduced herself and made her feel welcome. Rachael and Adam had rented a bungalow just down the road from Miriam and Mel. While their children played together, the two women talked through the warm summer days. Their children became friends, too. They were all within seven years of age of each other. Rachael had Steven, four, and Judy, two-and-a-half. Miriam had Harry, nine, Glenn, seven, and Sara, five. Rachael began to come over more and more frequently and soon Miriam forgot about going across the way to her friends. This "new" Rachael was interesting. Miriam could see that beneath the surface armor, there was a woman with warmth and sensitivity.

Two summers in the mountains went by and their friendship grew. They talked about the lighter things at first: their children, their shopping sprees, bowling, and later, their husbands, their disappointments, their pain. Rachael learned of Mel's unfaithfulness, and that he had threatened to kill her in one of his rages. Miriam had made him leave twice only to take him back for the children. Rachael learned of Miriam's need for marijuana in the bedroom.

Miriam learned that Rachael was tortured by her husband's lovemaking, that her body felt battered and she didn't know what to do. These tribulations the two women shared with no one else. Miriam did not recognize the significance of her growing love for Rachael.

Rachael knew that she had an underlying sexual desire for Miriam their third summer in the mountains. Rachael's kitchen window looked out on the road between two rows of bungalows. When she sat at the kitchen table, she could see everyone walking back and forth. She was idly looking out one day when Miriam came out of her bungalow wearing a dazzlingly blue bathing suit that fit her slender body perfectly. Rachael was transfixed. Miriam seemed to glow in the sun. Seeing Miriam's bare arms made her ache. Rachael says, "That day, the obsession took over." Rachael needed this woman, to be near her, to be touched by her, to feel close. Confusion, fear, desire, feelings! "My mantra then was, 'I don't need anyone.' An incest survivor's whole purpose in life is denying needs." But even Rachael's steely resolve could not stop her desire for Miriam.

When the summer was over, Rachael went to see Miriam in Brooklyn. When she couldn't see her in person, she made contact by phone. "I annoyed the hell out of her. I kept calling her. There was no such thing as 'no.' I had to be with her." Miriam was the true good thing that happened in her life.

Finally, Rachael confessed her addiction to Miriam and said that she was going to go away for the weekend and get off her pills, because she didn't want the drugs to come between them. Miriam would not let Rachael go alone. Miriam remembers, "She was in tremendous, tremendous pain, but she had no convulsions or hallucinations." That weekend sealed their close friendship. Rachael was so grateful for Miriam. "I had never known anyone so gentle, yet so strong." Miriam calmed her. Miriam felt protective and tender. Her own need to be near Rachael began to grow. After the initial withdrawal, Rachael saw an addiction counselor, but she didn't tell her counselor of her addiction to Miriam.

Miriam got used to Rachael's calling and coming over, began enjoying her company, and soon looked forward to it. Rachael was exciting and witty, yet something about her called out for care. Rachael told Miriam, "My therapist said that I need to learn to 'reach out.'" Miriam was glad to oblige. She held Rachael's hand—for comfort, and she exchanged warm hugs when they met and parted—friendly hugs, friendly hand holding. There were sensations in her body that Miriam refused to explore. They kissed once. Miriam remembers, "I was so stimulated that I thought I was going to lose my mind. I was a mother with three children, for heaven's sake!" Rachael laughs, "It's a wonder the whole couch didn't burn up!"

The women's husbands had become acquainted in the mountains too, and the four of them began spending time together. After the summer season, Miriam and Rachael planned their social events so that they could see more of each other. They hadn't planned on orchestrating the event that would truly bring them together—after ten years of friendship.

The foursome had gone out to dinner in Mel's car. Miriam explains, "The floor of his car was always full of junk. Passengers had to move it out of the way before they could be comfortable. When Rachael got out of the car, she tripped on a coiled wire and fell into the car parked next to them. She wrenched her back and neck and had to be helped into her house." Mel and Adam sat in the den watching television. The women were in the kitchen. Rachael was in agony even after several aspirin. Miriam asked, "Would you like me to rub you with Ben Gay?" If Rachael had said "No," it might have taken ten more years for Miriam to acknowledge her feelings for Rachael! Thankfully, when she began kneading Rachael's neck and shoulders, a little thrill caught in her chest. A warm, pink blush rose to her cheeks. She kept moving her fingers slowly over Rachael's back and Miriam knew that touching Rachael meant more than therapeutic massage. She tried to compose herself and assumed a casual expression, but it was too late. Rachael had seen, and Rachael knew that her prayers had been answered.

When the summer was over, Rachael picked up her daily routine. She missed seeing Miriam every day. It made it difficult to suppress the longing that had surfaced at the end of their summer in the country. Rachael had waited ten years for Miriam's touch. Miriam was such a tender, sweet woman, and Rachael knew her touch would heal her of more than her sprained neck. She must make sure of Miriam's feelings. She remembers, "I had been invited to go out to eat with friends whom I usually enjoyed. We would laugh, have a few drinks, and have a good time. This time, all I could think of was how much I missed Miriam. It was pining that brought physical pain." Rachael couldn't even manage to make the right responses in their conversation. A big invisible fist had seized her and started squeezing. "I couldn't think about anything but getting back to Miriam to talk with her. I needed to ask the question that would change everything, for better or worse.

Would Miriam remember what I asked? Would she remember the answer?"

The next day was Sunday, and that meant bowling league. Rachael knew that Miriam would be smoking pot that evening to get through sex with her husband, so Rachael chose that time to call Miriam. "I knew she would be stoned on pot, and I needed the truth. Maybe if she said, 'No' when I asked her the question, she would be stoned enough to forget the whole conversation." After several busy signals, the phone rang. As soon as Miriam answered Rachael asked, "Do you have sexual feelings for me?"

There was a quick intake of breath and then Miriam answered, "Yes."

"Oh, shit."

There was only a long silence from Miriam's end.

Rachael encouraged her, "Let's talk about it."

Miriam still couldn't speak and hung up the phone.

On Monday Rachael picked Miriam up to take her for a drive. "Miriam wouldn't look at me. I couldn't look at her." Rachael tried again. "If we were having a homosexual relationship, I could understand my feelings of missing you, but we're not. I don't know what's going on." Miriam looked at her then, but wouldn't answer. Rachael felt defeated. "When I didn't get a response, I accepted the thought that Miriam was just my friend, though I realized then that I was a lesbian. It was like all the pieces of the puzzle fit. I, at least, felt comfortable with that."

Miriam, however, was very uncomfortable. "After Rachael asked me if I had sexual feelings for her, I wanted to change my mind. I wanted to forget the whole thing. I was always a very practical person. I told her that I didn't want to lose my best friend. We both had separate lives and children. I truly thought that my husband would kill me. I really had a hard time with it. I couldn't figure out how we could possibly live our lives differently. I was so closed minded. I thought my unhappy marriage was going to be my life, my struggle. I didn't know any way out of the maze." Miriam decided that they should stop being so close. She thought, "What was there to give up actually, some intense hugs, hand holding, marathon telephone conversations? But there was that one kiss. . . ."

Miriam found that she couldn't turn her feelings off. Rachael was everywhere. Rachael never agreed to a slowing down of their relationship.

She continued to call and to come over. She wanted to think about the possibilities.

It didn't take Miriam long to at least think about how she could have a life with Rachael. Even though Miriam knew that Rachael had never had a sexual relationship with a woman, she began to bombard her with questions. "How are we going to kiss? How are we going to live together? What will we do with our kids? How will we know what to do with each other?"

Rachael's reply was, "How the hell do I know?" But Rachael knew one thing: they needed to find the answers. She told Miriam, "I want to go away for the weekend with you. We need to spend some time together."

Miriam's initial reaction was, "I have to ask my husband."

"Are you kidding?"

Miriam continued to worry about the details. "You have to know I can't be nude in front of you. I'm frigid, so I can't guarantee I can respond to you. If you still want to go away with me under these terms, I'll try." She was also afraid that Rachael would tire of her. "This is a novelty to you, and for you, the novelty might wear off."

Rachael's aunt had a place in Upstate New York where all of Miriam's fears vanished. From the moment their lips touched, they knew what to do. Miriam never remembered undressing. She had never felt such sensations, such loving in her life. Rachael couldn't get enough of Miriam's touch, the thrill of being so close. The weekend went by too quickly, a dream too quickly ended. They became aware of the seeming hopelessness of their lives, and they knew that nothing would ever be the same. In spite of the dangers, they had to be together. There weren't any other options.

When they got home, they started making plans, long-term and short-term. Miriam had the youngest child who would be twenty in five years, so at that point they would leave their husbands and begin a life together. They began collecting household items and hiding them in a large, out-of-the-way closet in Miriam's house. "My husband never looked in there." On their shopping trips they would buy extra towels, sheets, dishes. The short-term plan was to be together as much as possible. They had plenty of time to be together. Rachael says, "We weren't supposed to work. We were JAPS—Jewish American Princesses."

Rachael's husband, Adam, had given them part-time jobs putting labels on bathing suits in his swimming suit manufacturing business. He felt they needed something productive to do. However, Adam often told Rachael to go home early to take care of the house, always telling Miriam that she could leave too. He would have been surprised at how fast his house was cleaned. Miriam reflects, "We would go to her house, clean her house together in half the time and then we would make love the rest of the time." Still, their times together were stolen and not a real life with a real home together. Luckily, they had found gay friends with whom they could share their problems.

They both lived within twenty minutes of Manhattan. That part of New York City was progressive enough to have a support center for gays and lesbians. It provided recreation facilities, a place to meet, counseling, a bookstore, and information about the gay/lesbian community. It answered all of the questions Miriam and Rachael had. Rachael says, "We needed to learn about the lesbian lifestyle. How do you tell if someone is a lesbian? Where do you find them? Are there many in New York?" Miriam and Rachael became part of a large network of gays and lesbians. Miriam says, "We'd go over to the gay center regularly." Rachael adds, "All of our friends were gay. They helped us get through the hard times." But even with the support of friends, they began to realize that five years was too long to wait to be together.

Miriam divorced her husband first. Thanks to her father's foresight, the house they lived in belonged to Miriam, a wedding gift from her parents. When Miriam filed for divorce Mel, "raged for days." Miriam feared for her life. "He threatened to burn the house down. He threatened to kill me. He took the telephone cord and wrapped it around his neck in front of the kids and told the kids he was going to kill himself. My daughter, Sara, was sixteen and my son Glenn, was eighteen. Thank God Harry, twenty-one, was in California. It was terrible. If he thought he would win their sympathy, he was wrong. They knew what their father was. To this day my daughter will have nothing to do with him. Glenn thought, 'Even though he's crazy, he's my father.'"

Mel refused to pay her anything yelling in court, "You lesbian, let your girlfriend support you!" She had the house, but no income. To make matters worse, her father found out she was gay and cut off the money he was giving her. Her mother secretly gave her money every month to help, but it wasn't enough. Miriam got a job as a telephone operator at Arthur Anderson. With frugality, she got by. Money wasn't the only problem. Her middle son, Glenn, guessed what was going on between his mother and Rachael and was furious. Miriam remembers, "Glenn had been experimenting with drugs and was in no condition to be understanding. He left the house to stay with his addict friends, and then came back when he ran out of money. He started threatening me." Miriam took the threats seriously because Glenn had guns in the house. Rachael was worried. "I was afraid that I would come over some day to find Miriam dead."

Rachael helped Glenn overcome his addiction. She reached him through the love and friendship they once had. Rachael says, "Glenn was the boy who would come over to my house to have me style his hair before a date." Rachael made herself available any time he needed her. With her help, he beat the addiction. Glenn and Rachael formed a powerful bond. Now Miriam can joke about it. "He always comes to Rachael for advice. He doesn't ask me anything."

In the two years after Miriam's divorce, Rachael continued to spend all of the time she could with Miriam. She was a comforting presence when Miriam's mother died. She was supportive to Miriam's whole family when Miriam's father deserted them, married his mistress, and moved to Florida. Miriam was worried about him, but after a year of trying to contact her father and getting nowhere with his mistress, Miriam and her children gave up trying.

Rachael was getting comfort from Miriam, too. Miriam didn't push Rachael to end her marriage. She knew how much Rachael loved Adam. Rachael nods, "I didn't want to hurt him. He was the first person who really loved me. We had been married for twenty-three years. I love him to this day, but the terrible part for me was, I'd be with Miriam, feeling her tender love, and I'd have to go home and be hurt by him and pretend I liked it." Adam's and Rachael's marriage ended in bed. Rachael says, "Finally, I had to tell him, 'No more, I can't do it any more.' I was sorry to hurt him, but I was hurting myself more." Soon after telling him, she called Miriam. "I think I just ended my marriage." Miriam couldn't believe it. "I didn't know if she would ever reach that point."

When Rachael moved in with Miriam they had few problems adjusting to living together. Miriam says, "We had been in each others' houses so much already." Now they were free to do something that they never would have been permitted to do when they were married. As caged birds they couldn't stretch their wings. With the freedom to obtain jobs and to educate themselves for advancement, the ex-Jewish Princesses were learning to fly. Miriam's job at Arthur Anderson was going well. She suggested that Rachael apply for an opening there in another department. With two incomes and the sale of Rachael's house, money was less of a problem. Miriam found she had a special gift with people. She worked her way up until, by the time of her retirement, she was supervisor of personnel. Rachael was also finding that she could do well in the business world. She started at Arthur Anderson as a file clerk and worked her way up to a job in human resources. She later left the firm for a job at an advertising firm, then became a human resource manager for a large armored car company that employed fifteen hundred workers.

Through the gay/lesbian center, Miriam and Rachael learned about a gay temple on 50th Street in Manhattan. From the time she knew about it, Rachael wanted to marry Miriam there. She asked Miriam on a regular basis, but the answer was always no. Miriam says, "I was afraid. Everything was going so well. For some reason I thought that marrying Rachael would change our relationship." Rachael says, "I think she thought I was going to just change my mind and run away like I did my whole life. Anyway, on our tenth anniversary in 1980, she agreed. I guess she thought that after ten years, I was going to stay." They went to the gay temple and talked with the rabbi. Rachael says, "We told him our story, and he invited us to come to the service on the Friday night, before we were to be married. The rabbi honored us by calling us up before the whole congregation, and asking us to read from the Torah." Following Jewish custom, Rachael and Miriam provided cake and coffee for the whole congregation.

On Saturday, they were married. They didn't feel comfortable sharing this milestone in their lives with their children, but Rachael's sister and brother-in-law walked her down the aisle, and Miriam's cousin and her husband walked with her. Miriam wore an elegant white dress and Rachael wore a black slack suit. They stood under the canopy, according to Jewish custom, and repeated their vows, with thirty-six close friends in attendance. Rachael says, "I was a wreck. I was more nervous than when

I married my husband. My hands were shaking. I was very emotional." When they exchanged rings, Miriam held Rachael's hand to steady it. Rachael says, "We were the first lesbian couple to be married in the gay temple. We knew it wasn't sanctioned by the State of New York, but it was sanctioned by us." After the wedding, Miriam and Rachael followed another Jewish custom and took all of the wedding guests out to a Chinese restaurant! In the months and years after their wedding, Miriam's worries faded away. There were no problems between them.

What problems they had came from outside the circle of their love. Rachael's son, Steven, wasn't speaking to her because she divorced his father. Miriam's daughter was still living with them. Rachael's daughter, Judy, who came home from college on weekends, was homophobic. Rachael remembers, "Judy came home one weekend saying that there were two lesbians living in her dorm. Judy yelled, 'If God had wanted women to be together, He wouldn't have made men!' For my daughter to say God this or God that, it's a wonder the walls didn't come down. We had never been a religious family. We only went to Temple on high holy days, Yom Kippur and Rosh Hashanah. Miriam and I were sleeping in the same bedroom in the same bed, and she never made the connection that we were lesbians!"

They were beginning to juggle the various personalities pretty well, and their finances were improving when Miriam got a call from Florida. Miriam says, "It was funny how it all played out. My father started showing signs of dementia in Florida. When it got so bad that his mistress couldn't take care of him any more, she just moved out. Luckily, one of his neighbors found my number and called. They said that he was out wandering around and his wife was nowhere to be found. She later committed suicide. The short story is, we flew down to Florida, brought him back to our house, and ended up taking care of him until he died." During that time Miriam's daughter, Sara, finished college and married a fine young man. Rachael's daughter, Judy, finished college and later married. Glenn married, had a lovely daughter, Jennifer, and was on his way to becoming a successful businessman.

Since everything seemed to be going well, they didn't want to upset the peace by coming out to their children. They thought that only Miriam's son, Glenn, knew for sure. As long as the subject never came up, they thought that the rest of the children couldn't or wouldn't notice that their mothers were lesbians. Their silence ended when Glenn got a divorce. His wife got his house and Glenn came to live with Miriam and Rachael. He had his own living space in the finished basement. He had joint custody of his daughter, Jennifer, who would come to visit every other weekend, much to the delight of her grandmothers. One day Glenn called from his work in a panic. "Lucy is not going to let me have Jennifer anymore because of your lifestyle." Miriam's first response was to call Rachael to the phone. Rachael said, "We will take her to court. We have our rights. That's it. We're coming out to all the kids. We will fight this!" When Miriam told her daughter, Sara, she replied, "Oh, Mom, I've known all these years." Glenn already knew, and her other son, Harry, wasn't involved, because he was living in California.

Rachael had more trouble with her son and daughter. She took her daughter to lunch and after their meal Rachael told her.

"Don't tell my husband."

Nothing else was said about it. Judy chose to deny the truth, but she didn't reject her mother.

Since Rachael's son, Stephen, wasn't speaking to her because she divorced his father, it was no use trying to talk to him. Later, Steven's rift with his mother was bridged by his wife—a very liberal woman who was the first podiatrist in New York to treat AIDS patients. With her influence, he became more tolerant. All of Miriam's and Rachael's children had been friends for years. They had grown up together in the mountains at the bungalow colony. They saw each other when they got home. Their daughters were the same age and in the same group at camp. Their "coming out" had a happy ending eventually, and was worth the uproar, but it proved to be unnecessary for the custody of Jennifer. Glenn's wife dropped the custody suit when she found out they were going to fight.

The best part of Rachael's life was being close to Miriam, but even the power of Miriam's love could not overcome Rachael's subconscious memory of her childhood. Rachael had stopped taking drugs, but she could not completely escape the need for alcohol. She had literally been through hell trying to free herself from her addictions to alcohol and narcotics. She stopped taking drugs the night Miriam had stayed with her, but with alcohol it was another matter. Rachael remembers, "I joined AA and NA, and would go for ninety days clean and sober, then crash again. I didn't know why. I just couldn't shake alcoholism." The cause of Rachael's problems was still locked in her subconscious.

But the "cause" broke free when Rachael and Miriam went to see Barbra Streisand in *Nuts*, a movie about overcoming the horror of incest. Rachael remembers, "During the movie, I had a flashback to my father in my bedroom. It shocked me." She felt again the violation that was so abhorrent and degrading that it had once taken away her soul. "To this day I have problems with it. I came close to having nervous breakdowns several times."

Miriam knew something was wrong. While the credits were rolling, Rachael was rigid. Rachael says, "I didn't cry. In those days you could have run a knife through my hand and I wouldn't cry." Miriam slowly drew it out of her when they got home. Rachael didn't want to be held that night. She was too busy mustering the courage to tell her therapist. She had to give voice to the little girl she had been. After years of torment, her steely determination and Miriam's patience and understanding helped her begin the recovery from her father's treachery. Rachael says, "That incest really, for me, is the core of my existence. That's why I appreciate Miriam so much. She is a wonderful woman." Miriam was soft, kind and loving when Rachael needed nurturing; then determined and unwavering when she needed strength.

Years after Rachael healed she became a therapist herself. She started taking evening classes while she was still working at Wells Fargo, then interned at the prestigious Southbrook Psychiatric Hospital. To be sure she had every possible skill that would free others of their addictions, she trained in acupuncture and detoxification therapy as well as in counseling.

When Rachael successfully completed her internship, she became a counselor at Southbrook. Keeping her job at the armored car company, she worked two nights a week at the hospital. Later, she was with a private practice on weekends. Her personal experience gave her a window into her clients' minds. Her courses gave her the skill to heal others. Rachael was a counselor for six years, but then her work came to an abrupt halt.

Rachael had to retire because she contracted Lyme's disease. She and Miriam had visited some friends on their country property, and Rachael was bitten by a deer tick and didn't realize that the funny red ring on her arm was an indication of it. A year and a half later, she went to the doctor when she experienced flu-like symptoms that lingered for months. She also suffered short-term memory loss, and arthritis pain. Now, medication is helping to control it, but she gets tired quickly.

When Miriam retired after thirty-two years at Arthur Anderson, she and Rachael moved to Florida, so they wouldn't have to deal with New York winters. They had a home built on a lot that overlooks a lake. They are still very much involved with their families, traveling to the East Coast for special occasions. Recently they attended Rachael's grandson's bar mitzvah, babysat for Glenn's daughter, then stayed to wait for the birth of Rachael's niece. All of their children and grandchildren have let love overcome their ignorance and prejudice, and have welcomed Miriam and Rachael into their homes. Miriam and Rachael fly up North to visit, and are provided a car by the children or chauffeured to the next stop. Rachael says, "We go from kid, to kid, to kid. We travel from New Jersey, to Connecticut, to Long Island to Brooklyn." Rachael adds with a grin, "Every bedroom we sleep in has a double bed. We always sleep together. Miriam's grandchildren call me Grandma Rachael, and mine call her Grandma Miriam." All of the children and grandchildren come to visit them in their home in Florida.

Even though neither Miriam nor Rachael is strongly religious, they still observe some Jewish customs. Miriam explains, "We wanted to have mezuzahs on the doors of our home." A traditional mezuzah is a small decorated cylinder that can be nailed to a door post. The cylinder contains a parchment scroll on which two verses from Deuteronomy are written. Miriam explains, "Every time you pass through a door with a mezuzah on it, you touch the mezuzah, and then kiss the fingers that touched it. That is to express love and respect for God. We use the mezuzah in the newer way. We put mezuzahs in different rooms of our house filled with messages that have special meanings for us. There is a special ritual performed by a rabbi for each one. We remember how important our love is and how much we should appreciate each other."

Miriam continues, "We had plenty of problems on the way. It would take days and days to tell them all, problems with our children, problems about living together. I was very introverted and Rachael was a therapist. Rachael always pushed me to talk, and so she taught me how to communicate. That is the strength of our relationship. We've known each other thirty-two years. We've been together for twenty-seven years, and we always talk problems out."

Rachael adds, "We can't say that everything is wonderful all of the time, but the communication line is always open, and it makes us a success. I don't have the words to tell you how much I love this woman. I wouldn't be here without her."

As Miriam reaches for Rachael's hand, she says, "We wouldn't be complete without each other."

Louise and Carol

Carol and Louise have been together for forty-three years, and at first it is hard to separate the qualities which make them individuals. Both thoughtful, they lavish generosity on their friends. If anyone needs help, they will be there. Age has not dimmed the eagerness for life that shines in their eyes. They love having friends around them, traveling together, going to movies, and taking care of their yard and the abundant ducks and songbirds that visit there. Four cats and a Miniature Schnauzer keep them entertained if there is a lull in their life. They love making each other happy.

Their differences are complementary. Louise enjoys competition; Carol likes to watch it. Louise can be volatile; Carol is calming. Unblemished by age, Louise's skin seems to glow and she still has that knockout appeal that fluttered the hearts of many a young woman in the bars of San Francisco when she was a natural blonde. Carol is quiet and unassuming, but under the modest cloak of shy reticence lies the heart of an adventurer, a risk-taker, a person with inner strength. Her sweet smile and bear hug will signal that she loves you. What they have in common is their foundation; love is the cement that sealed their union.

Louise grew up in the Midwest in the late '30s and early '40s with all of the perks and luxuries that her upper-middle-class parents could provide their only child: expensive stylish clothes, vacations to Florida in the winter, a grand home surrounded by manicured grounds. A live-in maid took care of Louise, and she was both loved and indulged by her parents. Her conservative, society-conscious parents would have been upset at the fascination their daughter began to develop for women.

Louise didn't suspect that she was a lesbian even though she realized while attending high school that she much preferred checking out girls in the hallways while her girlfriends watched the boys. She didn't meet any girls she thought she could approach, so stayed in the background. Louise's introduction into the gay world began when, in her junior year, she became friends with a flamboyant popular young man named Greg. He was a light-hearted, talented dancer, and they became good friends. Finally, he trusted her enough to confide that he was queer. Louise says, "I was somewhat surprised, but I thought that accepting this would make me oh, so sophisticated, so grand and wise to accept Greg. He would invite me over, with other friends, to his mother's house. I met a lot of young gay men there and loved their good manners, humor, and flash. I would like to have met a girl, but none came on the scene. Anyway, I didn't know what I would have said or done without revealing myself."

During her senior year, the not-so-shy Jennifer approached Louise, ensuring that by the time Louise finished high school, Louise definitely knew she was a lesbian and what to do about it. After Jennifer, she had another affair, though nothing serious. She was careful to keep in touch with some of her straight girlfriends from high school so they wouldn't question why she had dropped out of their circle. She simply maintained two sets of friends.

After she graduated from high school in 1950, she took some college courses and got a job but lived at home, as was customary then. At twenty, she met an "older" couple, two women in their forties, who owned a lesbian bar on the rough side of Indianapolis. The bar was small, dark and unattractive, but she risked hanging out there from time to time, listening to a women's combo and having a few drinks. It was the only place she knew where lesbians could gather.

It became harder and harder to explain to her parents where she spent her time. "Where are you going?' they would ask.

"Out with some friends."

"Who?"

"No one in particular."

The stress of keeping all of the stories straight began to wear on her nerves and her conscience. "I didn't want to get into a position of telling one lie after another. Telling lies was like rolling snowballs down a hill. They would get harder and harder to manage." Louise met the answer to her problem at one of Greg's parties. Michael, a man she already knew as the son of one of her father's business associates, was there. He mentioned that his parents wondered why he wasn't bringing his girlfriends home to meet them. Louise approached him with a suggestion: "Oh, wouldn't this be nice. We can pretend we're dating and get away from our parents." Michael agreed.

This worked well for several months, so in 1950 they took it a step further and got married. They had a big church wedding, complete with satin, lace, bridesmaids, and cake. "The next day, we headed for Cincinnati where we met our gay friends to party," she says. "After that we all drove to New York City. I think Michael spent most of his time at the famous Everard Baths, one of the places where Barry Manilow and Bette Midler got their start, playing to gay men who came to the baths for entertainment and to cruise. The women in the group and the men who weren't interested in the orgies at the Everard saw *Gentlemen Prefer Blonds* starring Carol Channing."

Louise's midwestern eyes and ears were keen on catching every sight and sound in the big city, but the high she had felt there came crashing down when she got home. The arrangement she had with Michael quickly turned sour. In a few months, he revealed the ugly side of his personality. "He was too handy with his fists when he was drunk. I couldn't stay with him. After the divorce, I was back home and back to square one again." She couldn't tell her parents about how Michael had become too drunk to drive to a party. Louise had driven, with Michael sitting behind with his boyfriend. When they arrived at the party, Michael became angry and tried to kick her through the back seat. When her friend sitting in the passenger seat protested, Michael hit her, then got out of the car yelling, pulling Louise out by her ankles and hitting her. Before others arriving at the party could stop him, he had badly beaten Louise. She left the party, stayed with a friend that night, and went to her parents in the afternoon. "I downplayed my injuries because I didn't want my father to go after Michael and find out that we were gay. I did tell them that we had an argument in the apartment and he hit me several times." A quick divorce followed and Louise took back her maiden name.

Louise lived at home and continued to see women on the sly, then rented a house with three other lesbians. She fell in love for the first time with Betty, whom she dated for two years, always in secret, which was difficult because Louise's love for Betty compelled her to travel 100 miles to Fort Wayne to see her. Louise thought that they would be together someday, but Betty had other ideas. She met someone else and moved to Illinois. Just like that, it was over.

Louise was stunned. Her sense of equilibrium was off. The worst part was she didn't have many friends left to confide in, because it was the late '50s, and the land of the Golden Gate Bridge was calling. The stories of the gay nightlife — the bars, the Castro district, the restaurants, and baths — had reached the Midwest. Most of her friends had followed the lure of San Francisco. She was comforted by the fact that they all kept in touch and urged her to come join them. Friends Avery and Steve invited her to stay with them until she got settled. Louise needed a new start more than anything. Nothing at home could relieve the pain of Betty's abandonment.

Desperation pushed her. Now was the time. She would have to go or be stuck with her parents. She says, "For me, having lived such a sheltered life, it was a big decision. I didn't believe I could do it. A young woman alone was unusual in my social circles." But desperation pushed her to act. She got up the nerve to tell her parents that she wanted to move to San Francisco. "They, of course, didn't know that I knew a soul out there. Since I was 21, I really didn't need their permission, but for their feelings and out of politeness, I asked." Louise cringed at her mother's response: "But haven't we been good to you?"

Louise knew that Avery would be coming back to visit his family soon, so she planned to fly to San Francisco with him when he returned. She knew her parents would be seeing her off at the airport, so she told Avery that she wouldn't talk with him until after she boarded the plane. She had just said her goodbyes when a familiar couple approached. Peter and Metta Van Arsdale were old family friends. Metta exclaimed, "Oh, Louise, how wonderful to see you. I didn't know you were taking this flight out! We'll be flying to Chicago, too. We're linking up with a plane to Mexico City." Peter added, "Maybe our seats will be close." Louise tried not to roll her eyes.

Louise adamantly did not want any of her parents' friends to know that she was meeting someone on the plane. Louise led the way down the narrow aisle and when Avery rose from his seat to look for her, she

IN SPITE OF EVERYTHING....

quickly put her finger to her lips, teacher style, and begged him with her eyes to be quiet. Avery sat back down. Mr. and Mrs. Van Arsdale found their seats several rows farther on and Louise buckled in with a sigh. When they reached O'Hare, Louise graciously and happily parted company with the Van Arsdales.

The rest of the trip was uneventful until the plane banked to land. Louise gasped at the beauty of the bay, the Golden Gate Bridge, and the white-capped water of the blue Pacific. When the plane settled on the runway, Louise began a twenty-six year adventure in one of the most beautiful, exciting, liberal cities in the world, where gay culture and entertainment flourished.

After a heartbreaking letter from home arrived a few weeks after Louise was settled, she would need diversion to avoid guilt. Betty had written to her parents and told them that Louise was a lesbian and that they had been lovers. "I could have wrung Betty's neck. My parents were always so nice to her. Betty said that she told them as a friend. Some friend."

Louise stayed with Steve and Avery, both hairdressers, until she got a job and an apartment, which was right around the corner. She didn't have to buy a car right away because the streetcar stop was down the block; the public transportation system was good in San Francisco."

After a few interim jobs, Louise got a well-paying job at Holt House, an import-export company. Her responsibility was to see that the documentation was in order for customs for her clients who shipped thousands of products to many of the countries of the world. The job was very demanding, but she enjoyed her colleagues at work and would go out to lunch with them. It was the underground nightlife with her gay friends that she really enjoyed, though.

It was 1954. Louise arrived at an exciting time for gay rights in San Francisco. To see the sheer numbers of gay bars was amazing. When they were in the North Beach area, they weren't in the minority; that in itself was uplifting. This was Paradise compared to Indiana. Louise says, "There weren't many bars in Indianapolis where homosexuals could meet and socialize, and none that served a good dinner. Bar clientele were harassed by the police and sometimes beaten and hauled off to jail. The next morning they would find their names in the paper."

San Francisco had gone through a long period of evolution in its treatment of homosexuals, and between the early 1950s and 1961, many gains were made: a law that made a gathering of homosexuals illegal was struck down; police were prosecuted for extorting money from bar owners; and José Sarria, a popular drag performer, helped to start a "gay is good" movement by running for city supervisor and becoming the first gay man to demand respect in the politics of San Francisco.

"I couldn't get over all of the sheer numbers of gay people there were and the choices there were for gay entertainment. You could go to the Beige Room and see wonderful female impersonators. There was a lesbian bar called Mona's that featured women impersonating men. It was very popular, but it wasn't my cup of tea. There were high class restaurants down to motorcycle bars. My gay friends and I mostly went to the gay restaurants and bars that catered to the business set. They were the only places at that time where gays could gather and meet people. We were never outlandishly dressed and our behavior was always conservative and proper."

Louise liked a particular restaurant. "Gordon's was first class, with soft lights and thick carpet. The food was always excellent and served with finesse. It was mostly a men's bar but women were welcome. Men came in suits and ties right from work." She also liked The Nines, where there was a painting of the Duke and Duchess of Windsor behind the bar. "Dressed to the nines" was an expression of the Duke and Duchess of Windsor which meant "dressed to impress." There was a piano bar in the corner where Louise and her friends could sit with their drinks and sing along with the music.

It didn't take long for Louise to meet other women. She dated a lot, making up for the drought in Indianapolis. "In those days people really dressed up," Louise remembers. "For example, I wore things like blue and white sling-backed spectator pumps and a skirt and blouse. That was the time before pantsuits. The butch women wore men's suits and ties. You couldn't tell some of them from men. They could go anywhere but usually went to the bars that catered to them, like Mona's."

"When I started going to the bars, it was up to the bar owners to keep order and make sure that their bars would not be closed for serving 'sexual deviants.'" Certain standards of bar etiquette had to be met or the police could shut them down. There were signs in the windows warning that the bar was off limits to service personnel. Louise says, "We weren't allowed to touch or to dance. We couldn't lay a hand on someone's shoulder or give a polite hug. There were people, matrons, who would watch and come around saying, 'No touching.' The cops would come in and walk around to show us they were on the job enforcing the sodomy laws, but we didn't consider them threatening. They couldn't stop us from flirting and picking someone up with our eyes." Even with all of these restrictions, the atmosphere was lighter than she remembered it at home, and there was a sense of freedom.

One night, Louise was sitting in a booth in The Paper Doll with Gene, when she noticed an attractive woman sitting at the bar with several men friends. Their eyes met and in Louise's words, "Zap! We'd turn away and look again, and give each other that 'I'm checking you out look,' then we'd turn away, the whole cruising bit. Then Gene said in mock alarm, with a flip of his wrist for emphasis, 'Oh, *my*, I'm embarrassed, like I *shouldn't* be watching. It's so *hot*. I've never seen cruising like *this* going on and I'm *right* in the middle of it!' She and I had never said a word until we left the bar and talked over coffee." That was how Louise's romance began with Frannie.

Louise liked Frannie, but they didn't have a lot in common. Still, they lived pleasantly together for several years. One year Louise's parents decided to spend their winter vacations in San Diego to be near her. Her father's health dictated a warmer climate, so they couldn't live in San Francisco. Louise enjoyed seeing them and flew down to be with them on the weekends. She introduced them to Frannie and nothing was said about their living arrangements. Louise says, "We were from the Midwest. We never talked about anything personal or embarrassing. We just pretended it wasn't there."

Louise's father died in San Diego in 1965, when Louise was thirty-five. Her mother went back to Indiana for a year and by the time she decided to come back to California, Louise was living with another woman, Carol. Louise found a house for her mother about twenty minutes away, and when she came to visit, Louise introduced her to Carol. Her mother asked, "Did you break up with Frannie for Carol?"

Carol is a native San Franciscan born in 1932. As a teen and young adult she was crazy about movies and movie stars. Her friends in high school were people who shared her love for movies and the stars at MGM, Universal, and RKO. Even before she knew she was a lesbian , she didn't care if some of the boys were homosexual.

She and her friends would collect autographs at the places where the stars met the public, stars like Frank Sinatra, Katharine Hepburn, and Judy Garland. But getting autographs wasn't enough for her fan club; they wanted to be where the stars lived and do what they did. "We were all crazy about movies and we would go to Hollywood on the Greyhound bus for the weekend and see if we could get into their houses and look around. We didn't want to take anything, just see it. There weren't any walls or gates around the houses in the '50s. Often the houses would be empty. One night we were in Judy Garland's swimming pool and someone saw us and called the police. They came, but because of our young age, just shooed us away and said, 'Behave yourselves.'"

Of course, they didn't behave. There were other close calls. Carol remembers, "We walked into Katharine Hepburn's house and while we were looking around, she came into the living room. We were petrified. She looked right at us, and said, 'I'm no damn giraffe.'" Before she could add, "Get out," they had disappeared.

Carol's biggest thrill of those times was being an extra in *Singing in the Rain*. The second best memory was her job as a messenger at one of the big studios. One time she delivered a memo to a working movie set — heaven for a film addict.

As Carol matured, she gave up childhood things, but retained her sense of adventure. When she was eighteen, she joined a group of young women who bicycled through Europe, staying in youth hostels. The trip was grueling for Carol, who didn't have the stamina for so many miles each day. "It was all right; I kept up, but it was hard." Much more to her liking was a trip with two Canadian women, Brigitte and Charlotte. In 1956, they traveled to Italy, purchased Lambretta motor scooters, and began six months of touring. "I put 10,000 miles on the little scooter and never had a problem until I was on my way home. We went to Scotland, England, France, Germany and Switzerland, Italy, Sicily, Spain, and Portugal." They brought their scooters home with them on the boat. Charlotte went back to her university studies, and Carol stayed with Brigitte's family in Toronto to rest for a while. Her stay was so satisfactory for all that Carol was with them for a year. She rode the Lambretta to work and, when Brigitte's father needed a ride, would carry him behind her.

Eventually Carol decided that she needed to look for work at home and rode the Lambretta from Toronto to San Francisco. Carol says,

"In 1957 it was not so dangerous for a woman to travel alone. I stayed in motels along the way and had a great time." The scooter broke down in the mountains near Lake Tahoe. She got help from some men on motorcycles who took turns towing her behind them. That provided some exciting moments, because at one point there was slack in the tow line and the Lambretta's front wheel went over it. When the tow rope suddenly tightened, Carol was flipped over backwards. Despite many scrapes and bruises blossoming all over her body, Carol continued and managed to get to her friend's house in Lake Tahoe. After a short visit to rest and heal, she rode the bus home and had the scooter delivered when it was repaired.

In Toronto she had worked at a business which sent merchandise abroad. She learned how to prepare their exports for customs. Thinking that her meager experience would prepare her for a job at an import-export clearinghouse, she answered a classified ad in the *San Francisco Tribune*. When she got the job, she realized that she knew very little, but she was a quick study and caught on with the help of a sympathetic supervisor.

Carol liked the gay bars, restaurants, and the drag shows for tourists at Finocchio's. She went often, sometimes with her mother, who, like many San Franciscans, was very open-minded. Carol says, "There was a particularly attractive bar in North Beach called The Paper Doll that we frequented so much that the hostess learned our names. Later, when Louise and I went there together, Louise was surprised that she called me by name. I can't tell you exactly why I liked it so much there. It was pleasant and the hostess and waiters were so friendly. In some ways, it was like home."

Carol lived in an apartment for a while until her mother decided to buy a house as an investment. She wanted Carol to live there. Sadly, soon after Carol began to feel at home there, her mother died. She missed her mother terribly and threw herself into her work to dull the pain, becoming a most valued employee and making top salary at W.C. Boyd House. Carol explains, "Shipments from multi-million-dollar companies would come through the ports in San Francisco, dropping off thousands of pieces of merchandise. All of the documentation of that merchandise had to be reviewed, then new documents prepared to present to U.S. Customs. We determined how much duty was needed to be paid and then added that to the cost of ocean freight and air freight for our services which included sending each to its final destination. Besides dealing with customs, depending on the merchandise, you had to be involved with the Department of Agriculture, the Environmental Protection Agency, and the Food and Drug Administration."

Customs clearinghouses were very competitive, and landing and keeping an expert employee was at the heart of their business. Reputations of efficient employees were known around the competitors' houses. Louise, like Carol, was one of the elite. Her friend, Tom, inadvertently introduced Louise to Carol by encouraging her to get a job at W.C. Boyd House where the salaries were much better. She was accepted as soon as she applied and found a prize worth much more than the thousands in her raise. She met a shy, quiet woman with a paradoxically mischievous twinkle in her eyes. They worked in the same area separated by partitions. Their firm represented F.W. Woolworth, Caterpillar, and many other multimillion-dollar-companies. There was no room for mistakes. Getting to know Carol would have to wait until after work.

Louise says, "Several of us in the office would go across the street after work and have drinks before going home. I thought Carol was straight, like the rest of them. Even in San Francisco it wasn't wise to broadcast your orientation, so I wasn't going to ask." Louise didn't care at first; she just liked spending time with Carol and they were developing a warm friendship. "We loved to go to the movies and talk about this and that. We had a lot of fun laughing and enjoyed one another's company. One place we loved to go was the famous Red Garter where there was a banjo band. You could drink beer, eat peanuts, and throw the shells on the floor."

There was openness and sweetness about Carol that Louise found very appealing. She needed someone like that, because she was sometimes short tempered and demanding. Sometimes they would have what Louise calls "little arguments" and Carol would melt her anger with her calming presence and occasionally an armful of flowers. Carol chose to ignore the outbursts because, she says, "They were nothing compared to all of the many, many ways Louise showed her love for me."

Louise had decided that whether Carol was gay or not, she wanted to be close to her. "She was the one, no matter what." In 1967, when Carol went with her aunt and uncle to the World's Fair in Montreal, Louise

In Spite of Everything....

took care of her car for her. "I washed it up and did special little things to impress her." They were getting friendlier and friendlier.

Louise wanted to hold Carol's hand, but didn't know how she would react. Weeks later, after they enjoyed a movie and a late dinner, Louise drove Carol home. They were parked in front of Carol's house for some time, but neither wanted to end the evening. They sat in the darkness listening to the crickets and the fall of surf on the distant beach. Was there a slight earthquake? Two hearts beat faster. Without thinking, Louise had reached for Carol's hand and had felt the gentle pressure of Carol's response. A simple thing to cause such a thrill, but it gave Louise hope.

Carol wondered at the pleasure in this wordless communication. They sat quietly for some time, and then Carol surprised herself and Louise by kissing Louise on the cheek and quickly leaving the car. Later that night, lying in her bed staring at the ceiling, she wondered how she could have been so bold. It still didn't occur to her that she might be a lesbian!

There were more hand-holding sessions and kisses after that. Instead of taking Carol home one night, Louise asked Carol to spend the night with her. That night the women both found out: Carol was a lesbian. Carol says, "I didn't really try to analyze the way I was feeling. I just liked being with Louise and missed her when we weren't together. I was so glad that she felt that way too. She was the first person I ever felt that way about, and I've never been attracted to anyone else in forty-three years."

Louise says, "Carol was different than any of the women I had known before. She was sweet and gentle, so interested in everything. There was an innocence about her that was so appealing. I didn't want to go too fast and frighten her away." On that first night when Louise invited Carol to sleep in her double bed, she was happily surprised that Carol came into her arms willingly. Carol realized for the first time that her attraction went beyond friendship. She wanted to lie close to Louise, but had no idea what might follow. Louise took charge of that. She began carefully and slowly with tender caresses. Carol's body was quick to respond, as if it had been waiting for this a lifetime. After, she cried with release and joy.

In time, Louise moved into Carol's spacious house in the costal town of Pacifica. They had a spectacular fifteen mile drive into San Francisco on the Coast Highway which had views of ocean waves crashing on the rocky cliffs below. They loved being close. Carol says, "One of the things I loved the most were the showers we took together." The warm cascading water of the shower massaged away their stress. Louise adds, "On weekends, we were grateful to come home together after enjoying the many advantages of living near San Francisco." They attended San Francisco Symphony concerts and went to the theaters, museums, book stores, and the abundant gay bars and restaurants.

Everything seemed to be going so smoothly. Carol was easy to live with, but still, Louise was worried. She says, "I thought that Carol might object to the amount of time I needed to spend with my mother. My mother couldn't drive and didn't have many friends in California, so I would take her to the grocery and stop by and visit on my way home from work." Carol ended Louise's concern by coming with her. She would take Louise's mother to the grocery while Louise straightened up her house. Carol enjoyed going out to eat with Louise and her mother once a week and, occasionally, Carol's father would come along. They tried to encourage a match there, but there was no kindling for the fire.

Louise says, "We just lived a regular life, went to work everyday, cared for our parents, and had time to go out to the bars with friends on weekends. We would get a drink at one, maybe The Paper Doll, and go to another with a piano bar, get some more drinks and sing, and then end up at Gordon's for coffee about two 'o clock in the morning." Louise remembers, "We just had fun — we laughed, drank, and laughed."

Carol says, "There was a bar called the Black Cat in North Beach, and every Sunday afternoon a drag performer, José Sarria, would dress up like an opera singer and perform the whole opera in drag. One time he did *Carmen* and we thought we would split from laughing. He was so campy and outrageous; he came out wearing a mantilla and a rose behind his ear, prancing or flirting or breaking out and singing high C. Right in the middle of an aria, he would say something funny and the house would roar. The place was packed. Straight people would come too, and José would make fun of them, treating them like they were gay. No one seemed to care. He closed his act by singing 'God Save Us Nelly Queens,' and the audience would shout out the words with him." Carol says, "There's nothing like it now. It was closed down a long time ago because people were afraid in the early days of AIDS. They didn't know how it was contracted."

Louise hadn't known anyone like Carol who loved the adventure of traveling. Carol made all of the plans for trips to interesting and exotic lands. She would look at the tour magazines and find places of interest to visit. They loved traveling by ship, train, plane, or car, just as long as they went together. Because Carol and Louise were valued at W.C. Boyd House, they were not allowed to take more than one week together. Not wanting to limit their travels to one week only, Louise got a job at another company, and Carol could finally realize her dream of traveling the world with Louise.

Unfortunately, their parents' health began to deteriorate. After Carol's father, James Cartwright, had been in assisted living for many years, he had to go into a nursing home with last stages of dementia. Carol said, "He no longer knew me and that was very hard to bear."

In 1980, Louise's mother, Mrs. Neilson, began to grow weak and confused. She became so debilitated that Louise got a portable commode and put it beside her bed, then started spending nights with her. One night she heard her mother cry out. When Louise came to comfort her, she was sitting up in bed, eyes wide with fear and confusion. Louise knelt by the bed and took her hand. Her mother searched Louise's face, "Are you my mother?" Louise could barely answer, "No, Mother, I'm your daughter. It's all right. I'll take care of you."

After many tests, doctors found that Mrs. Neilson had internal hemorrhaging, but they couldn't find the source. The only treatment was blood transfusions. Unfortunately, after several years, the transfusions stopped helping, and her mother grew weaker. Louise hired a private nurse to stay while she was at work. "It took most of my paycheck. I couldn't help Carol with the expenses." Carol says, "It was fine. I didn't mind, anyway. Money wasn't important. Her *mother* was important."

Louise says, "We had a wonderful doctor, very understanding. He took charge and told me, 'Your mother needs constant care which you aren't skilled to give. Exhausting all of your strength and money will not help. She needs to be in a nursing home where you can visit as much as you like. Live your life and you will have the energy to visit your mother and not become ill yourself.'"

Since they could no longer get away on long trips because of their parents, Carol and Louise began to take overnight trips to places within a few hours drive from the nursing homes. They called several times a day to see how each parent was getting along. On a couple of weekends they went to the Russian River surrounded by redwood forests. The town of Guerneville on the river had a huge gay community, with gay resorts outnumbering the straight ones. One of their friends convinced them to go camping with a group. They had fun, but Louise didn't like sleeping on the ground. She did like backpacking once, but that wasn't her cup of tea. "I like to be comfortable." She did like the freedom to walk the grounds of the resort arm in arm with Carol and to be at ease in the restaurants there, not worrying about the conversation.

They also liked going to Carol's aunt's beach house in Santa Cruz on weekends. How romantic to lie together and hear the surf caressing the sand. When her aunt and uncle grew older and needed their help getting to the beach house, Carol and Louise drove them there and took care of the maintenance and housekeeping chores for them.

Louise took Carol to a resort called Harlow's Haven in Palm Springs, 500 miles from San Francisco. She says, "Jean Harlow, a famous actress at the time, bought it for her mother for income property. It was gay and so nice. We sat by the pool and ordered drinks, dozed in the sun and rested from staying out 'til two o'clock in the morning. There were other gay resorts in Palm Springs, some for men and others mixed."

Louise retired in 1982. Carol says, "It's a good thing too, because then she had everybody to take care of." Two months after she retired, Louise added Carol to her list of patients. At four o'clock in the morning Carol woke Louise up. She had made her usual night trip to the bathroom and noticed bright red blood in the commode, lots of blood. The bleeding continued. Louise called their doctor and broke records getting to the emergency room at St. Francis Hospital in San Francisco. When they heard the words, "cancer of the kidney," neither flinched. They both possess remarkably positive natures and were never burdened with scenarios of doom. The kidney was removed with the encapsulated tumor while Louise sat in the waiting room praying. Louise says, "We were fortunate to be close with the doctor. He treated me like I was Carol's spouse with all of the privileges. We never talked about it, but Carol and I thought he was gay."

Louise says, "When Carol came home it didn't take her long to recover, and she has never had a recurring problem."

Carol adds, "You might call us 'tough old broads.'"

"Carol was easy, because she recovers fast. She wasn't any trouble. I just had to fluff her pillows and make sure she was comfortable."

While Carol was recuperating, Boyd House asked Louise to substitute for her. Carol was soon well enough to do some of the paperwork that Louise brought home.

Two years after Carol's recovery, both of their parents began to deteriorate. Mr. Cartwright got along well in assisted living until he fell and broke his hip. Even after extensive rehabilitation, he needed nursing home care. At one point, Louise would visit both her mother and Carol's father in their respective nursing homes. She would pick her mother's laundry up and visit with her one day, and then visit Carol's father the next. Louise's mother died on Friday and Carol's father died the following Sunday in 1984. There was no joy in the sudden freedom they had gained, only a profound sense of loss. Their greatest comfort at night was in the warmth of extended hugs and sweet caresses that lulled them into a healing sleep.

In time, Carol began perusing travel magazines and leaflets again. One of their most memorable trips was to Germany in 1988. It came about because of their natural generosity toward friends and strangers. Louise had made friends with Christa Hoffmeister, a young German woman she met, while visiting friends in Ft. Lauderdale. A few years later, when Christa and her mother were in San Francisco, Louise and Carol showed them around and made sure they had a good time. Mrs. Hoffmeister said, "If you ever come to Germany, you must stop and visit us."

Years later, Christa invited them to visit her parents in Hanover, Germany. Christa parents welcomed them into their home in Hanover and showed them a wonderful time. They went on an excursion to Munich to celebrate at the original and best Oktoberfest which resembles a huge American state fair, complete with rides, merry-go-rounds, and carnival booths. It became a tradition to set up fourteen huge tents each sponsored by Bavarian brewers. The tents are filled with tables end-to-end, from front-to-back. Louise, Carol, Christa, and her parents sat at a table with other revelers and watched the waitresses, dressed in authentic

Bavarian costumes, carry eight, one-liter-tankards of frothy beer and set them on the tables. Louise says, "I can't imagine how they could carry that much weight, let alone not spill a drop. The food was good and plentiful: sausage, cheese noodles, sauerkraut, roasted ox tails." Carol adds, "Each brewery had its own tent and many had bands playing polkas and waltzes. It was loud and full of fun."

They thought Oktoberfest would be the highlight of their visit, but Mr. Hoffmeister had other ideas. After a day of recovery from the festivities, he announced, "I want to fly you to Berlin for breakfast and have a tour of East Berlin." Louise and Carol looked at each other. Nearly 100 people had been killed trying to escape from East Berlin since the wall went up in 1961. Through the years the evening news had few reports of successful escapes: people who had hidden in false bottoms of buses or under stacks of cargo. Seeing their apprehension, Mr. Hoffmeister said, "You will be safe, because the Russians allow tourists to come through a checkpoint to sight-see and visit for a few hours. We will be separated for a while at Checkpoint Charlie, but will come together after we are through."

The reality of that separation was chilling. The wall loomed ominously above them. The length of the wall was lined with watchtowers, a patrol track, bunkers, and a corridor with watchdogs. Louise says, "We got into one tour bus, while Mr. Hoffmeister had to go to another one. Even before we started, Russian border guards walked through the bus looking us over. They took off a dark haired, Middle-Eastern-looking man. We pulled up to Checkpoint Charlie. I couldn't believe we were there. As we drove through the checkpoint, I could see there were actually two walls with a strip of land between. It was the place called 'Death Strip' where most of the people had been killed when they tried to escape. When we got out of the bus on the other side, we saw beautiful gardens and gigantic statues of Russian leaders." Carol says, "They had one of the best Egyptian museums I have seen in all of my traveling, but beyond the museums, you could see some of the rubble still there from bombed-out buildings, lying untended for thirty years. Everything looked like an old black and white movie with old cars and buildings on the streets. It was depressing. The Russians had just put on a good show. Before we could go through the checkpoint again, the soldiers tramped through the bus trying to see if the floor was hollow. They put big round mirrors mounted on long handles under the bus. Finally, we got back. That was a trip of a lifetime."

Their trip to Hong Kong was a close second. Carol won the trip for two from her company. Each employee put his/her calling card in a large container and Carol's was drawn. They enjoyed all of the sights, sounds and smells of the crowded city and decided to have jackets tailored. Carol says, "They took our measurements and by the next day the jackets were done and fit perfectly." Louise adds, "We paid extra for a day trip to China and saw part of the Great Wall."

In their forty-three years together, they have traveled to Guadalajara on a tour, enjoyed the ruins and the architecture of Rome, and seen Lipizzaner stallions in the mountains of Yugoslavia. In Dubrovnik, Yugoslavia, they met a woman from Menlo Park, California, who introduced Louise to lawn bowling. Louise didn't consider herself particularly athletic, but when they returned to California, Sally invited Louise and Carol to attend a game in Palo Alto. The game appealed to Louise's sensibilities. "It was dignified and civil. You can play on your own or with a team of two, three, or four." That led to another shared pastime, Louise winning trophies and Carol cheering her on. There was a picture taken for the *Palo Alto Weekly* in 1988 of Louise kneeling in perfect position to deliver the bowl.

Louise loved San Francisco from the time she arrived in 1954, and she still loves much about it. Louise remembers, "The vistas, the ships going through the dark blue water of the bay, the white fingers of fog that reached in to touch the city, just beautiful. But in the twenty-six years that I lived there, things changed. By the '90s it became very expensive to live there. That was all right when we were working, but after retirement it became more difficult. It also became more crowded. Sometimes we almost missed dinner reservations because we couldn't find a place to park." Carol adds, "Parking costs twenty dollars. Who wants to spend that? You just have to take a cab and that's expensive, too. San Francisco has an excellent transportation system, but we lived in Pacifica and didn't have access to it."

San Francisco also began to have a problem with vagrants. Carol says, "If you wanted to go downtown to the theater, you'd have to step over the drunks lying all over the sidewalk. Many of the homeless were living in Golden Gate Park. The city needed to build shelters where they could go.

Union Square, right downtown across from the St. Francis Hotel, Saks Fifth Avenue, and Macy's, was occupied by sleeping addicts, drunks, and vagrants." Besides this growing discontent, some of their best friends, the men who had led Louise to San Francisco, were returning to Indiana.

Louise began to have fond memories of the rich foliage, green lawns, and neat neighborhoods of her home state. She and Carol took several vacations to Indianapolis to visit Avery and Steve, Gene and others. Carol says, "It was very pretty and the people were so welcoming and polite." Carol, as always, was amenable to a new adventure. When it was time for Carol to retire, they found a lovely home with a big yard in a quiet neighborhood and moved to Indianapolis.

Carol says, "Exactly one month after our move, something was happening to Louise's vision, so I took her to an ophthalmologist." It didn't take long for him to ask two of his secretaries to escort Louise and Carol to a heart specialty group in St. Vincent's Hospital across the street where they saw that she was admitted to the hospital. Within an hour she underwent surgery in her right carotid artery.

It was a good thing that the doctor who performed the carotid operation was also a heart specialist, because while Louise was convalescing, she had a heart attack. Further tests showed blockage in four arteries. Before Louise had time to worry about it, she was in the operating room for quadruple-bypass surgery. She was afraid, but she never let anything spoil her sense of humor. She said to the doctor, "You know where everything is, so I trust you to do a good job."

The operation was a success and after a week of recovering and doing exercises and treadmill tests, Louise left the hospital with the only pain medication she consented to use, Extra-Strength Tylenol. They also gave her a bottle of nitroglycerin, which she has never used in sixteen years, and orders to walk as much as possible. She took up golf and after some preliminary warm ups, hits a wicked ball straight down the fairway. Don't bet against her when she tries to sink a long putt. She recovered remarkably well and looks back on her other operations, as well as another carotid surgery and major vein replacement in her leg, as small events in the whole scheme of things.

Carol and Louise don't dwell on troubling times by rehashing them. They relish their lives and simply keep on going. Even with painful back problems, Carol still won't compromise. She refuses to buy a riding mower for her large back yard because, "It's good exercise to walk."

They have loved one another through good times and bad for forty-three years. Louise says, "We have everything in common. There could be no one else. We are wonderful together. Whatever we do, no matter what, we have a good time. Carol is still so thoughtful and tender. She kisses me good-bye when she leaves on errands, sometimes when she leaves the room!"

Carol says, "Forget Christmas and birthdays and Valentines' Day. It's the every day wonderful things she does for me that matter. Small things like little notes or touches. From the time we met, I loved her and there has never been any one else."

Erin and Dena

As a baby born in 1925 in Boston, Massachusetts, Erin had the complexion of a porcelain doll — transparent, pale skin with rosy cheeks and eyes as blue as an Irish sky in summer. Her complexion and light brown hair made evident her Irish heritage. Her parents, Marilyn and James Kilpatrick, had hoped for a child for twenty-two years before Erin was born. Since she was forty-two at the time of the birth, Mrs. Kilpatrick took special care by going to a private hospital for a caesarean delivery. Marilyn would always give her daughter special care, protection, and all of the opportunities.

Erin didn't participate in the rough and tumble games of childhood — never ice-skated, camped, hiked in the woods, or threw herself down on her sled to sail down the steep hill at the park. But she was very outgoing and did have many friends in her neighborhood. Her mother was there to push and encourage Erin in everything.

Her parents were intensely religious Catholics. Erin grew up loving the music and ritual of the church and being surrounded by the mysteries of Christ's birth, miracles, and resurrection. She was taught by nuns who lived in the convent next to her grammar school. Part of her schooling from first grade through high school included going to Mass every day, then to a class on religion before other subjects were taught. She learned about sin: original sin, venial sin, and mortal sin — the one that would send you to Hell. She and the other students went to confession once a week. Erin began to accept the principle of St. Paul, "The flesh is weak, but the spiritual life will lead to salvation."

At age eleven, she began playing the piano, and music became a passion that burned within her for seventy years. "My mother had taken me to visit with some friends of the family," Erin says, "They had an open piano in the living room and my mother played a scale for me. Without hesitation, I played just as she had, crossing my thumb under my hand to complete the eight notes." Everyone was delighted. The friends gave Erin the piano and her mother enrolled her with Sister Mary Claire, a nun who taught voice, piano, and organ. Erin couldn't get enough of practicing and performing. By the time she was seventeen, Erin was an accomplished pianist and had won a three-year scholarship to the prestigious New England Conservatory of Music. Twice a week, her mother would take Erin the hour and fifteen minute drive to Boston for her lessons. After the lesson they would dine at one of the fine restaurants on Newbury Street near Boston Commons.

"I didn't have time for dating. The boys I was acquainted with made me feel maternal. I wanted to be their friend and nurture them. Voice, piano, and organ were my life. I was attracted to other women. Not in a physical way, but I preferred the company of women." Erin dismissed the kisses she shared with a girl who dressed like a boy when she was fifteen. "That was just playing." One girl, Leslie, who was twelve — two years younger than Erin, captured her interest, at least in a sisterly way, but Leslie had a crush on Erin. Over the protests of her older friends, Erin would let Leslie tag along. She was sympathetic to Leslie because it was her nature to be sensitive to others. As the years passed, Erin and Leslie became close friends. They both loved classical music.

Leslie knew where she wanted their platonic love to go, but something more important was beginning to foment in Erin's soul. She began to feel that something essential was missing. Not her mother's love, nor her close friendship with Leslie, or her devotion to music could satisfy the growing torment that began to consume her. Erin reflects, "I have come to believe that the human soul thirsts after God. At age eighteen, I felt a calling to serve God. I was on fire to give myself up to a Maryknoll convent, where they mission out nuns to Africa and remote places to do God's work." Leslie was in despair when Erin told her of her calling. She couldn't accept the idea that their intimate friendship meant so little to Erin.

But Erin knew she must follow her calling, even though it was not influenced by her mother. When she applied to the Maryknoll order, however, she was turned down. The foreign missions could be dangerous and the church didn't want a family to lose an only child. Erin chose to enter a teaching convent which would enable her to share the blessings of music with students. Saying good-bye to her parents, Leslie, and her beloved piano teacher, Sister Mary Claire, Erin turned to walk the narrow path toward God.

In 1943, when Erin was eighteen, her parents dropped her off at the Bethany Novitiate School in Framingham, Massachusetts, where she would take the first step on her spiritual journey. "As soon as I stepped into the building, I felt that I was home. I had no regrets about leaving my mother, or father, or Leslie. Once you turn toward Christ, you easily leave other loves." Here, she could put away earthly things and attain purity of body and soul.

A very kind, soft-spoken Mistress of Postulants led Erin and forty-three other young women to two dormitories on the third floor. Each dormitory housed twenty-two postulants and their accommodations: a small bed, a dresser, a bookcase, and a white screen for privacy which pulled around their assigned space. Communal showers and toilets were down the hall. Erin filled with joy. The simplicity was a gift, and to be in the company of women, all striving for the purity to be a bride of Christ, was ecstasy. She soon adapted to the rigorous, Spartan life that would lead her to her goal.

One of the rules of the convent was: "No particular friendships, and no ownership of anything." There was little time or privacy to cultivate friendship, let alone romance. All of the postulates slept in dorms. They were trained to get up like a shot to a bell at 4:30 a.m., kiss the floor — an act of humility — and go to private mass given by a priest who would also give communion. After chapel, they ate breakfast in silence, and then each went to her "charge." Some would wash the walls or floors. Others helped in the kitchen, garden, or laundry. They went to school dripping wet with perspiration. Erin remembers, "We wore long underwear and stockings which we could wash, but we were not allowed to wash the postulate's black dress and veil for six months. Then we would become novitiates and receive a habit. It got pretty rank in that dormitory before the time was up. It was a penance, I guess. When I look back, the life seems impossibly hard, but we were young, full of energy, and could do anything."

Meals were eaten in silence while one of the nuns read scripture. There was evening meditation at five. "We studied from seven to nine and went to bed observing Night Silence. I wouldn't have broken Night Silence if you'd threatened to kill me."

While Holy Rules prohibited particular friendships, the women did form close bonds. Erin met several young women who became lifelong friends. One of her favorites was Sister Bertrando whom she nicknamed Birdy. Birdy was nearly six feet tall and big boned with flaming red hair. Another was Sister Mary Bernadett. Erin's eyes crinkle with laughter as she remembers, "Mary Bernadett was a devil. She got me into a lot of trouble. She would get me to do something with her, and *I* would get caught. I got in trouble all by myself, too. I was always arriving at dinner by the skin of my teeth. One day I had the bishop's room for my charge, the room where the bishop was received. I had a little carpet sweeper and a duster. I was running late and left the carpet sweeper and the duster in the bishop's room."

When the bishop came into the chapel, Erin, unfortunately, knew why. He said, "Here's a carpet sweeper." Mother Superior came to the front and added, "Will the nun who has the bishop's room step out?" Erin stepped forward. "Kneel, Sister. You will carry that carpet sweeper and that duster until I tell you to give it up." For two weeks she carried it where ever she went — into the shower, the toilet, the classroom. Erin laughs, "Of course, my friends were singing, 'My Buddy, My Buddy,'" a popular song at that time.

After completing six months as a postulant, the young women who wished to continue became novices and would receive their full habits in a ceremony after a Mass conducted by Cardinal Cushing of the Archdiocese of Boston. Part of the ceremony was getting their hair cut by their sponsor. Erin's long, light brown hair surrendered to the scissors wielded by Sister Mary Claire, her former teacher and now her sponsor. Erin smiled as her shiny hair piled up on the floor. It wouldn't be long until she was a full nun. Later, her head would be shaved, but for now Sister Mary Claire carefully snipped it close to Erin's head. A starched linen cloth was draped over her head and under her chin. This was followed by a stiffer band of cloth around her forehead which fastened in back. The habit was made of black serge wool and covered her from neck to ankles. The veil was placed on top of her head and draped around her face. A bib went round her neck. Only the front part of her face, from her shining eyes to her chin, was visible. The cincture, a soft rope, which was tied around her waist, and a large rosary, which hung from it, completed her habit. She was a novitiate at last. It was a day of joy for all, celebrating the young women's accomplishments and reaffirming their future in service to Christ.

In 1944, Erin and Bertrando, who had been friends as postulants, entered St. Agnes in Arlington to take college courses in music education. They also continued instruction in their specialties — voice, piano, and organ. There was a great need for nuns to serve as teachers, for the parishes had huge, well-attended churches which supported the Catholic schools.

"There was physical work to do as well as their studies in college. We still got up at 4:30 a.m. and followed a schedule. I was very strict with myself. I absolutely believed in the discipline and do 'til this day." In time, though, Erin's focus on self-discipline would nearly destroy her.

Two books, *The Lives of the Saints* and *St. John of the Cross*, greatly influenced her. She became particularly interested in the mystical saints, many of whom had fasted to purify their flesh. "After one year in the convent, I began to fast. I wanted the ecstasy of purity, experienced by the saints. I sat at the far end of the dining room where I wouldn't be easily seen. I took very little food and no one noticed. There were no mirrors in my room. My habit hid my weight loss from my parents when they visited every six weeks. Through the course of four years, I got thinner and thinner. My enthusiasm and stamina held up for three years and during that time I felt I was getting my body under control by fasting."

She was stimulated by her sacrifice and loved her life among the women in the convent. After completing her education courses she and Sister Bertrando were sent to Mount St. Joseph, a teaching order for advanced studies in piano, organ, and voice. Their charge now was to teach in the elementary school near St. Joseph's. Erin loved teaching music during the week to all the grades in a Catholic school in Boston. After school and on weekends, she would study with Sister Olivia and practice in order to perfect her voice, piano, and organ techniques. Sister Olivia was a professor who not only taught piano and organ, but also conducted a full orchestra made up of nuns. Her reputation as genius was widely accepted. People from all over the United States came to study with her. Erin enjoyed listening to Sister Olivia at concerts, where she would dazzle the audience with her artistry. Erin sighs, "I was thrilled with her music. She would play a Rachmaninoff concerto and follow it with a light and airy Mozart piece, changing her technique with ease."

Erin had a commanding presence in spite of her four-foot, ten-inch frame, soft voice, and quiet demeanor. She spoke slowly and deliberately, with a ring of authority. Six foot tall, Birdy was a gentle soul and easily led by her diminutive roommate. Erin talked her into helping her take Sister Olivia's charge of preparing the Thanksgiving turkey and the breakfast for the sisters who remained at school for the holiday. Sister Olivia needed time to rehearse the orchestra for the holiday concert.

Erin and Birdy were staying on the third floor dorm which had no heat. Erin remembers, "In order to help with the turkey, we had to get up at one o'clock. We helped one another dress quickly and were thankful, for once, for the heavy wool gowns. I got a flashlight and we wended our way down the four flights of stairs to the kitchen." The cook, who could have played right guard for the Notre Dame football team, had already put an enormous turkey into the oven. The last instruction she gave was, "Don't touch the turkey!"

After about an hour, Erin said in her slow, deliberate way, "Birdy, I remember that my mother always basted the turkey. We have to baste it with the juice."

"She said not to touch it," Birdy replied. Not to be deterred, Erin walked to the institutional-sized, iron oven. It was very close to the floor and she had to stoop to open the heavy door. Erin ordered, "You get on one side and I'll get on the other and we'll just baste that turkey." Birdy obeyed, the quiet assurance in Erin's voice making it seem like the only thing to do. They must have moved the pan a little too far forward in order to reach the twenty-seven pound bird, because the next thing Erin remembers was, "That turkey flew out of that pan and slid on the fat the whole length of the tile floor of the kitchen. I was so scared that I wet my pants. I said, 'Birdy, oh my God, my God, help us. What are we going to do?' Birdy's mournful reply was, 'The fat, we're swimming in fat!'"

Erin came to her senses. "Wait a minute. Fill a tub with boiling water and soap. We have to get the fat up." This was done while the turkey rested against the far wall, fifteen feet away. Erin continued giving orders, "Next we get the pan. Come with me now to set the pan down by the turkey. We'll get some big forks and you'll go in the rear end and I'll go in the stomach and we'll lift it gently into the pan." When Erin tried to steady the tottering turkey by holding on to the leg, it came off in her hand. Luckily the turkey slipped into the pan, which still had enough fat roiling around in it to make the trip back to the oven perilous. Once it was back in the oven, Erin said with confidence, "Stick that turkey leg in there and they will never know the difference." It was now 3:30 a.m., time to make breakfast.

A miracle of sorts occurred and the preparations for breakfast were successful in spite of Erin's mistake of breaking six eggs *with* shells into a pot of boiling coffee. The eggs were no help in keeping the coffee grounds down, because they were being poached on top. Erin saw her mistake and said, "We have to keep calm. We have to keep calm. Birdy, get those eggs out of the coffee. We haven't got time to make another pot so we'll strain the grounds with cheese cloth." They made bacon, scrambled eggs, and toast for thirty people without further mishap. As far as the Thanksgiving dinner went, no one ever said a thing about the turkey leg.

In spite of her grit, by the end of her stay at St. Joseph, Erin's body was closing down. Her periods had stopped after three years of fasting. She didn't see this as a sign of poor health, but she became frightened by her shortness of breath and fatigue. No one noticed her distress because she was missioned away to studying music and teach. After four years, she finally told the Mother Superior what she had been doing. Erin explained, "Every one of the saints fasted rigorously as a punishment to their flesh. I wanted to be like them. I have to tell you that I have been fasting and I finally realize that it is damaging me."

"My child, the Lord would never ask you to harm yourself. Why didn't you tell me about this?" Erin couldn't think of an answer to that. All she wanted was rest.

Mother Superior called Cardinal Cushing, who came to see Erin and said, "I don't want you to do anything drastic. Begin eating little by little until you are digesting full portions. I want you to stay another year until you complete your first vows." Erin stayed one more year and then asked to leave. "I felt that I couldn't go on," she explains. "The functions of my body began to break down. It was a terrible disappointment to leave the convent."

Erin's mother was shocked when she saw her daughter's wasted body. Her spiritual strength was evident, but her body was fragile. At home, Erin began to experience panic attacks, convulsions, and heart tremors, so her parents sent her to the Heart Institute in Boston. They found nothing wrong with her heart and diagnosed her as having a nervous breakdown. After one of the staff psychologists interviewed her and learned of Erin's background and close relationship with her mother, she told Erin, "I think you had a symbiotic relationship with your mother, that you were everything to each other. Your fasting may have been a form of anorexia."

Erin replied, "I wasn't homesick for my mother when I was in the convent."

"Maybe it was a relief for you to get away. Sometimes love can be overpowering. Right now, you need to relax and take care of your health. Reconnect with friends. Enjoy your music."

Erin didn't think her mother's love had been suffocating, but then, she didn't know what to think. She was too debilitated to work it out. Luckily, she had a friend who came to help her heal. Leslie still loved Erin and when she found out that Erin was ill, she came to visit and later took her out for rides in her car. Sometimes she would take Erin to her house and hold her. Leslie's care began to have an effect. Erin began to gain weight and her periods started again, but her light brown hair grew in white.

With her health returning, she was able to take a position as organist with St. Michael's Church. As she continued to improve, she began to sing at church and for weddings and concerts. Not making enough money to get her own place to live, she considered a career in teaching, but she didn't have the energy for it. When a friend mentioned there were job opportunities at General Electric, Erin applied and got a job at their plant in Lynn. It was 1950. She was twenty-six years old.

Erin underwent a transformation that, to this day, she finds inexplicable. "I had never felt the comfort and softness of a woman's body or the desire to possess it," she says, "But now Leslie's and my friendship bloomed into a physical lesbian relationship." Removed from the confines of stone walls and no longer separated from human contact by yards of

In Spite of Everything....

wool, mandated silence, study, work, and penance, she now experienced the allure a healing touch could arouse, the seduction in gentle kisses. Erin's experience with Leslie launched her into a world of women so different from the quiet order of the convent where she had desperately wanted to attain purity of body and soul. "I was fascinated by the night life in the lesbian bars. I loved having a great time, the laughter. I didn't feel that it was sinful to be a lesbian. Love was love, a gift from God, whether for straight or gay. The women I met were not so different from other people. They just happened to love women." She loved to dance and meet new people. The irony of the juxtaposition of playing the organ at high Mass and then dancing in lesbian bars on weeknights, never occurred to her. Suddenly she was free to have "particular" friendships. "I never thought that being a lesbian was wrong, so I never tried to hide it. It seemed so natural for me to love women."

Erin and Leslie never lived together and their physical relationship dissolved in time, though they did remain friends. Erin moved on to taste more of the forbidden fruit from the tree of knowledge. She met Eileen. "We went to bars together and had a little affair," Erin confesses. "Later, I met Connie at a party in Boston. She was the first person that I wanted to live with." When they began going out together, Erin introduced Connie to her mother. When Erin's mother saw them kissing on two occasions, she just laughed. Erin took that to be a demonstration of tolerance and asked if Connie could come live with them. Her mother said, "No."

Erin then said good-bye to her mother, who made no protest even though she was sad to see Erin leave. Erin was making a good salary at GE then, and could afford to pay for half the rent for the house she and Connie found. Erin and Connie often visited her parents who, though they were only in their late sixties, both had health problems and couldn't easily get out.

When Erin started at GE, she did general office work, working in a large room with many others with desks just like hers. She was well liked by her acquaintances at GE, because when the boss left the room, she would treat them to the sound of her beautiful voice. Her songs lifted them out of the monotony of their jobs and made the day shorter.

In the thirty-three years that she worked there, she moved up to supervisor over the key punchers, then to the production room near the factory where she was in charge of ordering all of the fuel control parts for the engines being built by GE. She had to order the parts a year ahead and estimate future needs. She later worked in the production control office and visited the factory floor to check on production. The military officers who came to check her paper work never guessed she was gay.

Because she was a good organizer, she was often asked to be on planning committees for staff parties. One of these was for a bridal shower for a woman named Dena, whom she had seen around the building. Erin says, "I thought she was attractive, but she was getting married and I had a partner. Any interest in her was not an option."

Dena O'Connell was born in 1927. The youngest of ten children, she came from a gregarious, Irish Catholic family from West Lynn, Massachusetts. Dena's father, Dennis O'Connell, died before she was born, so her mother had to raise Dena and her four siblings who were still at home. Through her husband's hard work and foresight, she owned a three-story apartment building where the family lived, so they had enough money to get by.

Like most Massachusetts natives, Dena's family was a hardy bunch. The whole family went sledding, skating, and skiing together. There was no whining about the cold or the accompanying bumps and bruises that were sure to be a part of the fun. If you fell down, you got back up. It was that simple. They loved being outdoors. Their motto was, "If it's going to be nasty, you might as well get out and enjoy it." Dena, now age eighty-two, says, "I started skating when I was just a little kid. In our family, the skates were passed down. I started on a pair that clamped on to your shoes. My mother could waltz and cut designs of flowers into the ice with her skates."

Dena was a daredevil and had adventures with friends that she would never confess to her mother. "When we were kids, I was about nine, we'd run buckeys, in the river. You know, when the ice breaks up in the early spring on a river? Those pieces of ice are buckeys. We would stand on them and ride them for a while, then jump from one to another to the other side. We'd fall off a lot of them, too. The water was cold, so when we got out we'd stand by the fire 'til we'd stink of the smoke. If I had a kid of my own I'd never let them do that. If my mother had known I did that, she'd have whooped me good."

In the summer her family would go to the coast and swim or sail. Dena loved all of it and more. She and her brother, John, sold sea worms for bait. After the tide went out, they would carry their buckets and clam shovels out to where the water met the mucky sand. They dug deep and turned the sand over to expose the worms. They had to be quick to pick them up before they disappeared into the sand. They hauled their catch to Ken Hurley's house and emptied their buckets on a newspaper he had spread on the floor. Together they would count and sort the worms. Ken gave them two cents for the regular worms and three cents for the bloodworms. Dena wasn't afraid to hold the slimy, squirming worms in her hands. "It was different. I liked to do things that were different."

Their circle of love grew as the family grew with in-laws and grandchildren. When the upstairs apartments became available, two of Mrs. O'Connell's daughters moved in with their husbands. Mrs. O'Connell's bright warm kitchen became more crowded and the dining room table was extended. Tangles of hugs, laughter, and the smell of rich food cooking filled the house, their church and Irish heritage the cement that held them together. Sadly, it was their religion and heritage that drove Dena from their circle of warmth.

"I think I was in the first grade when I fell in love with my teacher. At reading time we would sit around her in a circle. I can remember pressing my book on my full bladder to get a tingly feeling. I didn't know it then, but I'm sure it was sexual." Miss Peterson married and moved away before the semester was over. Dena felt a sense of loss like homesickness. She didn't know then that her attraction for women was one she would agonize over in her young adulthood.

"I was ten when I first read *The Well of Loneliness*, the first widely read book about a woman who loved another woman. I found it in my sister's hope chest. I knew that Stephen, the female heroine, and I were very much alike. I was very grateful that I was not the only one who felt like she did, because I was so ashamed of my feelings." Dena wouldn't tell the priest in confession, because she knew he would say that her attractions were works of the devil. She didn't want to be known as a bad person, so she began a life of secrecy and duplicity. The power of Catholic doctrine weighed heavily, a staggering load for a child. "I felt as though my whole life was playacting. I would present one side of me to some and present others another side." She continued to have crushes on girls throughout elementary school and had close relationships with girls in high school.

In 1950 when Dena was twenty-three, Dena's gay friend, David Gentry, introduced her to Sheila Thompson. It wasn't long before Dena began thinking that this woman would be her life partner. She didn't want her family to know that she was seeing Sheila on a regular basis, but it was nearly impossible to see Sheila without her family's knowledge. Her mother and sisters seemed overly curious about whom she was with. Dena decided to ask David if he would like to get married to end the suspicion of their families.

In 1951, Dena and David were married in the office of a Justice of the Peace in New Hampshire. Dena and her girlfriend Sheila could now see each other as much as they wanted and David could enjoy cruising. It worked splendidly until 1954. Sheila, who was in the Air Force, was shipped to Lackland Air Force Base in San Antonio, Texas. There she would train for deployment to Korea. Shortly after Sheila left, David joined the Army and was sent to training camp. Dena moved back home to her mother's house in Lynn, which was closer to GE, where Dena had been working.

"My family kept asking me where Sheila was. My sister Margaret asked, 'If you're such good friends, why doesn't she write to you?'" Dena says, "I *was* getting letters from Sheila, but she was sending them to our friend's address. No way did I want my family to see her letters." In her next letter to Sheila, Dena wrote, "Send a letter to me at Garden Street, my mother's address, so I can leave it on the coffee table. Make it one that my family can pick up and discuss or something." Dena paid dearly for that request. The letter Sheila wrote couldn't have caused more mayhem if it had exploded. Dena says, "She must have been bombed when she wrote that letter. It was very gay. She told me she loved me and all that and that she and another officer had married gay men, so they could live off the base and entertain gay friends. My sister Mary intercepted it and took it to the priest."

The parish priest requested an immediate meeting with Dena in the rectory. Dena remembers the chill when Father Michael handed her Sheila's letter. "I knew the jig was up." Father Michael said, "Your sisters wouldn't have given me this letter unless they loved you." Dena's icy response was, "They may love me, but they don't know me." She agreed to go to confession the next day, but when she got home, she packed her clothes and went to her friend Wendy's house. "Wendy was straight, but she knew I was gay and didn't care."

"I told my boss at work that I was going to leave and go to my husband who was in the service, but I took the bus to Lackland Air Force Base." A cab took her to Sheila's apartment off base. Sheila's home was crowded because she and her new friend, Lauren, were sharing it with the men they had married. Dena knew this beforehand and expected Sheila to be glad to see her. Instead, her reunion with Sheila was awkward. Lauren and Sheila seemed too close for Dena's comfort. She knew immediately that she wouldn't be able to stay with them. She rented a small apartment and stayed for a year until Sheila was shipped to Korea, never knowing whether Sheila and Lauren were more than friends. With no well-paying job and no place to live, she returned to Boston.

Not comfortable going back to her mother's, she lived with her in-laws while David was stationed in Germany. When he came home, they got an apartment together. She tried to get back with GE, thinking they would welcome her. She talked with a personnel manager who had resented her sudden resignation. She was told, "Why don't you go work someplace else for a while and come back when you can show us you're reliable?" That rejection meant good fortune for Dena. In 1956, she got a job at the Arsenal in Watertown, twenty miles from Boston. She impressed them so much that she was made the night supervisor in charge of running the world's largest computer. It took up a whole room. She and that computer made history. "I worked there five years operating one of the first computers this country ever had. It's in the computer museum in Boston now, Univac 1000."

Sheila continued to send letters, but Dena discovered through friends that she had a lover overseas and one in the States. She knew now that, for her, any close relationship with Sheila was over. When David received orders and left for another assignment, she realized that she couldn't bear to live alone. She missed her family but knew that they suspected that her marriage to David was for convenience. Her loving family now considered her a wayward soul. Her church, which had given her comfort in childhood, would not accept who she was. The only way she could come home was to live a "straight life." She was so depressed and lost that she was willing to suppress her need for the loving touch of a woman. Dena remembers, "I went back to my mother's house and stayed away from gay life. My only contact was with two lesbian friends whom I saw once a month. I lived that way for seven years. I wasn't happy with my life at all. I just went through the motions of living, going to work or church, and otherwise staying home."

In 1963, when the rumors began that Watertown Arsenal would be closing, Dena applied again at GE. This time, she talked to a person who remembered her qualifications and had heard about her success working with Univac I.

In the seven years Dena had been gone, Erin had been transferred to Dena's department, production control. She was still living with Connie, and their relationship had settled into a comfortable friendship. Sometimes, though, too much comfort can lead to complacency. Erin accepts the responsibility for their fizzling relationship. She says that she cannot share blame with anyone. She simply wandered away.

Erin began to look at Dena a little closer when she came back to GE. Dena had a slim athletic body and beautiful dark brown hair with reddish highlights. She moved gracefully, with controlled power like a cat. Erin could see that beneath her businesslike yet friendly exterior there was pain. Erin knew she didn't date or go out with people in the office and began to hope that Dena was gay.

Since Erin never had any doubt about being gay and never tried to hide it, she set about finding out whether Dena was gay the only way she knew how. Erin went to the sorting room where Dena brought the key punch cards she had coded. The sorting machine would tally all of the information. Dena was also walking toward the sorting room with a stack of 3,000 three-by-six-inch cards balanced between her hands. Erin was inside the door and got right to the point. "May I ask you a question?"

"Go ahead, but I have to keep working, because I want to get these done."

"Are you gay?"

"Are you gay?" The question echoed around the room as 3,000 cards went flying! Dena said, "I damn near died! All I could say was, 'Help me pick up these cards and I'll see you in the ladies' room.'" Erin responds with honest bewilderment, "How else would you ask someone?"

On a Friday two days later, Erin said to Dena, "I need a ride home. Would you give me one?" Dena was happy to say "Yes," but she didn't count on the time it would take before she would actually get Erin home. As she turned out of the parking lot that evening after work, Dena thought they might stop for a drink. Erin's soft chuckle accompanies Dena's next remark. "We bypassed the drink. Erin became very affectionate." Smiling, Dena continues, "We were gone for the whole weekend. We ran away.' They went along the coast to Gloucester and New Hampshire, then to Vermont, staying in motels along the way.

The memory of one particular night, forty-three years ago, lights a spark in Erin's faded blue eyes. "Oh that red blanket, I'd still like to go back and get that red blanket from the Buckingham Motel in Vermont. Oh, I loved that red blanket." In the Buckingham Motel, Erin's tender insistence finally released Dena from her self-imposed prison.

Slowly, with care, Erin awakened sensations Dena had long denied. Each part of her body came alive under Erin's hand, like the body of the adored statue turned to flesh in Ovid's *Pygmalion*. Little by little she surrendered, as stone had surrendered. Erin knew *her* statue had come alive when she kissed her neck and felt the racing pulse.

The next day, both glowing from the night before, they traveled to Stowe and had coffee and strudel in the hotel which had been the von Trapp family's mansion. On their way home after breakfast, their moods changed drastically. Erin says, "We had to face the music." The "music" was Connie, Erin's partner of seven years.

Dena carried guilt into her new relationship with Erin, "I felt terrible, breaking up someone else's home. I decided that I couldn't go through with it. I asked Connie if I could take her out for lunch and talk to her. It was driving me crazy." When Dena went to Erin and Connie's house, Connie had already left. Erin told her, "Connie has moved out."

"Why is she doing that?"

"I told her that I loved you." Dena remembers, "When I knew that Connie had left, I felt kind of lousy, not happy."

Dena had other problems, as well. Her family had been fine the seven years that she had been depressed, wearing her penance like shroud. She had given up living. Her sacrifice of abstaining from the loving touch of another woman had given her no comfort. There had been no one to relieve her anguish. Now, she was alive again and would not retreat.

Erin came with Dena when she went home to pack some clothes for the night. As they were coming down the stairs, they met Mrs. O'Connell in the living room. Her mother had seen the change in Dena in the last months, but fear that a woman was involved eroded the pleasure in her daughter's happiness. Her fears were realized when she saw how Dena looked at Erin as she said, "I'd like you to meet a friend of mine." Her mother's response was, "Get that woman out of my house."

"Okay, if you don't want her," Dena said, "you don't want me either." She vividly remembers the pain of that moment. "After I moved into the rented house that Connie and Erin had shared, I called everybody in my family and told them that I divorced them. 'You are no longer my family,' I said, 'I was never a part of you.'"

Guilt, anger, and fear came to live with them for a time. Neither could forget the sadness their joining had caused. Erin felt deep remorse for hurting Connie. Dena was angry with her family for expecting her to reject Erin and therefore the love she so desperately needed. Dena was afraid that the very act of living with Erin would cause her to lose her job at the GE.

Dena remembers, "I lived in fear for quite a while that my security clearance would be rescinded, or worse, that I would be fired. I worked in the part of the company that made jet engines, gears, and turbines for the government." While Dena was living with Erin, she was given top security clearance. Beforehand, her neighbors told her that an Air Force representative had come to ask questions about her character. None of her neighbors mentioned that she was gay. Pointing to Erin, Dena says, "This one has a large mouth. She doesn't care and never has cared who knows that she is a lesbian. Our boss, Kenny, knew she was gay and then I ended up living with her. Thank goodness he loved Erin. My security clearance stood."

Erin interjects, "She didn't want to ride with me to work. Dena is very quiet about being gay and I'm completely the opposite. It doesn't make any difference to me."

"At the office we never spoke about it," Dena adds. "I stayed with my crowd and she stayed with hers. I kind of purposely ignored her. They knew, but I wouldn't go down to talk to Erin."

In spite of the secrecy at work, when Dena moved in with Erin, she reconnected with some of her old friends and met Erin's. It was comforting and exciting to be surrounded by women's energy again. They enjoyed entertaining with cookouts and informal dinners, whether large parties or small gatherings.

Dena says, "We did a lot of things that Erin had never done. She was either working or pursuing her music career. Always her music had been first." Erin was still head organist at the church, sang for weddings and other events, and played the piano for them at home, but Dena wanted to introduce her to another world. Dena was an athlete and a daredevil, a combination that sometimes meant disaster. She laughed when Erin's mother told her that as a child, Erin couldn't throw herself on a sled and glide face down, that instead her mother pushed her to the hill while she sat upright like a princess. Dena says, "Erin would have been shocked at running buckeys on the river."

Erin had never camped, so Dena encouraged her to get a small tent trailer with a bed on each side, a stove, a sink, two tables, a heater, and a Porta-Potty. The maiden voyage was to Nova Scotia and Prince Edward Island. The scenery was spectacular, but Dena's greatest pleasure was seeing the expression on Erin's face as they drove. In a few years, they purchased a trailer and parked it at a campground in New Hampshire.

Dena encouraged Erin to go ice skating even if she was tentative, until Erin fell and hit her head on the ice. That ended Erin's ice skating career. Dena tried to think of a winter sport that would be more suitable. She says, "I had hurt myself downhill skiing so I couldn't do that any more, so long before cross-country skiing was popular, we went in to Boston and got skis and poles, pants, hats, the whole outfit. Erin belonged to the Audubon Society, so we used to go to different bird sanctuaries or parks." They'd pack a lunch with a thermos of coffee, which Dena carried in a backpack along with a piece of plastic to sit on. They would sit on a log, close for warmth, their frosty breath mingling as they looked for birds through snow-covered boughs. Sometimes they could only hear their songs delivered by the frosty air.

Erin liked everything Dena introduced her to except horseback riding. When she got her as far as getting up on a horse, Dena said triumphantly, "See, isn't that fun being up there?"

"Take me down."

"Just don't look at the ground."

"Get me down. *Get me down!*"

"Erin, you're in the damn stall!"

"I don't care."

Erin laughs as Dena rolls her eyes and says, "So much for horseback riding."

Dena thought living with Erin was grand, but even Erin's love could not soothe the ache from the loss of her family. They were her foundation. She missed them and so occasionally drove by the home that was the refuge of her childhood. One summer evening Dena and Erin stopped in front of the family home. Music drifting down from the second-story window touched her with sadness. Her sister and her brother-in-law lived in the second story apartment, so out of reach. A burly baritone shouted down to them. "Hey, you two, what are yuh doin'?" It was Dena's brother-in-law. She replied, "Oh nothing, just passing through. How are you, Michael?"

"I'm good. Say, come on up. We're havin' a party."

"What?"

"Come on up. We're havin' a party tonight."

Erin said, "I don't know about this."

Dena summoned her courage. "Let's go." She took Erin's arm and walked up the stairs to her sister's apartment. Together they stepped up to the threshold of a room teeming with conversation and song. The smell of a rich Irish stew permeated every corner. When the revelers saw who was standing at the door, all motion was arrested, sound stilled. All present focused on the threshold, waiting. In that moment of stillness, all pain was forgotten. Before the family could compose themselves and speak, Dena seized the moment, knelt down in front of her mother, and said, "Mamma, I love you very, very, much." Her mother took Dena's face in her hands and said, "I love you little lamb." Judgment fell away. Beer and Irish whisky flowed with the tears. There was embracing and laughter and singing. The family circle closed again with Dena and her partner inside.

When the family discovered Erin's clear pure voice, she became one of their principle entertainers. She harmonized "The Rose of Tralee" with Dena's mother and brother-in-law and brought tears to everyone's eyes with a haunting rendition of "Danny Boy." At Christmas, her flawless "Oh, Holy Night" brought peace.

Erin became one of Mrs. O'Connell's favorite "children." Dena says, "Isn't it strange how things work out?" Then looking in mock disgust at Erin, she continues, "My mother started introducing 'this one' as her adopted daughter. She would side with Erin and say, 'Erin's right, you know.'" Dena would complain to her mother and reply, "But Mama, I'm the baby."

Erin remembers, "It's funny, in the beginning her family was against me, but later on her mother began to love me. Her mother was a wonderful singer and we would sing all of the Irish songs in harmony. Her family all loved to sing. We took her mother to Nova Scotia with us when we had the little trailer. Through the years, we took her to Ireland three times."

Erin's mother was seventy-two and her father seventy-eight when Dena and Erin began their lives together. Her parents were both in poor health, so Erin and Dena visited them in Swampscott to help them with groceries and upkeep on the house. They both needed nursing home care in their early eighties. Erin and Dena visited them in their room every day for eight years. Erin says, "Dena shaved my father every day." Her father died of complications of an operation and her mother died a year and a half later. She was eighty-nine, Erin was fifty, and Dena was forty-seven. Erin remembers, "It was a very sad time for me. I know my mother and father had full lives, but it was hard to see them go. Dena was a big comfort to me."

Neither Dena nor Erin rejected the teachings of their Catholic upbringing. They disagreed with some aspects, but as a whole, they felt that following the teachings of Jesus, as presented by their church, would help them live a life acceptable to God. They try to have patience and generosity and to show compassion and love to each other and all of those whom they meet. They pray to have guidance and strength and Erin still finds time for meditation.

They rejected the idea that a loving lesbian relationship was wrong, but began to discuss and accept the Catholic doctrine that they grew up with: sex for any reason other than procreation is wrong for same sex couples and for male and female couples. They had a passionate love life for the first years they were together, but each in her own way came to the conclusion that something was wrong with having sexual pleasure. In the prime of their lives, before age and injuries, arthritis and joint problems made sex difficult, they made the decision to abstain from sex. It wasn't that they didn't enjoy it immensely. To this day Erin finds pleasure in the memory of that red blanket in the Buckingham Motel in Vermont.

Dena says, "I began to feel uncomfortable about sex. I felt it was wrong." She discussed it with Erin and found that she had reservations, too. They do consider themselves lesbians because they love a woman, but Erin says, "The physical part of gay life is wrong. I believe in celibacy. I don't associate a deep spiritual love of a person with sex. I don't see them as one thing at all. The only way sex is part of love is when a man and woman procreate, that's what it's for. I think it increases your love for a person to be celibate. I think it's stronger and deeper. I never felt the need to marry and procreate, so to fulfill God's will, I choose celibacy." Dena adds, "I feel the same way. In so-called normal people there's not so much love involved in sex as gratification. Rather than adding to a relationship, it takes something away. Sex becomes too important."

Dena and Erin are quiet about the choice they have made in living celibate lives. They are not interested in changing minds or expounding doctrine. They simply live a life that is right for them. When you are with them you know that, for them, it works. You can see those spiritual sparks between them, the tender way they care for one another.

Erin and Dena lived in their rented house for thirteen years before they bought a home in Wilmington, Massachusetts, in 1976. It was only twenty miles west of Lynn where Dena's parents lived and seven miles from the ocean. They lived in that house until they retired from GE, Erin first after thirty-three years. Dena retired a year later in 1988.

After they retired, they rented a house in Arizona for the winter and looked around for a place to stay permanently. They were very impressed with Sun City. Dena says, "There was a big clubhouse for each section of homes. There were seven recreation centers and beautiful swimming pools and golf courses." Even though Dena was concerned that the neighbors would find them out, she agreed that Sun City was the best choice. In 1988 they bought a home on a golf course and moved down in the fall.

A lesbian friend from Massachusetts gave them the names of a gay couple who lived in Sun City and they were happily surprised that there was a large group of gays and lesbians there. They made many friends, some they stay in touch with today, though they left the area in 2000. Dena says, "We had some really good parties there." Erin adds, "If the straight residents knew they were gay parties, they didn't say, but if you are giving a party attended by thirty-five people, and two guys are coming out of some cars and two women are coming out of the others, you should know what was going on."

Life was good. Erin and Dena also took advantage of the seven beautiful recreation areas. They swam, played pool, bowled, and took lessons in crafts. Connie, who is a good friend to both of them now, came down to visit them, staying a month from time to time. Other friends came down in the winter. The couple made eleven cross-country trips pulling their car behind their thirty-two foot motor coach, seeing the wonders of the United States.

In 1996, eight years after they moved to Sun City, Dena began to bump into things. At first she attributed it to not paying close enough attention to where she was going. It became more serious when she began falling. Dena was strong and healthy at seventy-two in spite of two knee replacements, and this turn of events was alarming. Thinking that she had had a stroke, her doctor made an appointment at the Heart Institute in Phoenix. Dena insisted that Erin stay home when she went to the doctor. She says, "I didn't want Erin to hear any bad news." She wanted to buffer what might be an alarming prognosis, because Erin's body had never fully recovered from near starvation and her nervous system was fragile. Dena wanted to tell her at home where they could have the privacy to gain strength from each other. Unfortunately, the news was grave. The MRI and MRA showed a dark spot at the back of Dena's brain.

After more tests, Dr. Harrington, the brain surgeon at St. Joseph's Hospital, met with Dena and confirmed her fears. Dena took the news without flinching, but her thoughts sprang to the early death of her father and wondered if she would die the way he did. To Dr. Harrington Dena said, "You keep quiet about this. I'll tell who I want to tell. It's my brain." When she told Erin, her partner was calm, summoning the strength to take them through whatever journey lay ahead.

Later in the week, they sat in front of Dr. Harrington's desk in his office, ready to hear his plan. He began by telling them about his recent trip to Ireland, calming them with a conversation about places familiar to all. Then he said, "As you know, you have a tumor at the back of your brain. We call it a meningioma, but the good news is it's not malignant. I feel that I can remove the tumor without damaging adjoining brain tissue, but it will be a tricky operation. The tumor is connected to the balance center. I will have to leave remnants of the tumor so as not to invade the brain with a scalpel and do damage." With an engaging smile, he looked directly at Dena and said, "I've done a few of these before. You're going to be fine." He walked them to the door, said good-bye, and started down the hall. Erin called after him, "Dr. Harrington, Dr. Harrington, I'm so glad you're Irish." Dena's color showed her embarrassment. "Erin, why did you say that?"

"I don't know. I'm just so nervous."

Once home, the magnitude of the surgeon's words filled the room. They held each other and cried, then began to prepare themselves to fight another battle together. In the week before the operation, Dena revised her will and made Erin her legal power of attorney and power of health attorney. She didn't want anyone to deny Erin access to her in the hospital. They had learned from a tragic situation in which a friend, Elaine, was blocked from seeing her partner, Janice, in the hospital because Janice's family was homophobic. Elaine did keep the house that she and her partner had lived in for ten years because it was in joint ownership with right of survivor, but the family took Janice's personal possessions and had her buried in the family gravesite. Janice's gay friends knew that she wanted to be cremated and have her ashes spread with Elaine's over Booth Bay Harbor on the coast of Maine. Elaine never recovered from this travesty of compassion.

Erin prayed constantly that week. The operation began at twelve o'clock in the afternoon. Erin kissed Dena as the orderly wheeled her down the hall to the operating room. She didn't see Dena again until she was allowed to go into the recovery room at three o'clock the next morning, fifteen hours later.

From the recovery room, Dena was taken to radiology. She was barely aware of the cart carrying her along the corridor as she watched the blurry lights on the ceiling float by. Then Erin's hand was in hers and friendly faces appeared one by one as she passed them. When the orderly stopped the cart, Dena could see eight beautiful women lining the hallway to greet her. They had flown to Arizona from Massachusetts to wait all night with Erin. Their encouraging voices began Dena's recovery. "Hey, Dena how're you doin'?"

"We've been missing you, girl."

"Welcome back."

Dena gave them a weak smile and said, "It looks like you're getting ready to line dance." They all laughed, relieved that their friend was alert and could still talk.

Dena was not out of danger, however. On the first day out of intensive care she woke up from a nap with her pillow covered with blood. Some of the stitches had come apart and she was bleeding through the back of her head. She was rushed back to the OR to have new stitches and a temporary shunt put in.

The surgeon told Dena later that she needn't worry that the tumor would grow back. "I liberally doused the area with RU486, the French abortion medicine. It's not legal to use for abortions in the U.S., but it's very good on this kind of tissue. It will really slow down the growth. It won't come back to bother you."

Dena went around telling her friends, "I've had a brain abortion so you'd better watch out!"

Erin says, "Dena recoups very quickly. She's had both knees replaced and has had spinal surgery for relief of back pain. We just keep going." Then she brags, "I'm responsible for Dena's quick recovery from the brain operation. When she tasted the dinner I made her, she got up and started cooking."

Dena fully recovered, but arthritis and degenerative discs gave her constant pain. She definitely couldn't do as much as she used to. She began to worry about Erin, as well. "Erin was having a difficult time with her eyes," Dena says. "She couldn't go out in the wind and her night vision was deteriorating." Dena began to realize that Sun City was not a place to be vulnerable because her family was far away. She thought, "If anything happens to me, Erin would be alone. Although we have made good friends here, everyone in Sun City is an import. They might move away." When Dena's mother died, she left the first floor apartment to Dena, so in 2000, when it became vacant, they sold their home in Sun City and returned to Lynn.

They had hardly unpacked their boxes when Erin's primary care physician from Phoenix called and told her to see a pulmonary specialist immediately because of a test he'd run before the women had left the state. The next day they drove to Mass General for X-rays and an MRI, after which the doctor took them into a private consulting room. He pointed to the X-ray illuminated by a bar of lights. "See the two spots there? I'm very sorry to tell you but you have stage one lung cancer." Erin's face was serene. At seventy-five, she looked as fragile as an aging porcelain doll, with delicate wrinkles around her eyes, intricate creping on her cheeks, and slightly sagging smile lines around her mouth. She had never looked strong enough to withstand trauma, but she surprised Dena with her fortitude.

Dena says, "That whole month before her operation was spent traveling from doctor to doctor and test to test. I never once heard her cry." She asked Erin, "What's wrong with you? Sometimes you cry at nothing and then the house can fall on top of you and there are no tears." Erin simply smiled.

It was Dena's time to wait in the operating room and pray now, and her prayers were answered. She says, "When they operated and took out the mass in Erin's lung, they found out it wasn't cancer at all. It was a Valley Fever spore from Arizona soil that had lodged in the tissue." It was a rare occurrence for this to happen, though desert spores did sometimes cause a high fever with flu symptoms. In order to remove the spore, the surgeon had to make an incision from the scapula around to the base of her breast. Then he moved the scapula and separated the ribs in Erin's back. Through the space this provided, he reached the lung and excised the spore. Erin was in such excruciating pain after the operation that she consented to take morphine, even though she never took pills unless she had to. By the time she was ready to go home, she refused anything but Extra-Strength Tylenol. It took Erin months to recover, and she had the best private duty nurse in the world.

After Erin was well enough, they started looking for a place to go for relief from the cold winters in Massachusetts. Dena called several resorts but didn't commit to any. Before long, Dena received a phone call. From out of the past a familiar voice said, "Why in the hell aren't you at Heron's Cove?"

"What?"

"You know, you go through all of that winter weather up there and everything else. Get down here, rent a place, do something." It was Sheila. Dena says of her old girlfriend, "We became friends again after a time — not kissing cousins, but friends." They took Sheila's advice and rented a home near her. Erin says, "We've been going down to Florida for the past four years now and have made friends of our own. You'd be surprised how many senior lesbian couples come south."

Erin is eighty-six now, and Dena is eighty-two. Erin has angel-white hair, which fluffs in waves around her face. She's ethereal as a snowflake melting in your hand. Dena is lean and still has the wiry frame of the aging athlete, her bones and joints damaged by strenuous use, but she is still quick with the comments that make Erin laugh. Her voice is low, straining through vocal chords and emerging as a gravely whisper. Their love is like a tightly woven mantle, sheltering them both.

As they look back through the years, they have few regrets and accept the mistakes they made in life as learning experiences. They have never had a derisive argument. Dena says, "Once in a while we'd cross swords but held no grudges. Holding a grudge doesn't accomplish anything. It's unhealthy. We've had no time for that. We may have had some silent moments or silent afternoons, but they usually ended by one of us making a joke. We have concern for each other."

There are still challenges on the horizon. Dena says, "I'm so worried about Erin's eyes because she has macular degeneration. There is no way to stop the onset of blindness. She can't play the piano like she used to. She was taught to go by the book, and has never played by ear." Erin, as always, is positive: "I have a media enlarger now. I can read opera magazines that I haven't read in years." Erin is concerned about Dena, who will need another operation on her back soon.

The wide world they used to inhabit has grown smaller, and yet their inner world of grace, love, spirit, and friendship has expanded. Their lives are full. Whatever happens, their faith will be true. Their love is strong and their friends are near to give a helping hand.

Suzie and Leila

For as far back as I can remember I had a deep unconscious longing and a sense of not fitting into the scheme of things in the world. I felt an aggressiveness pushing forward in my preadolescent years. It surfaced as being competitive in sports, especially wanting to be better than the boys in my neighborhood. I knew I wasn't like the girls; still, I felt protective towards some of them. In our pretend games, I wanted to be the hero, not the damsel in distress. While others raged with hormonal instincts through high school, I drifted through with attachments to certain female teachers. Not able to bond with the flighty, breathless girls and not affected by the strutting boys, I had few real friends. I was on the sidelines watching a confusing drama.

My home was a refuge where I had the comfort of caring parents. My mother was a practical woman with a wry sense of humor and my father was a minister, a gentle man who lived a life of service and truly believed in the wonder and abundance of God's love. By example, my father showed me the importance of a spiritual life. I have many memories of my parents, but one of my father is particularly fixed in my mind. What I experienced on a trip to the kitchen for a midnight snack gave me more comfort than food. Surrounded by darkness, Papa was sitting at the kitchen table, facing the glow from a candle. His folded hands, serene face, and bowed head were illuminated by the flame. Looking back, I think of a painting by a Dutch master. For a nine-year-old child, the scene was filled with mystery and wonder; most of all, it made me feel safe.

My parents encouraged me to go to college. I didn't know that I had lived a protected life until I began my college career at Butler University in 1957. It was an eye opener, to say the least. I was glad I commuted to school. From what I heard of dorm life, I wouldn't have liked it. I was serious about studying. I liked early morning hours and rarely stayed up past eleven o'clock to study. "Nerd" and "prude" were the labels I escaped by living at home. I pledged a non-Greek sorority and appreciated having a support group. Belonging to a sorority enabled me to participate in intramurals and other school activities. I loved the liberal arts classes and devoted much of my time to study. I also dated. It was part of college life. I was repulsed by groping hands and searching tongues, feeling like flesh given in sacrifice to the almighty college man's ego. I went out with a variety of boys, but very few were interested in me as a person. Time spent with them made me unspeakably lonely. Even the low-key fraternity parties of the late fifties were disturbing to me. Everyone else was having fun. I didn't know why I wasn't.

In September 1958, at the beginning of my sophomore year, I met Sue Ann Ritter, who would end my confusion and my loneliness. I had been waiting for her all of my life. She came to my sorority's rush party, and I was attracted to her from the beginning. Her collar length, dark blonde hair had golden highlights from the summer sun. There was a quiet reserve about her, yet energy generated even in repose. Above all, her blue eyes hinted a sweet vulnerability. I forgot about introducing myself to the new prospects. I talked with Suzie most of the afternoon.

I would learn later that Suzie had been popular in high school and was an honor role student, an athlete, and a member of many clubs and organizations. She dated and had friends, but the one she loved was Julie. Their young love blossomed as only high school-age passion can, full of emotion and wild dreams. They met discreetly, keeping their "perverted" love a secret. After Suzie's mother found a note revealing her daughter's passion for a girl, the young lovers' world came crashing down. Suzie's and Julie's parents agreed that the girls were never to see one another again. Suzie's mother sent her to a psychiatrist to find out what caused her abnormal behavior. Suzie endured the pain of separation, the anger of her parents, and the stupidity of a psychiatrist who intended to cure her of *love*. She sat, stared at him, and said nothing, her stolid, self-assurance already intact. In her loneliness, she withdrew to her room and to her precious music — Brahms, Franck, Beethoven. She held on to her sense of self and confided in her best friend, Carla, who was also struggling with the awakening of her own sexual orientation.

So it was that Suzie came that day to the rush party filled with the pain of loss, expectations of a student's life, the hope of a brighter future, and wounded and aching for the softness of a woman's touch.

When she was accepted into the sorority, circumstances brought us together on a regular basis. I was assigned as her "big sister," the person who would help orient her to the sorority and to college life. I met her parents and was welcomed into their home as a wholesome influence, which, of course, I was. I was the seasoned sophomore smoothing the way for my little sister. We saw each other frequently in gatherings with our other sisters, playing intramurals, and studying together. I began to feel my pulse rate soar when I saw her. She made me feel so full of joy. We began to spend more time together, going to the local drive-in for Cokes in her father's '55 Chevy or sitting in the campus club talking, lingering longer and longer.

One of the activities for the new pledges and their big sisters was a slumber party at the home of one of our members. Our hostess, Nancy, lived in a three-story restored Victorian home with her parents. The house had six bedrooms. We played cards, made pizza, ate snacks, and drank Cokes and Nehi sodas. We talked about our lives, hopes, interests, professors, and frat boys. After the night was nearly gone, the girls drifted toward the bedrooms and sofas. Nancy directed Suzie and me to a room on the second floor. Suzie closed the door. I hugged her and got into what I thought was my side of the bed. I hadn't been asleep long when my eyes opened again with a start. Suzie's body, close to mine, was so deliciously warm and exciting. I must have been talking in my sleep, the faint memory of a disturbing dream evaporated. I was in her arms. I nearly melted from the sweetness of it. I breathed in the fragrant smell of the summer sun from her skin and felt that this was strangely wonderful and wild, brand new, but as old as my subconscious yearnings. I put my arms around her and held her close. We went to sleep entwined.

As time went by, I gathered bits and pieces of her childhood. Her father had taken her hunting and fishing, but they had established no strong emotional bond. He was limited in his ability to understand her need for respect. He was quicker to use a strap than reason, trying to dominate a child who had an indomitable spirit. They clashed. He felt college was a waste for a girl, but her mother disagreed and prevailed. Her mother loved music, literature, and theater, but was restricted by a rigid set of values and was unable to communicate warmth. Suzie grew up with little tenderness and learned to use silence for protection.

In my naiveté I could only think that my surging emotions were expressions of "sisterly love." My arms ached to enfold her, to draw her to me and let her know the comfort of my embrace. So it was with my most motherly, big sisterly intentions that I took her in my arms and stroked her hair. It was I who first said, "I love you. I will always be here." Slowly, I began to realize that I was needed in a quiet, desperate way, not flesh to be fondled or lips to be parted. I thought of her as a golden child, my treasure, so intelligent and sensitive, one who saw in me strength I never knew I had. In my young mind I was suddenly Woman, Nurturer, Giver of Life. I suppose many straight people consider a lesbian to be a pale imitation of a male. It wasn't until I loved a woman that I became free to express the deepest part of a woman's emotions.

We saw each other as much as possible that fall and winter. Suzie was always wary of her mother's watchful eye and quick reproof. "Time to be home" was a burden. I loved the drives we took in the country holding hands. Sometimes she would stop and show me one of her childhood haunts. So much of her was connected with nature.

All winter long, I felt an urgency to be with her all of the time. With no words to voice my feelings, I felt a building pressure that had no safety valve. Suzie could see that I didn't fully comprehend what was happening between us. She wondered about the nature of my love, my capacity to love a woman in spirit, mind, and body. She hesitated, not wanting to trespass into forbidden territory. She wanted and hoped for complete love, but kept her passion hidden. I was consumed with thoughts of her. After holding hands in the car during our drives in the country, I went to bed at night with the fragrance of her lotion on my hands, taking the sweet scent of her into my dreams.

Spring arrived, green with promise. The earth warmed in the sun. Small wildflowers appeared through last year's autumn leaves and the unfolding buds dappled the ground with their shadows. Suzie took me to her favorite woods, another place where, in her childhood, she had spent many hours enjoying solitude. We spread a blanket on the ground and lay in the sun. Bird songs filtered through new leaves. The scent of the fertile earth hung in the air. Hours passed, but our small world stood still.

Suzie summoned her courage. She rested herself on her elbows, held me with her blue eyes and said, "Kiss me."

"Kiss me?" What an incredible idea! My family didn't give friendly greetings on the lips. I'd never thought of it. "Kiss me?" I was frozen, not from fear or repulsion but mainly because it was an idea that hadn't occurred to me. I didn't know what to do with it, so I said something really stupid like, "I don't want to have that kind of relationship with you." She quietly looked at me. Her full lips were slightly pressed together in a wistful smile. The buzz of insects punctuated the silence. Shortly after that, she drove me home. All the way home, I caught her lips out of the corner of my eye and wondered.

I don't know how I made it through my sophomore year. There was so much churning emotion. I did eventually kiss Suzie, and her mouth left a soft impression on my lips that lasted for hours. It made me weak. Our hand holding and kissing progressed to caressing arms, backs, and breasts. At this point even an inexperienced young woman from a protected childhood was getting the idea that something was really different about our friendship. I was suspended in that once-in-a-lifetime glow, before the awakening of sexual desire and all of its accompanying joys and complications. Our caressing was an expression of our love and as uncorrupt as Eve before she bit into that apple. We longed to be in each other's arms, taking every opportunity possible to be together. I didn't know there was more than that until our first summer together, ten months after I met her.

My summer job was counseling at a camp where Suzie got a job as lifeguard. The main lodge had two wings, one for boys eight to fourteen, the other for girls eight to eleven. In the center were the dayroom, dining hall, and kitchen. I was in charge of the older girls, twelve to fourteen, who stayed in a cottage two hundred yards away. Attached to the cottage were a craft room and a small bedroom for two counselors. It held a pleasant smell from old timbers baked for years in the sun. At last, we had a place to ourselves and some privacy. Our bedroom had two small single beds, an end table, and a dresser, with room for little else. We didn't care. We snuggled in the sagging mattress and wove our legs together. When our toes touched, the top of Suzie's head fit under my chin. We didn't get much sleep that summer. We would talk, sometimes just nonsense. Suzie said, "I love your hazel eyes. They change color with the light."

I said, "I love your eyes. I've never seen any so blue."

She teased, "I love those freckles that show up on your nose in the summer."

I answered, "I love your nose." We would laugh at that. Suzie's nose was wide at the bridge and slightly curved, a substantial but not unattractive connection between perfectly shaped lips and expressive eyes with long lashes.

We could embrace and caress all night. We grew accustomed to going to sleep in one another's arms. One night she began to kiss me differently, intensely, leading me toward an awakening need. I felt the tingle of her warm breath in my ear as she whispered, "I love you." Then her lips were on the hollow of my neck, then down, and then, "I love you, Leila."

"Yes," and I was lost but found.

After that summer, my life turned from black and white to Technicolor. There was brilliance in life I had never known before. All of the old clichés about falling in love applied. So young, eighteen and nineteen, and longing to be together always. It would take three years before she would graduate from college. Until then we spent every moment we could together. A lot of that time was spent in that '55 Chevy. Like most cars in 1955, the Chevy Bel Air hardtop she was driving had bench seats. That meant on remote roads, we could sit close with no gap between. With its sky blue body and white top, chrome bumpers and white wall tires, it was a sporty car. The gearshift was in the steering wheel. I operated the gearshift so we could put our free arms around each other while she drove.

One night after we had gone to a popular drive-in in Indianapolis called the TeePee, we parked in the alley behind my parents' garage. My mother would flash the porch light if we lingered in the front of the house. The alley was dark and we didn't think anyone would see the car. Suzie was sitting in the driver's seat, and I snuggled into her arms with my back to the wheel. I pressed as close to her as I could. Johnny Mathis was crooning "Misty" through the radio and we were content to drift with the music. We tried to stay alert to neighbors who might see the strange car and come to investigate, or worse, call the police. Our lovemaking usually started with warm hugs and gentle touches until we crossed that imperceptible line between pleasure and overwhelming desire. On this night we came to the brink of a panting, heart throbbing release when the crunch of a foot stepping in the gravel beside the alley froze everything. I stopped breathing, and then dropped to the floor beneath Suzie's feet, my legs sprawled on the floor of the passenger's side. I heard a man's muffled voice above me and Suzie's steady reply, "I'm just waiting for a friend to come out of the house next door." I don't know how she managed such composure. When I heard his receding footsteps growing fainter, I eased my cramped body onto the seat, head below the window. We moved with as much dignity as possible out of the alley, weak from frustration and fear. Later, high from the near exposure we laughed until we cried.

Our love was not sanctioned by society, nor approved of by parents. Discovery would have meant serious consequences for us. Suzie's mother would have cut off her funds for school. Although Suzie had a part time job to help with expenses, she couldn't make enough and stay in school full-time. I didn't want my parents to know. I felt sure they would still love me, but I did not want them to carry the burden of having a queer daughter. That was the last time we parked in the alley behind my parents' garage.

We were always watchful, always cognizant of the lowly place assigned to us by society. Suzie would make a joke of it and say, "Lesbians are one step lower than prostitutes on the social ladder." I didn't even know what a homosexual was until, to my great astonishment, I found out that I was one! I looked it up in the dictionary and when I took a sociology course was astounded to find the type of behavior that was expected of me and "my kind." I never saw any masculine women eyeing me in restrooms. I thought that Suzie and I were the only ones in the whole city, maybe the whole United States!

My love for Suzie shone through all of that ignorance and derision, and I knew our love was a beautiful sanctified gift. Because Suzie helped me realize who I was, I could finally have fulfillment with another human being. Without her, I would have married, because that was the course of a woman's life in the '50s and '60s. Before I met Suzie, I was dating a man whom I respected and probably would have married. Meeting

Suzie saved me from living that extended period of emptiness so many lesbians have suffered during marriage, not understanding why they felt there should be more. Suzie also saved my friend, Carl, from being with a wife who could not be fully engaged in a marriage. Suzie was the person of my dreams. We were ready to accept all the risks involved, to accept a life of secrecy and deception, if necessary, to obtain the dream of living together, forever.

I was undaunted when during our second summer at camp, Suzie gave me some troublesome news. While the campers were having afternoon rest period with another counselor, Suzie took me to the old barn in the clearing. In the confines of the ancient building, we were surrounded by hand hewn beams and light that streamed through damaged shingles. Crickets chirped from the shadowed corners. It would have been enchanting except for the expression on Suzie's face. Her eyes held pain, yet looked directly into mine. It seemed as if she couldn't speak at first. Then, "I should have told you this last year, but I didn't know where this would lead. Before we live together you have a right to know that there is a hereditary disease on my mother's side of the family. I have a fifty-fifty chance of getting it. It's called Huntington's chorea. I won't know until I'm about forty-five years old if I have it." She described her grandmother, who lurched and stumbled when she walked and who had trouble thinking and speaking.

"My Aunt Lenore committed suicide. When they began noticing the symptoms, her husband left her."

"I love you, Suzie. I will never leave you. Whatever happens to you will happen to me. If we don't have much time, we will make the most of every minute together."

We were young and eager to devour all of the time that would be given to us, even if that time was short. "You are so beautifully honest, Suzie. I admire you for that. It only makes me love you more." I realized the terrible chance she took in telling me that she might be flawed, my golden girl. We sat down on the warm straw, content in the silence and a comforting embrace. We would be together. That's all that mattered.

In the winter of Suzie's junior year, 1960, her mother became particularly suspicious of our relationship and refused open access to the car. We met on the campus but were mostly with others. One snowy night when the roads were slick and the snow was piling up in the city's yards, I went to bed wishing, again, that she was with me. I awoke from a fitful sleep to tapping on my window. My dream come true was there, standing outside in the snow. Snowflakes rested on her lashes and hair. I opened the window. She climbed in. She slipped into my bed and I wrapped her cold body with my arms and legs and warmed her. I can still feel her cool hands around my waist. It was so precious having her there in the warm cocoon of my bed, cozy and secretive and above all, thrilling with my parents in the next room.

After graduation, I lived at home with my parents while Suzie was finishing her senior year. I taught in an elementary school and began my graduate work. My first purchase with the salary from my new teaching job was a car, but I couldn't go to her house to pick her up. We tried to meet without her parents' knowledge and held on to the thought that our wait would be over in a year.

At the end of the summer after Suzie's graduation, she found a duplex in the city not far from either of our schools. She taught high school English and finally we could begin our time living together. Both of my parents enjoyed Suzie and came to visit us. Suzie's mother was angry at me for encouraging her daughter to move away from home. By living with me, Suzie took the chance of never seeing her family again. Her family's way of dealing with a problem was to walk away. She hoped time would bring them back.

We relished the idea of coming home to one another. I spent free time at work thinking of actually coming home and sitting at a table eating with her, preparing meals together, and sitting in our own living room reading books or listening to music. I looked forward to talking over the day's activities, planning what we would do on the weekends, doing those simple things that are the right of all people in love. The only other gay person we knew was Carla, Suzie's long-time friend from childhood, but she was at William Woods in Missouri.

There were the usual problems and compromises to be made when two people live together, when two independent women clash on the ways things should be done. We even cleaned house differently. I worked in a haphazard, random fashion. She was meticulous and ordered. Of course, *her* way was right, and I agreed since I wasn't much for housework anyway. I tended to leave drawers and cabinets open and clothes draped over furniture. She was particularly miffed when I would leave tools out after I fixed something. I just didn't notice the mess I left behind; it took years to correct that. She swallowed her irritation at my messiness and the chaos I left in drawers and cabinets, only shouting once or twice a week. There were compromises to be made on a number of things. I couldn't stand conflict, so I gave in on a lot of little things and was happy to have her lead and have a dominant role. She took care of me and cherished me and I made a safe sanctuary of love for her. Our nights were warm and exciting.

Six months in the duplex was all Suzie could take before her longing for the country became acute. Getting away from the city on weekends helped, but Suzie needed space, trees, open fields, water. She looked in the paper for a place outside the confines of the city. After we looked at several unsuitable places, she found a log cabin for rent on a twenty-acre estate. It rested on the brink of a cliff overlooking a creek. Large windows in the living room looked out on the creek and woods in the back and an orchard in the front. The cabin had a small bedroom and a kitchen with a brick floor. There was a fireplace in every room.

As soon as we moved in, we felt at home. We had privacy and peace away from the hum of the city. A new puppy and a kitten provided hours of entertainment. We were allowed to have a garden behind the orchard, my first. Suzie introduced me to all of the country things she loved: gardening, fishing, hiking in the woods, and hunting mushrooms. I loved them all as if they had always been a part of me. Our enjoyment was doubled with the sharing of it.

There was a chill in the morning air on the day she introduced me to gardening. We tramped to the site Suzie had chosen for our garden. She showed me how to slice through the roots of the sod and lift it away to expose the bare earth. Then she began turning over the soil and breaking up the dark loamy clods. She held out a piece of earth to me. "Smell this. You'll like it." I broke it in my hands and released the rich sweet aroma of the earth. "I didn't know that dirt could smell so sweet." She wanted to plant spinach. I was against it. "I can't bear the idea of swallowing the stuff."

She laughed. "You'll see. It doesn't taste anything like the slime in the can."

At harvest time, I had the great pleasure of tasting fresh, cooked spinach. I followed Suzie's example and topped it with a pat of butter and a little vinegar. It had texture and firmness. I loved the taste.

I had never thought fishing was very interesting until Suzie and I went to northern Minnesota to visit her godparents, Frank and Mary. Rugged people who loved fishing and camping, they had moved from Indiana fifteen years ago for that purpose. Frank took the four of us to a remote lake up by Bemidji. Swan Lake drained and made a river by the same name. In Swan River I discovered the excitement and thrill of hooking into a six-pound large mouth bass. I could barely hear Suzie shouting instructions as I struggled to reel it in. When the creature rose out of the water and shook its huge head, I stopped reeling. The fish spit the lure out and sent it winging back at me. It struck the side of the boat with a loud crack. I heard a gaggle of laughter behind me, then Suzie's voice choking, "Do you like fishing now?"

When I recovered my voice, all I could say was, "Wow!"

We went back to "Swan" alone in following summers, camping on an island living like natives, bathing in the clear river, lying on the smooth boulders to dry. We slept in a tent among the birch trees, ate fish we caught from a canoe Frank had loaned us, cooked over an open fire, and explored the tributaries of the Swan, watching the wild life along the way. The love of nature had been a part of me all along; I just hadn't had a chance to experience it. Suzie brought me out of the stuffiness of the city to the open fresh air of the country.

I had a gift for her, too: the thrill of the open road. My family had always taken long trips in the summer, and that wanderlust was in my blood. On cold winter nights, we liked to sit by the fire and look at seed catalogues or outfitter catalogues. It was a pleasant way to bring a little summer into the dark nights. "Hey, Suzie, here's an ad about an outfitter that will take people down the Middle Fork of the Salmon River in Idaho. They supply all of the gear and food. It's one of the premier trout streams in the United States. Want to go?"

"I don't know. I like it at Swan."

"I do too, but I'd love for you to see the Rocky Mountains. The open spaces in the West are incomprehensible. There would be so many sights to see along the way. We could load my station wagon with supplies, take the canoe and spend a month camping our way to Idaho. Think about it."

The next day I joined AAA and brought home maps, brochures, and tour books. It took very little explaining to teach Suzie how to use the tour book to find campgrounds and places of interest. We looked at the pictures of high mountain lakes and the Great Plains stretching to the horizon. Suzie didn't need to see more. "Let's go. Idaho or Bust."

In the years of our summer travel, we visited all of the major cities in the United States, but it was the western wilderness that called us back again and again. We camped and hiked in the national forests, rafted wild rivers, trekked up mountains, and made love in all of the states along the way. We thought there was nothing better than being the two of us alone to share those wonders. Two for the road. The trip to Idaho meant the most to us, for on the way there, we went through Montana. That state's open, wild, and pristine beauty left an indelible impression on both of us. We had been thinking about raising horses, and now we fantasized about having a ranch there. Even though we didn't act on it, the Montana dream stayed in our hearts.

Our life at the cabin began to settle into a comfortable routine. Suzie's parents came to visit, sparingly at first. They saw that Suzie and I were good for each other. I believe Suzie's mother even began to like me. She at least chose to close her mind to the nature of our relationship so she could enjoy her daughter once again. We began to play cards together, and eventually I was invited for holidays with their extended family.

Carla had returned to find a nursing job in the city. She and her partner, Jenny, were renting a house with a barn on ten acres. They invited us to keep horses there if we wanted. In their childhood, Carla had shared her horses with Suzie. We all loved horses, and when Suzie and I bought ours, we spent a lot of time at Carla's riding by ourselves and with Carla and Jenny. The dream of a farm of our own began to materialize.

We had a growing circle of gay friends and went to parties and enjoyed having company, but we never went to any of the gay bars in Indianapolis. Teaching in the '60s and '70s meant we could lose our jobs if our sexual orientation was revealed. We were secretive about our private lives. I never spoke to my colleagues at school about the person who was the most important part of my life.

After five years, our lives seemed secure and happy to me. I wasn't aware of a growing shadow of discontent in Suzie. Everything we enjoyed together shrank in significance to her growing doubts about my physical need for her. She needed me to be more aggressive in our lovemaking. She translated my lack of confidence in taking the lead to a lack of desire.

When our roles were reversed, it seemed uncomfortable and out of sync. What had been so fluid and magical became disjointed and awkward. It was my nature to be more passive, and she became impatient and rigid. She wanted me in a more dominant role but couldn't bear to submit. The womanly warmth I needed from her was locked deep inside. The silence which had protected her in her childhood and youth worked against us now and became a barrier between us. Lacking the confidence to break out of my own comfortable pattern of submission, I could feel her slipping away from me. She became convinced that I had no compelling physical need for her. She loved me still and bore the pain, but it began to flare into resentment. Her coldness put me off and kept me from feeling the very thing she needed most.

In the course of the next year, Suzie's relationship with Carla's partner Jenny seemed to get closer. I noticed a light flirtation, a concentration of care. I first saw it when Carla was called into work one weekend. Suzie and I decided to ask Jenny if she wanted to go swimming with us. We liked to go to Highland Lake, a private lake and beach developed from an old gravel pit. It was a lazy summer day. Suzie, Jenny, and I basked on the beach, smelling the hotdogs and mustard, tanning oil and hot sand. The Beach Boys blared from loud speakers at the concession stand. I wasn't a very good swimmer, so my entry into the water was to cool off or float. Jenny decided to swim for the float about one hundred yards out. "I'll race you," she called over her shoulder. Suzie was on her feet and running in an instant. "You're on." With arms flashing and feet churning the water, they arrived at the same time. They stayed there sitting close, feet dangling in the water. An uncomfortable length of time passed. I watched them laughing. They're probably resting, I thought, but something about that scene made me feel like crying.

A few weeks after we went swimming with Jenny, she hurt her shoulder and couldn't drive. Suzie offered to drive her up to visit her parents at their lake in Wisconsin, making it clear that I was to stay at home with the animals. My mind raced to grasp at a logical reason for me to accept this trip as anything but a lover's rendezvous. My worst fears were confirmed when she drove off in her convertible smelling of the cologne I loved.

Suzie confided in Jenny the things she withheld from me, and their friendship grew into an attraction. Weeks later when I realized that they had been seeing each other, I knew something was terribly wrong. The knowledge wrapped around me like an icy fog. I confronted Suzie. She confessed that she loved Jenny. In my own desperation and need I clung to her, which only made matters worse.

Four years after we moved into the cabin together, she left for the summer to housesit for a friend on vacation. She needed to get away. Even though at different times both Suzie and Jenny told me that nothing physical had entered into their relationship, I imagined them embracing or worse. Carla and Jenny came to assure me that they were very much a couple. Jenny felt that Suzie needed her as a friend. Suzie told me, "I will always love you." Her words were like blows to my chest. Nothing made sense to me.

Through the suffocating agony of separation, I knew I had to make some major changes. I searched for what could have gone wrong. I knew I needed to take the lead in many ways. I never wavered in the belief that we were meant to be together. I also knew that Suzie wouldn't be able to reach out. She needed me to come for her.

Love is not only kind and giving; love is power. I tapped into the power of my love, and it gave me the courage to believe that she would be mine, to believe that we belonged together and that nothing was going to keep us apart. At the end of the summer one evening, I called. "I want to see you."

"Do you want to come over tonight?"

She had made the friend's upstairs bedroom into a combination sitting room and bedroom. I followed her up the creaking stairs, smelled the old wallpaper of the one-hundred-year-old farmhouse. The single light in the room on the nightstand cast a warm glow over the bed. I led her to the bed, and pulled her gently down beside me. Time for talking was over. I would let my body tell her how much I wanted her. I kissed the top of her head and smelled the freshness of her hair. I kissed her eyelids and lips. My hands were firm, teasing, demanding. My mouth and hands led her into an ecstasy of intimacy that we would build upon. She would know that her love was the most important thing in my life, and that I wanted her — heart, mind, and body.

Suzie came home after her friend returned from her trip. We both believed that we could work everything out if we honored our love, but changing beliefs and behavior is not easy. Established patterns are hard to break. We needed time to repair the wounds we had caused each other, to reestablish trust. The memory of rejection threatened my confidence and Suzie needed to summon the faith to believe in me. The underlying mantra that kept us going was, "We belong together." We stopped seeing Carla and Jenny for a while and boarded our horses at a farm that was on the way to my school.

Subconsciously, we may have known that we needed a change of place. We had grown, loved, and almost lost in the little cabin. After six years there, it was time for a new start, a place of our own. We put aside money for a down payment on a place in the country with about twenty acres where we could raise purebred Arabian horses and have some space to ourselves. We had enjoyed having our horses at Carla's place, but we wanted the pleasure of seeing them from our own windows, running with tails held high like banners in the wind.

We spent a year driving through the country on weekends, looking at places realtors suggested. We saw many that were totally unsuitable, some that were tempting, but none gave us the special knowledge that, "This is the place." We both thought we would know it when we saw it. I would go to sleep at night wondering how the moonlight looked on "our farm."

Then one day in February, our realtor called and told us about a place that was a little farther out than we wanted, but had more land and a house with a long driveway and a fireplace. We went out to see the fifty-two acre property with a creek running through it. On a cold February day we asked the owner, eighty-year-old Ezra Johnson, if we could walk his place. Snow was on the ground. The ice on the creek was beginning to melt; little rivulets ran through the center and bubbled under the ice. As we walked through the woods along the creek and turned into the pasture, we realized that this would be our paradise.

As we approached the house to thank him, we saw Ezra at the door beckoning us in. We came in the back door through a closed-in porch. The smell of fried bacon clung to the knotty pine long after the morning dishes had been put away. Ezra was slightly stooped but moved quickly through the kitchen into the dining room where he had an easy chair in front of the picture window. He said, "I like to see whose comin' down the road." His eyes smiled from under bushy eyebrows as he talked with enthusiasm about the farm. He gestured with gnarled hands that had worked hard from the time when horses had supplied the power for his farm equipment. He was a delightful host and took to Suzie immediately. Her blue eyes shone with excitement at the prospect of living on this farm.

She asked, "Do you have a garden?"

"Oh yes, there's 'bout a foot er topsoil coverin' the back yard. It's planted mostly in strawberries right now. There's nothin' better then fresh Indiana strawberries with a little sugar and cream."

Suzie said, "We'd like to have tomatoes and lots of vegetables."

Ezra grinned, "You'll have tomatoes as big as pumpkins and radishes as big as yer fists. The rhubarb will be comin' up in June for your dessert."

I said, as if we already had the place, "We'll have you over for rhubarb pie."

Usually calm, Suzie could hardly sit still. "My dad used to raise chickens, and I'd like to have laying hens. We had Rhode Island Reds when I was a kid."

"There's room fer anything you want, but you'll have to build a chicken pen or the weasels or foxes or coyotes will git 'um. A weasel can fit through a knot hole in a fence and they'll kill every one they can git to."

We talked until the sun started for the horizon. Ezra pointed out the window. "Ya see that big tree 'cross the road in the fence row? That's where the sun sets in winter. You'll know it's spring when the sun sets right at the end of the drive way." We got up to leave just as the red sun touched the horizon. Ezra walked us to the porch and we all waved good-bye. Would we see the sun at the end of the driveway when it set in spring?

We were afraid it would be difficult for a couple of women to get a loan for a farm, and, indeed, were turned down by a big city bank. Ezra's realtor suggested a bank in the small town near the farm. That banker said we could have the loan if we could come up with one-third down. The $4,000 we had saved for a down payment suddenly looked impossibly small, even though in 1970 it would have been enough for a city house. We pooled our resources and were still $3,000 short. Ezra came to our rescue with a second mortgage.

One day after the closing, we brought some lawn furniture out and placed it in the backyard. Ezra was there, waiting to go with us to celebrate our communal good fortune. When he saw us unloading the furniture, he said, "Ya won't need that. You'll be so busy out here ya won't have time to sit. That's why living on a farm is hell----thy." He was right on both counts. For the first ten years, we rarely sat in those chairs, and living on the farm *is* healthy.

We adopted Ezra and he us. He used to say, "Someone has to take care of the widders and orphans.'" We were neither, but became known around the area as "the girls." In time, everyone in the vicinity knew where "the girls'" farm was. If anyone had any reservations about us living together, it was never spoken. We were accepted because we worked hard and loved the land. Ezra became a wonderful friend. Between him and Henry Dodson, who farmed our land, we learned all of the things we needed to know in order to survive in the country.

Our first project was the barn. With Henry's help we put in a hayloft and tack room. With many a bent nail and smashed thumb, we learned to build. Henry enjoyed showing off his skill and laughed at our ineptness. We were introduced to a new kind of humor, the gentle joshing between friends that implies, "Even if you're a little rough around the edges or wet behind the ears, you'll do." He introduced us to the local restaurant, a place where farmers gathered for "dinner," which was "lunch" when we were city folks. Here the food was flavored as much with friendly banter as salt and pepper. Henry helped us build fences and feed bins and Ezra helped us put in an automatic heated waterer. Later, Suzie and I closed in the three-sided pole barn and built six stalls with the help of friends. Henry sold us his old 1950 Allis Chalmers tractor and a sickle bar mower so we could cut our own hay. We never heard from either Henry or Ezra that we couldn't do a thing because we were women. They enjoyed our enthusiasm for farm life and our willingness to try everything.

With a little help from me, Suzie and Ezra built a 60 x 16-foot addition onto the barn with materials we got from tearing down a 100-year-old barn on a neighbor's farm. When I left for school one morning, they were beginning to nail slats to the rafters that would later support the metal roof. I was to cook chili for them for supper. When I got home, they were gone. I thought maybe they had gone for more materials, so I prepared the chili, set the table and waited and waited. I went out to the barn to see the progress of the day's work. Uncharacteristically, the tools were scattered on the ground. Something was wrong, but I could only go back to the house and wait. An hour later they arrived. Suzie came in smiling. "Sorry we're late for supper."

I was about to say, "Where have you been?" when I looked at her leg. One leg of her jeans was slashed at the thigh and a blood stained bandage showed beneath it. Suzie, who fainted at the sight of blood, had driven herself and Ezra to the hospital after she had cut her thigh with the electric saw blade. The safety guard did not retract as she drew the saw across her thigh to set it down. It took seventeen stitches to close the inch-deep gash. "It didn't bleed much and I wanted to drive. I didn't think Ezra would go fast enough." Her seven-inch scar was a topic of conversation for years.

As our skills grew with practice and Ezra's and Henry's tutoring, we decided we could build a room and a patio. With Ezra's help and that of my nephew who had just started working as a house framer, we built a 24 x 14-foot master bedroom onto the end of the house, complete with patio doors and windows on three sides. The east windows looked out on the pasture and woods beyond. Later, Suzie and Ezra added a brick patio. We hauled the bricks in Carla's pickup from the demolition site of an ancient building in town. They were paving bricks, each one weighing nine pounds. We must have loaded and unloaded ten times. I lost count after my body went numb. Our hands were blistered and we were covered with mortar dust. I was young, a mere thirty-five, but I couldn't stand up without great effort. Suzie and Ezra finished the job together in the weeks to come.

I was usually the one with the creative ideas, and Suzie, the meticulous planner, saw that the job was done right. We were a perfect team if she could remember to have faith in my ideas and I could remember to be patient while she thought through the plan. I could visualize a thing completed but didn't want to take the time to work out the details for getting the job done perfectly. Her motto was, "If you can't do it right, don't do it at all." I learned never to say, "You can't do that." to Suzie. Her only reply would be, "Get out of my way," and the car *would* be pulled out of the snowdrift, the impossibly heavy object *would* be lifted, or the hay *would* be cut in spite of the oncoming lightning threatening to blow her off the tractor! Her determination was legendary.

It was Ezra who suggested we put in a pond by damming up a ravine that had a flow of water running through it: "A feller could put a pond in here," he said. I took up the challenge and had the soil tested and began to look into getting government help to build it. Suzie was skeptical of the plan but kept quiet while Ezra and I proceeded. The soil conservation service paid for one-half the excavation and soon the huge hole began to fill with water. It grew to a two-acre lake. Suzie loved the water. She had spent her teenage years swimming and diving off the high dive at a pool near her home. She was a graceful, strong swimmer, at home in the water, and I was thrilled that my perseverance paid off in this gift for her. We not only swam; we got a canoe and spent many days casting our lures for bass. We often walked back to the house in the moonlight, because when I suggested we go back to the house, Suzie usually said, "I just want to hit that point off the dam one more time."

We wanted to try everything. We had a large fertile garden and invested in eight Holstein heifers in order to make enough money to buy our first Arabian broodmares. The cows were a whole education in themselves. We had no idea what cows were like. We chose young female Holsteins, because the local banker said they were a good investment. You feed them through the fall and winter, breed them to a bull in the spring, and sell them at the local sale barn. We liked the idea of having dairy cattle because we didn't want them to be killed. We thought cows just lethargically browsed in green pastures, gazing placidly up from time to time. We didn't realize that they could jump our sagging fences at a single bound and dodge pursuers at right angles or scale a five-foot creek bank.

The farmer who adjoined our property on the north called one spring evening. "There are some Holstein heifers in my barn lot," he said. "Could they be yours?"

I replied hopefully, "I don't think so." Further exploration revealed a mashed down place in the fence where they had jumped. We tracked them along the creek, under the water gate to his barn lot. I had seen plenty of movies with a country setting where the drovers just walked behind the cows with long sticks and so imagined a pleasant walk home by the creek through a sun-dappled woods. I expected our cows to walk back in a quiet line. Everything was idyllic until our neighbor opened the gate and we attempted to drive the cows home. By now the shadows were lengthening and the day cooling. We got about one hundred yards away from the neighbor's barn when our nice little line began to waver and break apart. One or two cows would decide to double back and we would have to run to the side to drive them into line again. The farther we got from the bull, the more obstinate the heifers became. That quiet spring evening became a test for me, a test of my strength and skill against the desires of our simple bovines. I armed myself with a long branch from a tree and used it to extend my reach, but I couldn't have *lifted* a stick that would have been long enough to divert those cows from their intended goal. Nothing seemed to work. Two hours of driving and dodging failed to get them home. Suzie was having no better luck than I. At one time I thought I had Bossy cornered between a fence and the high creek bank. "Now I've got you!" I saw disdain in her eye before she stuck her wet tongue into a nostril in an obscene gesture. She easily slipped down the embankment and trotted back to her bull. This was nearly the last straw for me. I felt totally humiliated and exhausted. I must confess I beat the nearest tree with my drover's stick, expending all of the strength I had left. Then I sat down on the flower-covered ground and cried. By the time Suzie and I caught up to the cows at the neighbor's barn, the heifers were wagging their tails contentedly, looking in adoration at that Angus bull. Our neighbor had to bring them home in his stock truck.

In time we learned how to mend fences and how to catch the cows to restrain them for medication. We had heated arguments over how much to feed them. Suzie fed them like beef cattle fattening for market. I saw our profits going through four stomachs. I could never get her to see it my way. She simply *liked* to feed them and see them glossy and fat — fatter than a milk cow should be.

We learned so much in those first years. We put our hearts and souls into the building of the place and we grew in strength, knowledge, and love. At last, we had enough for our investment in those Arabian broodmares. I will never forget the day that the two elegant grey mares walked sedately down the ramp of the trailer into our lives. When their delicate hooves touched the ground, another grand adventure began. It had been a goal of ours to raise the horses that dreams are made of, the legendary desert horse with bloodlines treasured for centuries. Many of the modern pedigrees went back to the original desert breeds. We felt it was our privilege to take care of such royal creatures, and we were determined to have the most beautiful, athletic horses in the United States. We pored over pedigrees, studied the offspring in horse shows, and spent ten glorious years raising foals, training young horses, and selling them to people we hoped would love them. The work was rigorous and demanding. The horses needed to be fed twice a day and their stalls needed cleaning every day. With fences to build and maintenance on everything, our vacations and social lives diminished. Some of our friends couldn't understand our obsession with horses. It really became a compulsion, neither of us rational enough to see it. More and more of our time and money were spent in search of the dream of the perfect Arabian. We hoped that we would be able to make enough money with the horses to retire from teaching and have the farm as a full-time business. It took us many years to realize that it wouldn't work out that way. In the meantime, it was a labor of love.

We were enchanted with the newborn foals every spring. We loved touching them and taming them, training them to the halter and lead, watching them run on stilted legs around and around in the pasture, kicking up their heels with the sheer joy of being little horses. It was pure delight watching them grow into strong sinewy yearlings, powerful, free as the wind. They blessed us with their beauty and we collected them like expensive paintings, cherishing everyone.

While we were building barns and fences, patios and rooms, and raising cows and horses, the love that we had rekindled grew and took on new dimensions. We had made the mistake in the beginning of falling into the pattern of dominant and submissive. One was afraid to yield, the other did not know how to take control, but slowly, slowly through love and commitment, through work and patience, the communion came. Our dance began to follow the rhythms of our hearts with tenderness and harmony, equal yielding and taking, urging and submitting.

We had purposeful work and beautiful, ever changing surroundings. We had come to that good, secure time in our lives when trust and respect were as natural as breathing, but we were often too tired at bedtime to make love. We kissed, curled up and went to sleep. No amount of work could sublimate the sexual tension that built up when days stretched into weeks. We were bitchy and I knew why. By this time I was much more aggressive and said, "Suzie, we take the time and energy to prepare and eat three meals a day. We have to make time at least once a week to make love."

"That sounds like a good idea. I've been missing you."

We made every Friday "our day." After work we fed the animals and had a simple meal so we could relax and get ready to go to bed early... really early. Sometimes Patsy Cline or Anne Murray would accompany us, but before the vinyl serenade was over we had usually lost awareness of the music, absorbed in our body's contours and hollows that we knew by heart.

We loved what the farm looked like in the moonlight and how it looked in the summer evenings when the fireflies rose out of the wheat fields, hypnotic lights floating through the dusk. We learned what spring smelled like. The perfume of freshly-turned soil filled our nostrils and in the summer it was the fresh cut hay, intoxicating in its earthy sweetness. We were awed by summer storms building on the horizon, darkening the land and rushing toward us with lightning cutting through the clouds. We learned the power of wind and rain, wind and snow, snow piling up in the driveway and covering fences, blotting out the view of the barn, causing hardship for the animals and for those who took care of them. We learned about backbreaking work, the joy of newborn foals, and the tragedy of losses that taught patience. We gained the wisdom of those wonderful farmers who had borne it all for generations and said of the hardest troubles, "That's part of it." We finally understood that we belonged to our place and that we, too, were part of it.

Some tragedies come suddenly, others with imperceptible progression. In 1979, after nine splendid years on the farm, Suzie had to give up teaching. The constant bombardment of the interaction with students grated on her nerves. She, who used to be the sponsor of the gifted students in academic competition, was having difficulty with lesson plans. Her evaluations were critical of her growing lack of sensitivity toward her students. I told her she didn't need to teach any more. "Suzie, we can get by on my salary until you get into the real estate business. I know you've been interested in that for years. You don't have to teach. We'll get by."

Suzie loved to walk the land, to look at farms and houses. She studied and worked hard to pass the broker's exam, an all-day test. She didn't pass the first time, missing by three points. It was a surprise to me that she didn't pass. In her undergraduate and master's work, she was an honor student. Her failure to pass was a sign of things to come, but it didn't fully register until later. She studied and reviewed again and when the test came up in three months, she passed. She became a real estate broker, meaning she could have her own business, but she went in with a local broker at first, to gain experience. She worked hard. It was a difficult time. Interest rates were high, crop prices were low, and farmers were not buying land. The gas crisis was on and people were not moving to the country. We cut back drastically on the things we did for ourselves. We stopped going out to eat, cut out magazines and newspapers, only bought bargains, and were careful about the groceries. I remember one exciting time when she sold a 100-acre farm and we had an $8,000 commission to celebrate. We still had each other and knew that was the most important thing, but we also had the expense of fourteen horses. We had some very lean times, but Suzie did the best she could and we got along.

I knew when Suzie quit teaching that something was wrong. I thought it might be the beginning of the disease she had told me about so long ago. I had seen the progression of the disease in her mother and knew what a terrible thing it would be. Neither of us mentioned it. She worked hard to make a success of the real estate business, and she did sell several farms around us. Her contribution helped keep us going. We knew we needed to sell horses now and worked harder at doing that. As I transitioned to the principle breadwinner of our household, Suzie took on the responsibility of running the farm. I had a bonus in that. I used to tease the teachers that I was the only woman who had dinner waiting for her when she got home. By the time we were in our forties, we had gotten tired of hiding. When I drove out of the driveway to go to work, she'd be at the window waving good-bye. She was there to welcome me home with dinner ready, laundry done, horse chores complete.

That winter our well pump stopped working because the well had filled with sand. We didn't have the money to fix it. Every morning Suzie would go to the neighbor's and fill containers with water so we would have enough to flush the toilets and wash. Most of our horses could drink out of the creek. We were coping with that burden when the weather changed. A heavy snow was predicted for the next two days and we knew we would be snowed in. We frantically worked out a plan. I bought extra containers on my way home from school for our drinking and cooking water. At the grocery I bought a week's worth of TV dinners so we wouldn't need to wash dishes. The snow was falling rapidly by the time I got home. We went to a neighboring farmer, who gave us five ten-gallon containers, the kind used by dairy farmers in the old days to send their milk to the market. We filled those ten-gallon jugs and put them in the kitchen. For three days we used that water to flush toilets and to water those horses that were pastured away from the creek. It was a hard time, but as always, we took courage from each other. We made it through four days of being snowbound. After it was over, I relented and borrowed money from my mother to have the well dug deeper and have a new pump installed. Our life went on.

The summer of 1981 marked a turning point in our lives. I had written an advertisement for one of the horses. As was our custom, Suzie would proofread it and add suggestions. While she was doing that, I went out to the barn to feed the horses. When I returned, I saw a rare thing. Suzie was crying. She showed me the paper. "I can't write. I can't hold the pen still." We knew. We had to face it then. It was beginning. I knelt down beside her at the table and held her in my arms. "My precious love, I will take care of you. We'll be all right. I will take care of you." We went to the bedroom and lay down. We held each other tightly and cried together. "Suzie, I will never leave you."

I had some idea of what to expect of this Huntington's disease. In a ten-year span of time, I had seen her mother lose control of her coordination, her speech, and her bowels. I saw her waste away in a hospital bed and finally die of pneumonia. I had no idea, however, of the mental and emotional turmoil the disease would cause. I had no warning that it would take away her sweetness and trust in me. I had no idea what terrible anger could be unleashed from her damaged brain, what fierce violence would boil over.

It began with verbal assaults and vicious accusations. She locked me out of the house, hurled things through the windows, and broke furniture. The part of her brain that could control the flaring of anger was being destroyed, and although I knew that this was the cause of her abusive outbursts, it still hurt me. I was pelted with hateful words day after day, month after month. I became so frustrated and angry that I wanted to lash out at her, scream at her that I could have her locked up, away from me.

I was cutting Suzie's hair one day as I had done for the previous ten years. Because the disease was destroying her motor skills, her body was always in motion now. It made cutting her hair a challenging task.

Her head would twist and jerk, and her arms would fly up periodically. I nicked her ear, unleashing a tirade. "You stupid son of a bitch. You irresponsible bastard. I hate you. I'll kill you." She punched me. I left the room shaking with pent-up rage and resentment, thinking she deserved to suffer in Hell for treating me this way. I cried out to God, "What would You do with a terrible monster like this?"

The answer came quietly into my mind, "I would hold her in my loving arms."

I was overcome with the realization that a power beyond my comprehension was with me, a part of me. I focused on Suzie's anguish. She was the ravaged one, not I. I was all she had to stand between her and death in a nursing home. That message stayed with me through the next ten years of our lives together.

Still, I had to be on guard, as I was in danger much of the time. I couldn't go out to the barn to feed the horses or clean the stalls without her coming after me in a fury for leaving her. She attacked me with a pitchfork and knives, a fireplace poker. She'd lock me out of the house or throw things through the windows, break up furniture, and drive away our friends. She wanted to die, because she knew what it would be like for her beautiful body to deteriorate, for her superior mind to become confused. She saw her fate in her grandmother and mother, and she rebelled against it with fury. I couldn't leave her. I wouldn't leave her. I loved her beyond all measure but did not know how to reach her or even how to survive living in that house with her. I realized her reason for trying to drive me away was she thought I would leave her. She took control and decided to kick me out first. I had to make her understand that her physical prowess and mental ability were not the main reasons I loved her. I loved her because she was decent, good, honest, and real. She was the most complete person I had ever known. Suzie could not see me as a person capable of dealing with the pain and work. She, who sought perfection in all things, would be a helpless, lurching cripple and, in her mind, inadequately cared for by a person who couldn't know what to do.

After two years of struggling with the rages and depression, Suzie realized that she desperately needed help and agreed to see a neurologist only because the doctor was a lesbian recommended by a friend. She had refused to go at first, because her mother's doctor, a family physician, had recommended that her mother be put in the state mental hospital. I found out later that, in fact, many Huntington's patients were confined to mental hospitals. Without the advances in medication we have today, it was nearly impossible to keep them at home. To her father's great credit, he cared for Suzie's mother at home for ten years. In our case, having a lesbian doctor was a blessing. She prescribed several medications that helped to regulate Suzie's temper and moods. They did not stop the steady decline of her motor skills, but for the first time in years, she became more of the person I'd known before the illness struck.

We had a reprieve when a relative peace descended on our household. She regained her buoyant sense of humor and avid interest in sports. She loved to watch her favorite teams on television and could recite endless information about the players, coaches, and history of the teams' losses and wins. When her favorite horse needed to be rushed to the local veterinary school's emergency room for an operation on a twisted bowel, it was Suzie who rode in the trailer with her, keeping the mare on her feet for the whole forty miles. She had trouble balancing her own body but she insisted that the horse knew her best and would respond better to her. I don't know how she stood up in the swaying trailer herself, but she did. It must have been a tremendous strain on her. Suzie was like that, giving her all for those she loved.

Nothing could stop the slow deterioration of her brain, and through the course of the next ten years we struggled to maintain what was left of "us." I built a large gazebo out at the pond where she could sit and look at the wildlife. When she couldn't walk over the farm anymore, I bought a golf cart to take her to all of our special places. When she couldn't chew her food, I pureed everything and fed her, and when she couldn't swallow pureed food I made liquid drinks from fruit and vegetables combined with protein supplements. She couldn't bear to have anyone see her in her diminished state. Only a few long-time friends were allowed to visit. I was isolated from the support that would have been so comforting in those years filled with distress and anguish. The stress was suffocating, oppressive, and I felt that I had reached the limit many times, but through prayer, my strength returned. We went on.

As the years passed, I began to lose track of my own identity. The only thing that was clear was my purpose in life. "We belong together. She will never leave our home." Our love drove the monster disease into the dark corners of the house and we lived life to the fullest in spite of it. I found a home health care service which sent an aide to care for Suzie in the daytime. If it hadn't been for the money Suzie received from her disability check, we would have lost the farm.

Seven summers passed in which I was the principle caregiver for Suzie. Gone were the roadtrips we had shared. I'm sure she missed them too, but she never complained. She wouldn't even visit friends, let alone travel across the country. I really needed to have some time away from caregiving. After seeing an ad for Montana land in a horseman's magazine, I told Suzie that I wanted to get away for a while. I wanted to fly to Montana and look at the property advertised, twenty acres at $1,000 an acre. It sounded exciting. I said it would only be for a weekend and that Carla had agreed to stay with her. To my complete astonishment, she said almost clearly, "I want to go."

That began the planning for the "original" incredible journey. I found that the cost of renting a big RV was prohibitive, so I converted my Toyota van into a camper. It had a bed for her to rest on and a Porta-Potty so she didn't have to use the public rest rooms. I planned the trip meticulously. Every motel was reserved. A blender and an electric skillet were essential, for all of her food had to be pureed and cooked in the motel. It was a monumental task, but we forgot the risks involved, took the challenge, and started out one bright June morning high on the realization that the two of us were on the road again. I drove between ten and twelve hours a day, cooked, fed Suzie, and dressed and bathed both of us, and I still had energy enough to enjoy the scenery and the wonder of what we were doing. She rarely used the bed in the back of the van. She stayed in front, smiling and laughing and dozing. Going to the bathroom was a major event because she had to get out of the van, and then step into the back to sit on the Porta-Potty. When she said, "Stop," I stopped, no matter how busy the highway, because her bathroom needs were immediate! We laughed about mooning a few people along the way.

We stayed in a two-bedroom cabin in Ennis, Montana, near the Madison River, and I drove us up into the mountains and put out a chair for Suzie to sit on while I walked around exploring, always keeping her in sight. She loved the mountains, too. They energized us. We picnicked in the mountains and by the river. I learned a valuable thing from sitting in one place with Suzie. I learned to meditate and absorb the beauty and silence of nature. The lesson has enriched my life. Now I can sit for hours on a mountainside watching the play of light from sun and clouds change the colors like a kaleidoscope. I see and hear the things most people miss in their hurry to move to another place. Thank you, my love, for teaching me to sit still.

We found that the land which was advertised in the horseman's magazine was unsuitable, so I checked out the local realtor and we went to see other properties. The parcels in the mountains were too expensive and too much like housing developments, even though they came with twenty acres. We wanted a wilderness experience, not a community of people in big homes with satellite dishes in their front yards. The land around Ennis was too arid for us, mostly juniper trees and sagebrush, so that first year we didn't find anything we liked. Our trip was so successful, though, that we decided to come back and explore farther north. I left my name with two other realtors, hoping they would find something for us.

Thinking about Montana was a way to restore our sanity in the hard times, the time of Suzie's increased difficulty in walking, her inability to eat even pureed food, and her almost total loss of speech. We coped with these terrible things and dreamed about being in the mountains again and fantasized about "our Montana land." I thought that I could pull a small recreational trailer to our land and we could spend our summers there. I never imagined what gift was awaiting us.

One cold January day, a catalogue arrived from Century 21 Realty in Livingston, Montana. An ad from the Recreational Properties' section was intriguing: "Cabin on Cottonwood Creek in the foothills of the Crazy Mountains." I wasn't looking for a cabin, but I had a compelling feeling that this would be worth looking into. We decided to start for Montana early in June to get a look at this property before others had a chance. We met Cheryl Bratvold, the Realtor and a kind and interesting person who became a good friend. We followed her car in the van, explaining that we might have to stop suddenly for a potty break. The trip along the highway was disappointing at first. It started in an arid, treeless valley.

"Suzie," I said. "I hope this isn't going to be another 'Mountain Views' place."

"Ya."

Soon after we turned onto a gravel road, the mountains grew closer. The foliage changed from sagebrush to verdant grass and then scattered

Douglas firs appeared. The blue snow-covered mountains began to grow and take form. We got closer and closer and I could not speak because it was so beautiful. We wound down and around the last hill and saw a small cabin nestled among the tall fir trees. The ground was covered with wildflowers; a small stream gurgled somewhere behind the cabin. We had stepped into a picture postcard. The delicate scent of flowers filled the air. The grass was bowing in the wind and above it all were the granite peaks of the Crazy Mountains covered with snow. To our great surprise and delight, the cabin had a ramp instead of steps. "That ramp is meant for you, Suzie." We wanted this place. Thirty-six thousand was much more than I had expected to spend, but then I didn't expect to buy a cabin in Paradise, either. I tried to conceal the excitement I felt, but it was futile. How do you hide sparks shooting out of your eyes? To Cheryl I said truthfully, "We really want this cabin, but I don't know if I can afford it."

"Take time to think about it and you can make any offer you want tomorrow."

We went back to our motel to think. I had saved money for my retirement, but I knew that this was the buy of a lifetime. We needed it now. Our time together was growing short and here was an opportunity to have a furnished cabin now instead of waiting for an uncertain property in the future. The owner lived in Maryland, so negotiations would take a while. That night after I got Suzie into bed and crawled in beside her, she managed to say, "Iee ope we geh tha cab en." It was time to take a risk. The next day, we met with Cheryl and I offered $30,000 with a $15,000 down payment and $5,000 each year for the next three years.

It wasn't until after we returned home and school had started that we received word that my offer had been accepted. Twenty-eight years after we first fell in love with Montana, we were able to buy a cabin in the mountains there. It would be ten months before we could return and spend our first summer in the cabin, a period that would turn out to be Suzie's and my greatest challenge yet.

I found a lump in Suzie's breast while I was bathing her one evening in February. The mammogram showed a fatty tumor, but the surgeon wanted to remove it for a biopsy. The lab found a minute bit of cancer inside the tumor, but all seemed well because it was all removed by a lumpectomy. Hard tissue began to form around the scar in the months that followed, so we went back to the doctor in May. He said it was a very aggressive cancer that had returned and that Suzie needed to have a mastectomy. It's strange how the mind works in times like this. We had been so fixated on the idea of spending part of the summer in the cabin that one of our first concerns was getting to Montana. How could we make the trip with Suzie recuperating from major surgery? But there were much graver concerns to deal with. The prognosis was grim. The surgeon came into the waiting room and said, "The lymph nodes had cancer and were removed. We will know in six months if it metastasizes to the bone." To my great relief, because of her advanced Huntington's disease, none of her doctors recommended chemotherapy or radiation treatment. I didn't want the rest of her life to be spent in hospitals and suffering through the tortures of treatment. We couldn't dwell on the negatives. We had a life to live.

After her lumpectomy, Suzie had arrived in her assigned hospital room smiling and alert. After the mastectomy, she slept all day and was in and out of consciousness that evening. I went home when she went to sleep for the night. For the second time in the long trial with Suzie's illness, I dared to rail at the Almighty God. In my despair, I felt I had been cheated into thinking the cabin was a blessed gift. "Why," I shouted, "is there a ramp up to the cabin if she isn't supposed to make it there?" I think that we are all tremendously blessed that God chooses not to listen to us sometimes.

Suzie woke up at six o'clock the next morning and somehow let the doctor know she wanted to go home. I picked her up at noon and twenty-eight hours after the operation, she was back at the farm. She had the radical mastectomy on May 26th and on June 29th we arrived at the cabin. Suzie did walk up the ramp into the cabin and we had the most colossal, extravagant, exciting, grand finale to our travels that could only have been Heaven sent. We sat on the deck, deeply inhaling the smell of the Douglas firs which surrounded us. Big Sky sunsets were nearly overwhelming. We called sunrises lightshows. The sun would appear above the mountain and weave long shafts of gold between the trees, then turn the grass translucent and the massive trunks flat black in silhouette. I drove her to the banks of Cottonwood Creek, where we sat and heard the power of the water rushing over boulders. She would get tears in her eyes from the joy of these things, as she did when she listened to a great symphony.

In Spite of Everything....

We came home exhilarated and full of thanks that we could share such a place. I had bought a video camera and we played back the scenery and the animals we saw for friends and for ourselves. We tried not to think about the cancer. It was enough to deal with the Huntington's disease. Suzie began falling. She had so little use of her arms that she couldn't break the falls and she got terrible bruises and cuts above her eyes and nose. Toward the beginning of the next summer, she needed help getting everywhere.

We still planned to go to Montana again, but my faith in that goal began to waver as I saw her deteriorating so rapidly. Just before school was out for the summer, she became incontinent and paralyzed from cancer in her spine. I rented a hospital bed and got seven-hour-a-day help to take care of her. I learned nursing care to help her the rest of the time. A long, laboring time began of clearing her lungs and throat, but her buoyant spirit prevailed. She smiled for friends, smiled for the sun on the patio, for tasty fruit drinks and for her favorite chocolate shakes. Suction tubes were inserted, catheters invaded, and still she held on to her own sense of self. Her beautiful muscular body wilted and shrank. She smiled at us or glared at us for our lack of understanding and remained Suzie. Breathing became more difficult. She turned yellow, but those blue eyes still sparkled with light. She began to refuse food because it was bitter and repulsive, the final affront. She had endured it all.

On Saturday the 17th of October, her body began to shut down. She dozed most of the day and all night, and by morning she was semiconscious, unresponsive except for her precious music, Brahms. She roused up for it and for her dear friend, Carla, who came to check on her after I called. A few hours after Carla left, Suzie turned inward and at last found the most perfect peace. The struggle was over. Quiet settled in the room — tangible, motionless. Her mouth and eyes, half open, were relaxed, no movement, silent, beautiful face, my angel, sweet spirit released.

We shared thirty-five years of joy, struggle, tragedy, and triumph. She showed those of us who knew her how to live life to the fullest and that we should never compromise the essence of ourselves ever, even to the end. I see her now, striding out across the land, vital and happy, blue eyes shining, and there is a smile on her face, just for me.

About the Author

Leila Peters received her bachelors and masters degrees at Butler University where she met Suzie, the woman she loved. They were both teachers. In their thirty-five years together they traveled, bought a farm and raised Arabian horses, and found a dream cabin in Montana. Until *In Spite of Everything* became her passion, she wrote magazine articles about the things she loved: farm life, nature, and horses. She has been published in *Outdoor Indiana*, *The Western Horseman*, The Writers' Center of Indianapolis periodical, *Flying Island*, and *Teacher Magagine*. It was Suzie's death that prompted the writing of their story which became the catalist for gathering stories of other women who have been in loving relationships for nineteen years or more. Leila still lives on the farm she and Suzie bought in 1970 and loves to ride and walk over the land. She also spends time at her cabin in Montana in the summer, where she does much of her writing. After living alone for seventeen years she was blessed for the second time with a wonderful woman. Another chapter begins.